SEX AND LOVE IN PORFIRIAN MEXICO CITY

Sex and Love in Porfirian Mexico City

A Social History of Working-Class Courtship

Michael Matthews

UNIVERSITY OF FLORIDA PRESS

Gainesville

This book will be made open access within three years of publication thanks to Path to Open, a program developed in partnership between JSTOR, the American Council of Learned Societies (ACLS), University of Michigan Press, and The University of North Carolina Press to bring about equitable access and impact for the entire scholarly community, including authors, researchers, libraries, and university presses around the world. Learn more at https://about.jstor.org/path-to-open/

Cover: *La Guacamaya,* April 1905 número extraordinario

30 29 28 27 26 25   6 5 4 3 2 1

https://doi.org/10.5744/9781683405016

Library of Congress Cataloging-in-Publication Data
Names: Matthews, Michael, 1978– author.
Title: Sex and love in Porfirian Mexico City : a social history of
working-class courtship / Michael Matthews.
Other titles: Social history of working-class courtship
Description: Gainesville : University of Florida Press, [2025] | Includes
bibliographical references and index.
Identifiers: LCCN 2024047972 (print) | LCCN 2024047973 (ebook) | ISBN
9781683405016 (hardback) | ISBN 9781683405221 (paperback) | ISBN
9781683405467 (pdf) | ISBN 9781683405344 (epub)
Subjects: LCSH: Sex customs—Mexico—Mexico City—History. |
Sex—Mexico—Mexico City—History. | Love—Mexico—Mexico City—History.
| Working class—Mexico—Mexico City—Economic conditions—History. |
Poor—Mexico—Mexico City—History. | Mexico City (Mexico)—Social life
and customs—History. | BISAC: HISTORY / Latin America / Mexico | SOCIAL
SCIENCE / Human Sexuality (see also PSYCHOLOGY / Human Sexuality)
Classification: LCC HQ18.M4 M39 2025 (print) | LCC HQ18.M4 (ebook) | DDC
306.70972—dc23/eng/20241210
LC record available at https://lccn.loc.gov/2024047972
LC ebook record available at https://lccn.loc.gov/2024047973

University of Florida Press
2046 NE Waldo Road
UF PRESS   Suite 2100
                Gainesville, FL 32609
UNIVERSITY
OF FLORIDA   http://upress.ufl.edu

CONTENTS

ILLUSTRATIONS

Figures

Maps

TABLES

ACKNOWLEDGMENTS

Having spent the past years (how many I am embarrassed to say) immersed in the lives of the Porfirian Mexico City residents who appear in this book, it is difficult to put them aside now. Trying to tell their stories and understand their motivations has proved a difficult task, but one that it has been my honor to undertake. There is much, admittedly, that I could not recover from the brief glimpses offered by the often tattered pages of judicial files. Yet even in the brief windows that allowed me to peer into the fragile and too-easily forgotten lives of the past, I encountered a world not sapped of its strangeness and with endless possibility and meaning. It's that very alienness of the past that brings such joy to historians as we attempt to uncover and reconstruct it while, at other times, it can be the cause of a gut-wrenching sense of helplessness. And so, I have tried my best to tell their stories, to capture their words and deeds and their moments of happiness and hardship. The errors and omissions I have made in so doing were surely not for a lack of encouragement from family, friends, and colleagues. William French, Kathryn Sloan, Robert Buffington, Richard Boyer, and Ann Cahill read various chapters of the book and offered generous, thoughtful feedback. I warmly thank you all!

My longtime *compadre* and colleague, Stephen Neufeld, read the manuscript in its entirety and several chapters more than once. His insightful and original interpretations of the past are unmatched, a talent he graciously shares with me. He was as unwavering in his support as he was unsparing in his commentary, helping me avoid grave theoretical and interpretive errors as well as too many run-on sentences. James Garza, Linda Arnold, and Víctor Macías-González were always willing to answer random questions on sources, archives, or terminology. Patrick Eberlein, kindly, has been my reliable proofreader over the years, taking a break from math to read about Mexico. My Elon University colleague, Ryan Kirk, was kind enough to dedicate his time and energy producing the outstanding maps used in this book. Student workers, over the years, helped proofread and organize my research notes. Thank you, Lizzie Weber, Shannon Rodgers, and Lucy Garcia. Any errors or omissions, though, are mine and mine alone.

Elon University's History and Geography Department bestowed me the honor of being the first recipient of the four-year O'Bryant Developing Professorship which provided two things always in short supply: time and money. The generous course releases and travel funding it afforded made the research for this book a possibility. Elon Faculty Research and Development grants also facilitated research and writing.

This book would be no more than an idea without the archivists who make the historian's work possible. As such, my deepest appreciation goes to the archivists and staff at the Archivo General de la Nación, the Archivo Histórico del Distrito Federal, and the Instituto Mora in Mexico City, as well as at the Benson Latin American Collection at the University of Texas in Austin, who shared their knowledge and expertise while also kindly catering to my relentless requests for documents. My gratitude also goes to the staff at the University of Florida Press, especially Stephanye Hunter who reached out to me, years ago, with an early interest in this project. She has proved to be a tireless advocate for the book and a consummate professional in all things related to publishing. I was fortunate to have dedicated and thoughtful peer reviewers who demonstrated a sincere interest in making my manuscript better. Reviewer 2 was *never* a Reviewer 2.

The Mehas family—Shayna, Paulette, and Mayze—were a much-needed support structure in tough times. Red wine and dance parties offered reprieve and distraction when I needed it most. Lydia Kramer's encouragement and kindness convinced me to continue with the manuscript at a time when I nearly scrapped the project altogether. Her steadfast support—in so many ways—made this book possible.

During the years working on this project, as always throughout my life, my mother, Rossana Castagnetto, has been my tireless cheerleader and champion. My father, Charles Matthews, passed away before the completion of this book. Although he rolled his eyes at the topic, I know he would have been proud to see it on his shelf.

Finally, I am deeply grateful to Montgomery and Nolan for bringing me so much happiness and for reminding me, every day, that no voice is too small.

Introduction

Santa, Federico Gamboa's 1903 naturalist novel about an innocent rural girl turned urban prostitute, is ubiquitous in Mexican society and culture. The book remains a perennial bestseller. Mexico's first novel selected for mass-market promotion, *Santa* has inspired popular songs, four movie adaptations (1918, 1932, 1943, and 1969), the second of which was Mexico's first talking picture, and, in 1978, was turned into a primetime telenovela.[1] Beyond the novel's fine prose, well-researched authenticity, and salacious storyline, literary critics have attributed its persistent popularity to its resonance with a Mexican psyche that divides women into "good mothers or bad whores."[2] The story tells of a young girl living in a rural hamlet of Chimalistac, on the outskirts of Mexico City with her mother and two hardworking brothers. Just a teenager, Santa is seduced by an itinerant soldier stationed near her home, impregnated, and abandoned. Her brothers, learning of her deflowering and dishonoring after a miscarriage, banish her from the family home. Santa makes her way to the capital where she falls into a life of prostitution, spiraling deeper and deeper into degeneracy. Even when she is offered opportunities to escape her fate—for example, by a bullfighter who falls in love with her—Santa, corrupted by the city and her life of prostitution, sabotages a better future through an act of infidelity. She spirals further into sexual degradation, working in brothels of worsening repute until, consumed by illness, she dies.[3]

Though the iconic theme of a daughter's fall from grace by sexual dishonor has long resonated with Mexican audiences, Gamboa's novel particularly reflects an elite assumption about how common people viewed virginity, sex, and honor. While his naturalist style allows for a near-cinematic rendering of fin-de-siècle Mexico City, Gamboa belonged to the highest echelons of Mexican society as a career diplomat, literary professor, and government minister. Shaped by the dynamics of Gamboa's class and professional identities, the sexual act and deception that serve as catalyst to the novel's plot reflect elite attitudes about how men's honor was tied, at the time, to the sexual purity of their female family members. Losing her virginity out of wedlock, Santa can no longer be a good daughter or, eventually, mother and is relegated to perdition as a so-called bad whore. Yet was this, truly, how common Mexicans at the turn of the century understood female sexuality and its relation to family honor?

In contrast to Gamboa's conservative vision of how humble Mexicans viewed sexuality, working-class penny press newspapers circulating the city around the same time his novel was published offer a radically different view about sexuality, honor, and the importance of female chastity. The penny press targeted lower-class Mexicans as a significant part of its audience, many of whom were recent arrivals to the city from the countryside. Among the editorials, advertisements, humorous dialogues, and didactic comic images found in its pages, several of the most popular and highly circulating penny presses offered readers short vignettes, in assonant poetic verse, titled "Romance Callejero" or "Street Romance." They chronicled the leisure activities, love affairs, aspirations, betrayals, infidelities, and squabbles that comprised working-class life.[4] While not exclusively treating romance and courtship, both were common themes in the "Street Romance" feature. Far from the conservative views of female sexuality espoused by Gamboa, the "Street Romance" dialogues openly acknowledged—in sometimes bawdy and vulgar innuendos and double entendres—a sexual culture among men *and* women. They abounded with examples of men acknowledging that their lovers had previous sexual partners; of women openly discussing sexual desire and self-pleasure; of couples engaging in blatant infidelities; and of promiscuous people forging and dissolving sexual relationships without moral misgivings. Indeed, the penny press offered a wide array of fictional fare that centered on a free and open view of sexuality devoid—or at least much less devoid—of the stigma surrounding sex in *Santa*.

The dichotomy that reduced women to either good mothers or bad whores does not emerge from a reading of the penny press that claimed to speak for the working class. If *Santa*'s popularity can be attributed to a national psyche that sees men as hypermasculine with an exaggerated sense of personal honor tied to the sexual control of women, or if its wide readership can be ascribed to a national audience for whom a story about the ostracization of unchaste women resonates, such a vision does not emerge in the penny press. This book questions those suppositions by reconstructing the sexual lives of Porfirian Mexico City's lower classes through an examination of criminal cases of *rapto*, the abduction of underage women from parental authority, and *estupro*, the initiation of sexual relations with underage women. It challenges long-held assumptions about aggressively masculine behavior—known as *machismo*—and female sexual subordination. What emerges from the pages that follow, I hope, is a more complicated view of the wide range of mores, beliefs, and behaviors held by Mexicans about sexuality.

The decades-long dictatorship of Porfirio Díaz, which lasted from 1876 to 1911, ushered in an era of Mexico's modernization. The nation had experienced, since achieving independence in 1821, half a century of civil wars, foreign invasions, and economic stagnation. A testament to the young nation's instability, the presidency had changed hands seventy-five times, and four different constitutions (1824, 1836, 1843, and 1857) had proclaimed the nation to be an empire, dictatorship, central republic, or federal republic, depending on the political hopes of various ephemeral regimes. Adding to the turmoil, the nation suffered four different foreign invasions by the Spanish, the Americans, and, twice, by the French. The Mexican-American War (1846–1848) left Mexico with half its national territory, and the second French invasion installed a European monarch as the nation's emperor from 1862 to 1867. A half-century of political tumult bred economic instability, which, in turn, only furthered governmental chaos and endemic banditry in the countryside. Ascending to the presidency, Díaz inherited a near-bankrupt treasury, a string of foreign debts, and an anemic mining and export economy.

Díaz's 1876 Revolution of Tuxtepec ousted Benito Juárez's successor, Sebastían Lerdo de Tejada, on a political platform of *puro* liberal policies that included the prohibition of consecutive presidential reelection, electoral reforms aimed at popular political incorporation, and local autonomy through direct municipal elections (known as *municipio libre*).[5] During his first term in office (1876–1880), his administration received national and international acclaim for its success in establishing the rule of law and political stability as well as nascent economic investment. Díaz appeared to lay the groundwork to achieve the positivist mantra of "order and progress" that guided his administration. Staying true to his political promises championing the Constitution of 1857, Díaz stepped down and handed over power to his ally Manuel González who pledged to build upon his predecessor's modernization program of railway development, economic reform, and material progress.[6] But, returning to the presidency after González's unpopular reign marred by political corruption, Díaz showed himself to be a liberal more in name than in practice. He jettisoned his constitutional principles and built a highly centralized regime where he did not relinquish power until the Mexican Revolution forced him into exile in 1911.

The political stability ushered in by Díaz's strongarm rule spurred a roaring economy driven by foreign investment.[7] It allowed the government to undertake large civic and infrastructure projects aimed at modernizing urban centers and improving public health. Beyond the exponential growth of railways across the nation, the construction of telegraph lines, steamships, and custom houses all served to reinvigorate the economy. Mexico City was the epicenter of the regime's modernizing vision that sought to restructure all aspects of society. The draining of Lake Texcoco, completed in 1900, for example, represented one of Díaz's most ambitious projects, seeking to end the capital city's centuries-long problem of periodic flooding—and ensuing disease—through the construction of a series of canals and tunnels as well as a modern sewage system.[8]

Such scientific planning characterized other public works projects that sprang across the country's urban centers. Street cars, public parks, city police, fire brigades, and electric light reshaped the urban environment while aiming to align citizens with the modern values espoused by policymakers.[9] Similarly, public rituals and holidays were redefined in their use to celebrate new values of sobriety, progress, civilization, and industriousness and to reshape social relations.[10] Officials, proud of the progress they made, showcased their nation's progress at international events such as the 1889 World's Fair in Paris where Mexico's pavilion—the Aztec Palace—commemorated its pre-Hispanic past while simultaneously defining itself as a modern, cosmopolitan country attractive to foreign investment.[11]

A Social History of Sexuality and Porfirian Modernization

In a range of different venues—the schoolhouse, the military, the prison, the workplace—new forms of discipline and surveillance aimed to mold Mexicans into ideal citizens who were hygienic, moral, and hardworking.[12] Such efforts were also promoted in attempts to curb the perceived lasciviousness of the poor. Public health officials, pedagogues, and policymakers, as well as new experts in the emerging fields of criminology and psychology, sought to control working-class sexuality and promote healthy families and a healthy social body.[13] New political and social strategies and technologies targeted popular sexual practice for reform in an effort to order, enhance, and secure life, reproduction, and productive power, an application of what Michel Foucault terms "biopower."[14] Policymakers forged institutions and strategies aiming to solve social, biological, and scientific problems, solutions they deemed crucial to strengthening a nation engaged in competitive global relations. The regulation and intervention by state agents in the sexual affairs of common people—for example, in the investigation and adjudication of crimes such as rapto and estupro—tied the sexual morality of the working class to the regime's civilizing mission and its goal to forge a modern nation.[15]

This book uses 234 criminal cases of rapto and estupro to examine the sensibilities of residents in and around Mexico City about courtship, love, and sex. These cases bring us into the world of ordinary people, illuminating their everyday struggles, conflicts, joys, and diversions. Beyond the information they provide on the multitude of romances that played out on the streets and in tenement buildings, rapto and estupro cases offer incredibly rich information about intergenerational conflict, family life, work routines, and gendered norms. A growing, yet nevertheless small, number of studies have used sexual crime cases to understand gender relations, courtship practice, and the legal system in modern Latin America. These studies, although focused on a diverse range of issues, make known the legal strategies that poor, young women used to exert agency and make independent choices about their spousal partners, romantic desires, and economic needs.[16]

Two book-length studies have used rapto and estupro cases to explore the courtship practices of ordinary Mexicans during the Porfiriato. In *Runaway Daughters*, Kathryn Sloan uses rapto cases adjudicated in nineteenth-century Oaxaca to argue that the growing power of the liberal state usurped parental power as the legal system increasingly emerged as the arbiter of family disputes over children's romantic decision-making. She shows that young women (and men) used the legal system to gain adult independence when parents called on legal authorities to restore family honor that had been lost when their daughters eloped or lost their virginity.[17] William French uses rapto and estupro cases, originating in the State of Chihuahua, to different ends. He examines alternative literacies as a social practice among marginalized groups and, in so doing, explores concepts of romantic love articulated in love letters that were entered into the judicial record. Although approaching rapto cases through a different theoretical lens, French also shows that young women were active agents who used the judicial system to their advantage to assert adult independence and make individually oriented decisions that often clashed with family expectations.[18] Both studies shed light on important aspects of Porfirian social and cultural life, especially the continued centrality of the concept of honor while also recognizing its contextual redefining by different individuals in different moments.[19]

This book builds on these pioneering works and shifts the focus to rapto and estupro cases adjudicated in Porfirian Mexico City. It presents a social history of lower-class sexual life in and around Mexico's capital at the turn of the century. As the setting to the interpersonal dramas that unfold in the pages of criminal cases, Mexico City offers the unique backdrop of a growing urban metropolis with modern accoutrements and diversions and as the showcase of the Porfirian modernizing project. This study, at times, refers to the individuals whose life stories we follow as "working class," yet as scholars have noted, Mexico City did not have an industrial proletariat comparable to the factory towns of Europe or the northeast United States.[20] Although the number of factory workers increased by 355 percent between 1895 and 1910 to about 10,000, one-third of whom were women, they only comprised about 4 percent of the city's population.[21]

The city counted on a sizable workforce of skilled artisans as well as individuals who earned wages in domestic work, service industries, street sweeping, sweatshops, commerce, and as day laborers. Over the course of the Porfiriato, the rise of factory work and new machinery used in workshops undermined older forms of artisanal production, especially in textile and cigarette production. This increased the numbers of unskilled and casual workers (*obreros*), among both men and women, and provided labor for the emerging service sector of hotels, restaurants, and entertainment.[22] Many, especially women, were self-employed market vendors who provided cheap, essential goods to the city.[23] Unregulated markets and peddlers provided food, clothes, tools, and household goods at low prices that allowed the poor to eke out an existence.[24] As a hub of recently arrived migrants from the countryside, who came to the city during their most productive ages, Mexico City's population was considerably younger than the national average with 56 percent of residents being between the ages of sixteen and forty-five.[25] The individuals whose lives briefly flash before us in the vignettes of this book, overwhelmingly, belonged to these social sectors.

In the outlying municipalities, workers labored on haciendas, on public works projects, and in nascent industries. The internal functioning of the hacienda, its use of the company store and debt peonage, limited the movement of free labor while simultaneously pushing people off their traditional lands as commercial agriculture grew, fostering an ecological crisis that put pressures on land, water, and forests.[26] Commercial growth taking place in the Valley of Mexico fostered its economic, spatial, and environmental subordination to the capital city whose population growth and infrastructure development relied on the constant provision of affordable, fresh food (much of it sold in the unregulated markets of poor neighborhoods). It also relied on the valley's canals and lakes to drain the city's waste water.[27] Railroads and canal systems connecting the city and its outlying municipalities allowed for the development of an internal market that facilitated the movement of goods and people.[28] Many of the legal cases examined in this book reveal the intimate connections between the capital city and the Valley of Mexico as workers moved between them looking for opportunities provided by the formal and informal economies.

This book argues that Porfirian Mexico City's working class had a freer and more liberated sexual life than their upper- and middle-class counterparts. While it would be too bold to claim that they rejected elite values related to sexuality, their words and actions reveal a culture of courtship, romance, and sex that could be ambivalent toward a wide range of norms such as honor, shame, marriage, love, and female chastity. Relatively little has been written on the sexual mores and practices of the inhabitants of Porfirian Mexico City.[29] This book addresses that lacuna. While elite observers from the era viewed working-class sexuality as licentious and immoral, this study seeks to map the motivations and calculations that defined lower-class sexual life. The archival record of sexually based crimes brings light to the lives of forgotten people whose economic precarity and daily struggle for survival shaped the nature of their amorous encounters. Although the jaundiced eye of moral reformers and government officials regularly identified popular sexual practice as animalistic and wanton, a contextualized reading of archival records and the working-class penny press makes known a far more complex and nuanced set of values and practices that often highlight a distinctly modern subjectivity.

Using sexuality as a lens through which to investigate Mexico City's poor during the Porfiriato offers a unique perspective on their shifting beliefs and practices in everyday life. Because sexual practice and behavior represent a focal point in the constructions of masculine and feminine identity, the study of sexuality is intimately connected to the history of gender.[30] Sexuality is thus inseparable from gender norms and identities as well as the distribution of power and privilege.[31] Judgments about sexuality expose and determine who wields power, who deserves it, and who is denied it.[32]

Yet, as recently argued for the history of twentieth-century Mexico City, sexuality as a category of analysis serves to decenter policymakers, allowing for an examination of the dialectical interactions between ordinary citizens and the state. Such an approach reveals how ordinary people accept, adapt, modify, or resist hegemonic ideals about sex and sexuality (articulated, for example, by policymakers, reformers, religious figures, or mass media) to meet their own lived realities.[33] This study utilizes sexually based crimes to examine the historically contingent nature of how ordinary people contested, co-opted, and consented to sexual norms.

Studies using sexually based crimes such as rapto to explore Latin American society, in both the colonial and modern contexts, have analyzed a range of significant topics: the construction and performance of honor; the social value of female chastity and virginity; the sexual mores and practices of different social groups; and the gendered worlds that shaped men's and women's capacity to exert agency over their own lives. Together, these are especially rich topics with which to consider the interconnections between gender and sexuality in the construction of social norms and identities. Since colonial times, the law has defined rapto as the abduction of an honest woman from her home to force or seduce her into sex, a crime that, aside from harming a woman, also brought dishonor to her male relatives.[34] Rapto, in practice, closely resembled elopement where young women and girls agreed to run away with their lovers to consummate their relationship sexually. By doing so, they put pressure on their families to repair their tarnished honor by accepting a daughter's decision to marry.[35]

Honor, in the colonial era, was central to how elite groups maintained distinctions among ethnic, cultural, and economic hierarchies.[36] And, despite its denial by dominant society, plebeian groups also made claims to honor but defined it through the lens of individual conduct and worthiness instead of a status acquired through privileged birth. Lower-class men asserted their honor through honest behavior and hard work, their control over female subordinates, and their demonstrations of strength and bravery.[37] Plebeian women did so by stressing their marital fidelity, modesty, and good housekeeping.[38] In so doing, plebeian peoples more often invoked *honra*, a notion of self-worth based on virtue and conduct, rather than *honor*, which referred to the status of an individual.[39] Sexual conduct was the benchmark of honorable behavior and, as such, virtue and chastity represented ideal characteristics that defined honest women.[40] Protecting the sexual honor of women was one of the few agreed-upon values that cut across different social groups of colonial society.[41]

The Catholic Church policed sexual morality for the majority of the colonial period as the Crown authorities showed little interest in regulating the behaviors of the lower classes. Church officials, like the colonial elite more generally, did not recognize a lower-class culture of honor and, thus, demonstrated more concern over people's salvation when adjudicating cases of heresy or sexual deviancy.[42] In the eighteenth century, the Spanish and Portuguese Crowns wrested away power from the Church to make the bureaucracy more efficient, the economy more productive, and the people more sober, disciplined, and governable. This portended the kinds of state interventions over morality that would define the national period.[43]

After independence, the formal abolition of special privileges based on birthright and racial purity by the newly formed republican nations failed to erode the culture of honor. Even though, in theory, honor would be determined by merit and not birth, colonial legacies infused the everyday practice and understanding of honor among the elite who continued to deny that an alternate system of honor existed among the lower classes.[44] The connection between honor and social hierarchies was, nevertheless, severely undermined by republican and liberal legal codes that emerged across Latin America, especially in the second half of the nineteenth century. Yet the concept and culture of honor remained tenaciously persistent. It informed modern notions of citizenship and the everyday workings of civil society as well as newly emerging scientific fields such as psychology and criminology.[45] Among the poor, honor remained a form of "social currency" to defend their reputations and autonomy in both the public and private spheres.[46] For all classes, honor also remained a highly gendered concept and, as such, was central to expressions of and conflicts over sexuality.

Scholarship on honor and its relation to sexuality has shown a persistent throughline in how families, especially among the elite, protected female virginity and chastity before marriage as a crucial stratagem in maintaining public respectability and ensuring a daughter's marriage prospects.[47] The control of female family members' sexuality upheld patriarchal honor because protection of racial lineage, legitimacy, and inheritance were crucial to family interests and the politics of marriage.[48] Nevertheless, in the colonial period, premarital sex was socially acceptable as long as a couple eventually committed to marriage.[49] And, in some instances, premarital sex could serve as proof of virginity to one's betrothed.[50] For the non-elite of the colonial world, virginity held far less value. As has been argued for colonial Venezuela, high illegitimacy rates and the frequency of concubinage suggest that for individuals not concerned over the inheritance of property and with little chance of acquiring wealth, the practical motivations for marriage and legitimate heirs did not exist.[51]

Virginity, in the nineteenth and twentieth centuries, continued to matter for the marriage prospects of the elite and was central to the defense of patriarchal honor. Yet, as this book argues, the elite hid familial battles over deflowered daughters from public view. In contrast to the colonial period, the well-to-do rarely used the courts to arbitrate matters related to the protection of virginity, marriageability, and honor. Overwhelmingly, it was poor families, instead, who dragged young suitors to court when a promise of betrothal went unfulfilled, seeking a commitment to marriage or financial restitution. This dramatic shift underscores—among the lower classes—a variety of views about the value of virginity across Latin American nations and time periods. Studies on nineteenth-century Puerto Rico and Brazil, for example, have argued that virginity was not central to marriageability among the poor.[52] In contrast, examining cases of sexual crimes between 1920 and 1940 in Rio de Janeiro, Sueann Caulfield maintains that working-class men did see virginity as a prerequisite for marriage although they continued consensual unions with non-virgin women. Moreover, she notes that most working-class women commonly married men to whom they did not lose their virginity.[53]

The scholarship on modern Mexico, likewise, has put forward a range of different conclusions about the social importance of virginity. Nora Jaffary argues that in the late-nineteenth century, among *all* social classes, women adhered to a "cult of virginity" and that lower-class women mimicked elite notions of respectability strongly associated with premarital virginity.[54] Ann Blum, on the contrary, argues that virginity would have had little value among populations where illegitimacy was high and where no stigma was attached to children born out of wedlock.[55] Although neither Caulfield nor Jaffary focuses specifically on cases of rapto or estupro, the Sloan and French studies on modern Mexico that do, likewise, put forward opposing claims. Examining cases of rapto in nineteenth-century Chihuahua, William French notes that male suitors were "preoccupied" with the virginity of their romantic partners when considering marriage suitability.[56] He finds that men expected premarital sex to confirm virginity in order to fulfill a marriage promise, highlighting rapto cases where men used a woman's failure to prove virginity as a justification to renege on a marriage promise.[57] Kathryn Sloan, examining Oaxaca during the same era, finds that men did not consistently demonstrate a deep concern about virginity when making marriage offers. And, for young women, she claims that virginity could represent a "form of capital" that they wielded to compel parents to accept their suitors.[58] This study, while closer to Sloan's conclusion, argues that in Porfirian Mexico City, the working class and poor held ambivalent views about female chastity because the material and social conditions of lower-class life made adhering to a "cult of virginity" untenable.

The sexual mores and practices of the poor has received some scholarly attention among Latin Americanist scholars.[59] In the colonial era, Sonya Lipsett-Rivera finds that a greater degree of sexual freedom characterized plebeian culture and that poor women would have several sexual partners over a lifetime.[60] Similar claims have been made about nineteenth- and twentieth-century Mexico.[61] In her examination of nineteenth-century Rio de Janeiro, Martha de Abreu Esteves claims that working-class women's values related to honor and virginity differed significantly from elite values and that the opportunities for leisure in the urban environment allowed for greater sexual freedom.[62] In her examination of nineteenth-century Guatemala, Catherine Komisaruk argues that a sexual permissiveness existed that allowed for an acceptance of illicit unions among the poor, especially in urban centers.[63] Nevertheless, a gendered, sexual double standard existed for men and women. Social norms marginalized sexually adventurous women while, for men, such behavior was promoted and celebrated.[64]

Robert Buffington contributes to the literature on the sexuality of Porfirian Mexico's working class through his examination of the penny press. He argues that periodicals targeting the working class demonstrate a sexual openness in their topics, humor, and social commentary. Far from a macho hegemonic masculinity, the penny press articulated a vision of working-class sexuality that was ambivalent, ambiguous, and, at times, highlighted the companionate nature of relationships, a phenomenon Buffington identifies as distinctly modern.[65] This book engages these claims insofar as it assesses, when appropriate, how the words and deeds of ordinary people found in the judicial record reflected or contested views about gender, sexuality, honor, courtship, promiscuity, and companionship articulated in the penny press.

If the lower classes lived lives more sexually liberated than those of their social higher-ups as this book argues, such freedom did not stem from inherent wantonness or lasciviousness as so many of the social reformers of the era maintained. Rather, to better grasp the factors that shaped the sexual culture of the poor, this study examines their social lives in the context of the material conditions and disciplining mechanisms that emerged as a result of Porfirian state formation and capitalist growth and development. This book underscores how a twofold process of Porfirian modernization reshaped workers' lives and the social conditions that structured the practice of courtship, romance, and sex. These changes, in turn, also reshaped value systems related to honor, virginity, and morality. First, export-led development tied Mexico to the demands of the global economy, altering labor regimes and landholding patterns that spurred migration, urbanization, industrialization, and ecological change in and around Mexico City. Workers—in both the formal and informal sectors—served as cheap, exploitable labor that fueled economic growth while they suffered the social conditions that accompanied rapid capitalist development: overcrowded tenement housing, financial insecurity, unsanitary conditions, and high crime rates. Second, the regime's modernizing vision shaped policies that sought to discipline and surveil popular groups to create a more reliable workforce to sustain economic development in an increasingly competitive global order. Government officials, social reformers, police forces, and public health workers increasingly interfered in the private lives of the poor to instill a middle-class morality understood as the bedrock of civilization. Rather than confront the lower class's existing economic conditions, reformers explained their unhealthy environment and poverty as rooted in immorality.[66]

Yet despite the government's increasing attempts to reshape people's productive and reproductive practices—most often through mechanisms of moral reform—and its increased capacity to do so, state formation represented a contested and limited process.[67] State initiatives targeting hygiene, sanitation, welfare, prostitution, vice, and public safety could meet people's acceptance, resistance, or ambivalence. These interactions and negotiations between ordinary people and the government often transformed the implementation and intended outcomes of the policies.[68] What was often the highly gendered nature of state programs has led scholars to refer to such campaigns, especially during the years of Revolutionary state-building (1920–1940), as the "modernization of patriarchy."[69] That is, a set of social reforms that aimed to modernize the productive capacities of the nation and its people and, in so doing, reinforce the states' paternal role and men's control over their families.[70] These social reforms created new institutional centers of male power while also entrenching traditional patriarchal structures.[71] While the state initiatives of the Porfiriato were not as robust as Revolutionary social welfare programs, they nevertheless appear to have laid the ideological groundwork for the Revolution's "modernization of patriarchy," an observation that bolsters recent claims that Porfirian and Revolutionary policymaking represent a continuation rather than a radical rupture.[72] It was the perceived failure of nineteenth-century liberal regimes across Latin America in solving the social problems that accompanied rapid economic development that spurred more comprehensive twentieth-century political projects aiming to connect nation-building and the nuclear, male-headed family.[73]

As the vignettes of popular street life in this study show, these broad governmental forces simultaneously created new spaces and opportunities for ordinary citizens to exert a more liberal sexual agency while they also experienced increased repression as the scope of state power expanded, becoming more intrusive in its attempts to control lower-class sexuality. These seemingly contradictory phenomena emerged because of the limits of state-building initiatives. The ongoing, everyday interactions between subordinate and dominant groups—at the family, community, and state levels—shifted and reshaped normative expectations about gender and sexual life as people adapted government policy, legal apparatus, social tradition, and cultural custom to meet their own ends. Within this context, developments such as sexual liberalization and women's emancipation do not represent a teleological history characterized by steady advances in the progressive modernization of gender relations. Rather, they demonstrate that patriarchal authority could be hardened in certain areas of life while, in others, men and women found opportunities to exert agency and experience greater sexual freedom.[74]

A Note on Sources

This study, in many ways, adheres to a format and structure more common to the judicial and Inquisition case-based research undertaken by colonial Latin Americanists.[75] Criminal cases, for social historians, provide a treasure trove of information about marginalized, subordinate, and, often, illiterate individuals who would be lost to history if not for their brushing up against the law. The defendants and litigants in the criminal cases examined here discussed a range of issues related to the crimes in question: courtship, love, sex, kinship networks, and family dynamics. But their depositions provide so much more. They tell us about patterns of work, residency, and movement as well as about the changing urban landscape of Mexico City, its entertainment and leisure activities. We learn about what and where people ate and drank, the clothes they wore, and how they spent their money. We get glimpses into the arduous life and grinding poverty that defined lower-class life but also the everyday strategies of survival people employed to make ends meet. We also find that despite the procedural apparatus and formulaic legal language, common speech and behavior bubble up from the sources.[76]

And we encounter women. Judicial sources make women visible and bring to light their absolute presence and centrality in the everyday workings of city life.[77] The abundance of female-headed households exposes the myth that the patriarchal, traditional family unit has been universal and transhistorical.[78] While the following case studies bring forward women from all age groups and walks of life, this study, in particular, because of the nature of the sources, focuses on the sexuality of young, heterosexual women from the most marginalized sectors of society. Criminal cases serve as a corrective to the vast array of historical materials and primary sources that too often have rendered women, especially poor women, invisible.

Yet a reliance on criminal cases also puts forward several challenges. They can present a reified vision of state power while making ordinary citizens appear uniformly unlawful, wanton, and lascivious. Beyond that, because judicial records were produced by middle- and upper-class judges, and because defendants employed strategic, gendered narratives before unsympathetic officials, criminal cases do not tell the "truth" as much as they tell *of the truth*.[79]

A statistical aggregate of working-class life is not the focus of this study. Instead, it seeks to put forward a moderate number of cases and examine them in as much detail as possible. Some statistical information is, nevertheless, worth highlighting to grasp the scope of how and where these everyday dramas took place and among whom. A sample of 234 criminal cases are presented that were adjudicated in and around Mexico City between 1884 and 1911. At times, the condition of the document or a criminal case's transfer to another deliberative body omits some pertinent information. The period between 1900 and 1911 weighs more heavily in the number of cases (61 percent), while the period between 1884 and 1889 and 1890 and 1899 represents 21 percent and 18 percent of the cases, respectively. The majority of the cases (77 percent) stem from the eight precincts that served as the hubs of police presence in Mexico City. Of these, just eight of the 181 cases that originated in the city were investigated in the 8th Precinct, the capital's most affluent sector, a reflection of the fact that it was, overwhelmingly, the poor who reported sexually based crimes. Only 12 percent stem from the municipalities that surrounded Mexico City but that

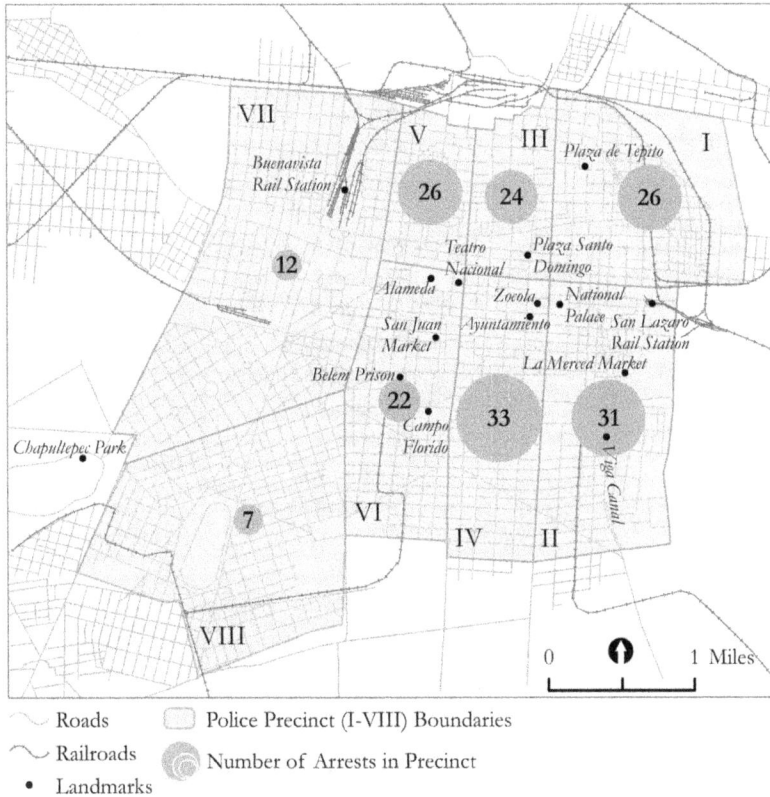

Map 1. Mexico City crime by district.

were administratively part of the Federal District. And just two cases (0.9 percent) originated in the neighboring State of Mexico. In 10 percent of the cases, the origin of the legal proceeding cannot be determined.

In terms of how the cases under examination here were legally classified, 128 were initiated as rapto (55 percent), eighty-six as rapto and estupro (36.5 percent), fourteen as *only* estupro (6 percent), and just six (2.5 percent) as *violación* or rape.

Categorization of the crime by legal authorities was often haphazard, especially regarding whether a case was filed as rapto, estupro, or rapto *and* estupro. It appears that legal authorities investigated both the abduction (rapto) and deflowering (estupro) concurrently regardless of how the crime was entered into the judicial register. Cases of rape, on the other hand, were instances of violent sexual assault. Such cases were rare as judges privileged deceit over violence as the defining trait of sexual crimes.[80]

Table 1. Cases by Decade

1880s	50
1890s	42
1900–1911	142
TOTAL	234

Source: Archivo General de la Nación, Archivo del Tribunal Superior de Justicia de la Ciudad de México and Archivo del Tribunal Superior de Justicia del Distrito Federal.

Table 2. Origin of Complaint

Precinct 1	26 (11.1%)
Precinct 2	31 (13.2%)
Precinct 3	24 (10.3%)
Precinct 4	33 (14.1%)
Precinct 5	26 (11.1%)
Precinct 6	22 (9.4%)
Precinct 7	12 (5.1%)
Precinct 8	7 (3%)
Azcapotzalco	1 (0.4%)
Guadalupe Hidalgo	5 (2.1%)
Tacubaya	7 (3%)
Tlalpan	11 (4.7%)
Xochimilco	3 (1.3%)
Estado de México	2 (0.9%)
N/A	24 (10.3%)
TOTAL	234

Source: Archivo General de la Nación, Archivo del Tribunal Superior de Justicia de la Ciudad de México and Archivo del Tribunal Superior de Justicia del Distrito Federal.

Mothers were most often the individuals who reported the abduction, deflowering, or rape of a daughter (55.5 percent), a reflection of the many female-headed households found throughout the city. Fathers, the next most common initiators of a criminal complaint, did so in about one-quarter of the cases (25.5 percent) Other family members, employers, and, even, one tenement building doorman represent the remaining complainants. And, in just two cases (0.9 percent), did the victim of a sexual crime report the case to authorities. In six (2.5 percent) of the cases, the original complainant cannot be determined.

The average age of the men accused of a sexual crime was twenty-three years old, and the female victims were, on average, fifteen years old. The oldest female victim was twenty-six and the youngest eleven years old. The oldest male defendant was fifty-five and the youngest fourteen years old.

This book attempts to reconstruct the everyday experiences of ordinary people by taking their testimony in criminal cases seriously as reflections of their thoughts, deeds, and desires. Yet it recognizes that using judicial records to find out what "really happened" proves a nearly impossible task. The young women and men who populate these cases often provided con-

Table 3. Criminal Charge

Rapto	128 (54.7%)
Estupro	14 (6%)
Rapto and Estupro	86 (36.7%)
Violación	6 (2.6%)
TOTAL	**234**

Source: Archivo General de la Nación, Archivo del Tribunal Superior de Justicia de la Ciudad de México and Archivo del Tribunal Superior de Justicia del Distrito Federal.

Table 4. Complainant

Mother	130 (55.6%)
Father	64 (27.4%)
Aunt	8 (3.4%)
Uncle	4 (1.7%)
Brother	2 (0.9%)
Cousin	1 (0.4%)
Grandfather	1 (0.4%)
Grandmother	2 (0.9%)
Sister	9 (3.9%)
Victim	2 (0.9%)
Employer	4 (1.7%)
Doorman	1 (0.4%)
N/A	6 (2.6%)
TOTAL	**234**

Source: Archivo General de la Nación, Archivo del Tribunal Superior de Justicia de la Ciudad de México and Archivo del Tribunal Superior de Justicia del Distrito Federal.

tradictory testimony and changed their stories in the course of the proceedings (sometimes repeatedly). Witness accounts also often differed, sometimes on minor points and other times wildly. Parents or guardians often proffered information that they received through neighborhood gossip. And, even when witness accounts did align with one side or another, the possibility of collusion or witness tampering must at least be considered as a (rare) possibility as plaintiffs and defendants could have ample time "to get their stories straight" before confronting legal authorities. At the same time, whether victims, culprits, suspects, or witnesses, those individuals who found themselves in the presumably intimidating circumstances of police or judicial interrogation did not want to be there. Scribes, most often, jotted down their words in the moments immediately after an arrest had occurred. While their version of events was surely strategic, and even scripted, they did not have "the same premeditation as the printed word."[81]

The couples involved in rapto and estupro cases fashioned their experiences and goals into coherent and, ideally, persuasive narratives.[82] How they did so also proves a complex matter. Crucial to putting forward a persuasive account was crafting a script that met the gendered expectations of how women and men in courtship and sexual scenarios should behave. Mexico's seduction law assumed that only men demonstrated active sexuality and, therefore, only men could commit sexual crimes. As such, male sexuality can often appear as unfettered in the criminal cases. Yet, as the following cases demonstrate, a wide range of factors—state repression, neighborhood gossip, cultural norms, or gender anxieties—could limit male sexuality and how masculinity was articulated.[83] Women consistently portrayed themselves as passive victims.[84] Men also reliably played certain scripts. For example, as Mexican legal discourse tied female virginity to male honor, men's testimony assumed female virginity at the outset of courtship or sexual relations (even in cases where such an assumption would have been highly unlikely). And as both women and men showed a great deal of knowledge about law, legal procedure, and punishment, it meant that they could frame or fabricate their testimony as they strove for the best possible outcome.

Judges and scribes played a principal role in shaping the narratives recorded into the legal record, beyond simply converting the words of witnesses from the first to third person. A suspiciously consistent narrative is striking when reading judicial cases. While scribes did not record the questions asked by judges, the almost universal format in which plaintiffs and defendants told their stories suggests that judges guided testimony using a set of standard questions that omitted superfluous information. For example, the records of parents or guardians reporting a rapto overwhelmingly followed a set pattern: the young woman had been found missing, a family member investigated the matter, they received information or did not receive information about her possible whereabouts, they did or did not find the missing woman or couple, and they demanded an investigation or punishment for the culprit. Both testimonies of the romantically involved couple, likewise, followed a strikingly similar formula: they noted the length of their relationship, the event that led to the abduction or elopement (and whether there was a marriage promise), the state of the woman's virginity, and, specific to the woman's testimony, the opinion on whether the man should be charged with a crime.

Despite the consistency of the story-telling format, criminal cases are characterized by conflicting testimony as defendants and plaintiffs sought to put themselves in the best position to accomplish their desired outcome. The often-conflicting testimonies among defendants, plaintiffs, and witnesses create one of the most difficult obstacles to reconstructing the events in question. When recounting a particular vignette where testimonies contradicted, I have tried to weave both accounts into the storyline.

Although such a presentation of a romantic drama can often read as a he-said-she-said dispute, it allows the reader to see the difficulty historians face when reconstructing events while also allowing the reader to draw their own conclusions about what might have transpired. At times, I venture to put forward my own conclusions. When witness testimony and corroborating information are overwhelming, I attempt to reconstruct events in a more streamlined narrative, explaining to the reader—when relevant—my thought process. Another challenge of crafting readable vignettes from criminal cases stems from the scribes who recorded testimony in the third person. To make the narrative more readable, especially when quoting the words of defendants, plaintiffs, and witnesses, I have translated their testimony back into the original first person in which they would have been delivered in an attempt to capture a more earnest version of people's voices.[85]

Like the testimony format, the word choice and phrases used by witnesses were remarkably similar and, perhaps, better reflected the middle-class diction of legal officials than the popular vernacular. Parents and guardians called for culprits to "cover the honor" of their daughters. The young couples, in the court records, most commonly referred to having sex as "coitus," "the carnal act," "enjoying her," and "dishonoring her." It might be plausible that the working-class individuals who found themselves in front of legal authorities employed language they believed would be expected from an educated elite and that would put their claims in the best possible light. Yet that Mexico City's poor spoke in the seemingly refined manner recorded in judicial records belies the informal language used by popular groups as recorded, for example, in the working-class penny press.[86] Indeed, one case that stands as an outlier, perhaps due to an ambivalent or novice notary, sheds light on how judicial officials might have reworked testimony into more appropriate and honorable language.

Jesús Medina, when arrested for the estupro of Romana Montaño in 1909, had a scribe record his testimony: "he went to visit her house every day and several days ago he told her that he wanted to fuck her (*cojérsela*) to which she replied that she loved him very much. The speaker fucked her (*se la tiró*), finding her to be a virgin." During her declaration, Romana Montaño described the sexual act: "he put in his thing where she pees" (*le metió su cosa por donde mea*).[87] The informal language found here—which I have kept in the third person to show readers how testimony is presented in the legal documents—is even more explicit than what we find in the penny press. While an extreme and rare example, it does highlight the possibility of how working-class and poor Mexicans might have addressed judicial authorities who then transmuted their words into what officials viewed as more conventional and appropriate language for the legal record.[88]

Organization of the Book

The six chapters that follow advance a social history of lower-class courtship and sexuality in Porfirian Mexico City. The first two chapters map out the spatial, social, and ideological terrain to contextualize the ways that the city and the state shaped the nature of courtship. Chapter 1 examines how the growing and modernizing metropolis of Mexico City offered new work opportunities, especially for young women, new forms of urban housing, especially the rise of tenement living, and new forms of leisure and entertainment that created novel venues for young couples to meet, woo, and, eventually, have sex. It thus considers how the city itself shaped sexuality. Chapter 2 explores how the increased capacity of the modernizing state to surveil, detain, and adjudicate sexual crimes—made possible by the growing political stability of the Díaz regime—manifested itself in instances where poor families called on legal authorities to arbitrate matters of courtship and intergenerational conflict. It focuses on how the city's most marginalized residents legitimized and empowered government officials to adjudicate their most intimate matters.

The next two chapters delve deeper into the ways that young couples defined their expectations of proper courtship and the diverse ways that they formed relationships. Chapter 3 uses the concept of will (*voluntad*) to consider how young couples demarcated the boundaries between force and consent during the courtship process. It uses accounts of coercion and rape, on the one hand, and expressions of willful intent by women, on the other, to make known the high stakes at play when young couples sought to justify or refute their romantic relationships to themselves, to each other, to their families, or to the community. Chapter 4 deals with the various types of relationships that working-class people chose and what those relationships meant to them. It provides an overview of consensual—but legally illegitimate—unions, marriage by the state and by the Church, and casual sex. In so doing, it considers how material conditions shaped the kinds of relationships forged by the poor.

Chapter 5 shows how the city's poor, and especially how young women, used sex in strategic ways as a form of self-management and survival. Initiating sexual relations offered a powerful tactic to weaken parental authority and claim adulthood. Strategic sexual self-management also could serve to mitigate the worst aspects of economic insecurity as well as create opportunities for self-fulfillment. Examining cases of rapto and estupro alongside the writing of the penny press, chapter 6 explores the ambiguous and ambivalent views about courtship and sexuality held by the working class. Yet, while seemingly nebulous, in their words and actions, together with the writings of the penny press, we find a much freer view of and approach to sexuality than was held by their upper-class counterparts.

The pages that follow attempt to visualize the social and sexual lives of the Porfiriato's most marginalized residents. It seeks to uncover, gauge, and interpret their views about family, courtship, romance, desire, and pleasure as well as how class and material conditions shaped the contours of their amorous encounters. Even if for a brief moment, I hope to give life to people too often rendered invisible by the historical record; to shine a light on the city's poorest residents who, amid grinding poverty and precarious circumstances, found moments of intimacy and tenderness—but, perhaps just as often, cruelty and contempt—in the everyday romances that took place on the streets of Mexico City.

1

City of Sexual Danger, City of Sexual Delight

The urban environment of Mexico City shaped the ways that young couples met, courted, and loved. The population grew by 50 percent during the Porfiriato, and the city experienced tremendous change spurred by the modernizing vision of the regime. Newly arrived railroad and streetcars—coupled with a much older canal system—connected the growing city to the outlying municipalities that, together, composed the administrative jurisdiction of the Federal District.[1] Both mule-driven and electric streetcars connected the city, allowing wealthy and middle-class residents to move to new suburbs developing on the west side. Tram fares, although steadily decreasing throughout the era, remained prohibitively expensive for the working class. As a result, by the 1890s, 65 percent of the city's population continued to live in the colonial center that extended from the Alameda to the streets just east of the Zócalo. From the 1890s onward, lower-class neighborhoods developed to the north, east, and south of the Zócalo, near the newly emerging employment centers, especially the Buenavista and San Lázaro railroad stations and textile and cigarette factories. The high cost of rent confined the laboring classes east of the Zócalo with more than one third of the city's population living on just 15 percent of its land.[2]

One way that many residents of the city experienced Porfirian progress was in the waves of migration that brought provincials to the city in search of work and wages. Spurred by agricultural demand and railroad construction, privatization and speculation drove up land prices and tax rates across the nation, driving an internal mass migration from the provinces to the country's major urban centers.[3] By 1900, two-thirds of Mexico City's population was born outside the Federal District.[4] Insufficient housing caused chronic overcrowding in the tenements as well as in the ramshackle *jacales* (abode buildings constructed with pilfered or discarded materials) on the

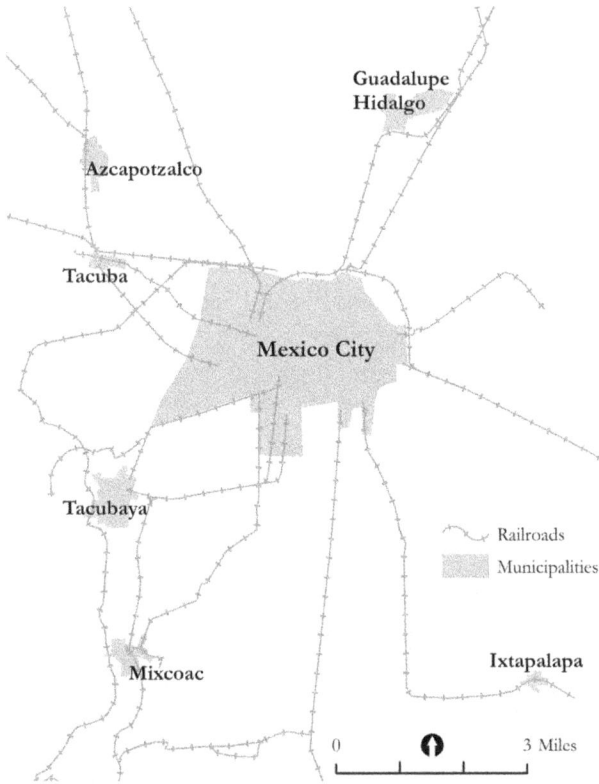

Map 2. Mexico City and municipalities.

edges of the city that served as the first landing spots for migrants.[5] The city's modernizing infrastructure programs, such as the draining of Lake Texcoco to end the cycles of periodic flooding that plagued the city as well as the construction of paved streets and the installation of electric lights and sanitation works, benefited the modern, wealthy neighborhoods of the west side, further segregating the rich and poor.[6]

During the early years of the Porfiriato, the rich inhabited the city's center on streets running west of the Zócalo to the Alameda Park. By the 1890s, many began to move farther west to the newly developing colonias of Cuauhtémoc, Juárez, and Roma modeled after European capitals and built by American capital. The affluent residential suburbs featured tree-lined streets of single-story houses, elegant apartment buildings, and opulent mansions, all designed in a diversity of European styles.

A small, but growing, middle class also lived in the city center at the start of the era but moved to the west and northwest colonias of San Rafael and Santa María where artisans, merchants, and professionals took up residence.[7]

The neighborhoods of the poor and working class were a world apart from those on the west side of the city. While some artisans and workers could perhaps afford humble homes just north of the Zócalo in the working-class suburbs of Santo Domingo and Guerrero, more and more settled in neighborhoods that developed on the outlying swampland to the east, north, and south of the city.[8] Rough barrios such as Tepito, San Lázaro, San Pablo, and San Pedro emerged around the many churches that ringed the old city center, absorbing the migrants who arrived daily. The respectable classes viewed these neighborhoods as dens of filth, vice, and crime, streets they dared not tread. But no area of the city held a worse reputation than Colonia de la Bolsa, an unauthorized settlement that arose on the swamplands northeast of the Zócalo in the 1880s. A mix of neglected tenement buildings and makeshift *jacales*, its inhabitants were deemed squatters and thus denied repeated petitions for paving, water, sewage, and police protection.[9] Newspapers described it as a slum where "the most horrible crimes are committed."[10] *Terry's Mexico*, a popular guidebook, described it as the "plague and crime spot of the city . . . a sort of native Ghetto with dirty and microbic streets, repulsive sights and evil smells." Colonia de la Bolsa, it concluded, was "just as offensive to intelligent Mexicans as . . . to foreign visitors."[11] While the well-to-do avoided these areas, the poor traveled from them to wealthy neighborhoods working as domestic servants, street sweepers, peddlers, carters (*cargadores*) and, more generally, day laborers (*jornaleros*).

Workers most often lived in crowded *vecindades* (tenements), colonial buildings that had once served as schools, monasteries, and palaces.[12] One- or two-room apartments surrounded a common patio where women hung laundry and children played among dogs, cats, and chickens and the din of street noise. Residents lived in small, windowless rooms and shared common toilets and washbasins.[13] The cramped, uncomfortable conditions of apartments (known as *viviendas*) meant that most women spent a great deal of time in the patio, not only washing clothes and utensils, but socializing and celebrating. This fostered community and solidarity and, also, at times, animosity and intrigue among neighbors.[14] Acts of sex, violence, and solidarity shaped public reputation in the tenement buildings where domestic privacy did not exist.

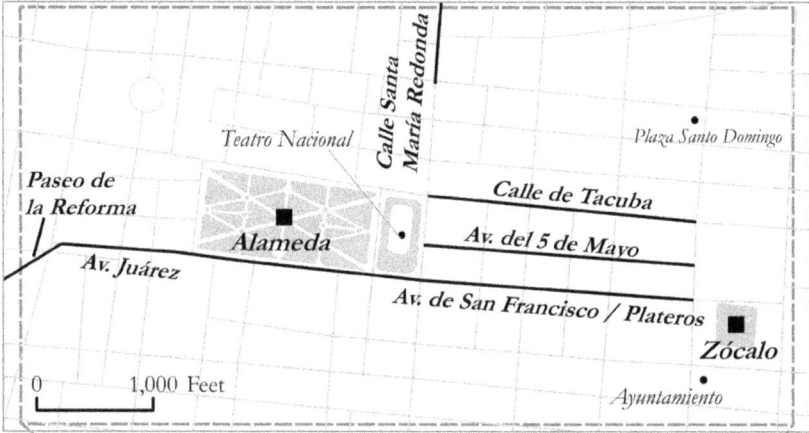

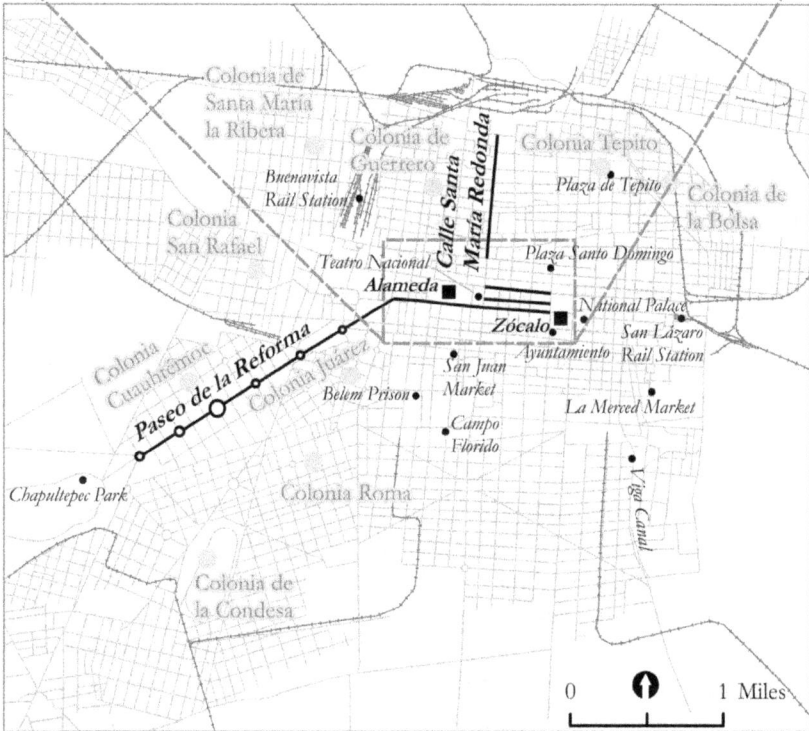

Map 3. Mexico City.

The city government targeted vecindades as hotspots of danger and disease. Stagnant water and perpetual dampness from rain, as well as lack of air circulation in rooms where people prepared and ate meals during the day and slept at night, made them the focus of health inspectors concerned that sicknesses such as typhus could spread to the entire city.[15] Expensive rents and low wages conspired to create overcrowding, worsening unhygienic conditions. Health officials found extreme cases where one-room apartments housed up to twenty people.[16] An 1895 study estimated that nearly a third of the city's population lived in tenements and that a single tenement building could house 600 to 800 people.[17] The vecindad's lack of privacy led reformers to conclude that it promoted promiscuity and moral decay among the poor.[18]

The elite's modernizing mission in Mexico City that equated material and moral improvement with civilization made it a showcase of Porfirian progress, luring eager foreign investors.[19] Glamorous new neighborhoods, feats of engineering, and the accoutrements of modernity (electric light, department stores, streetcars, police and firefighters, etc.) made the capital the outward face of the regime's mantra of "order and progress."[20] But there was another Mexico City hidden in plain sight: one of squalid neighborhoods and impoverished masses that threatened to expose, if not undo, the limited reach of the government's civilizing mission. Government officials, social reformers, moral crusaders, philanthropists, journalists, and a host of other critics saw the city as a den of vice, lasciviousness, and misery. The pastimes and proclivities of the poor, they argued, promoted sexual wantonness and perversity.

Mexico City was a den of sexual danger or delight, depending on one's perspective. Government officials accepted prostitution as a "necessary evil" that provided sex-seeking men, both married and single, a form of libidinal release that prevented more serious social disorder spurred by activities such as masturbation, rape, bestiality, pederasty, or sodomy.[21] The social hygienist Dr. Luis Lara y Pardo, in his 1908 study *La prostitución en México*, estimated that 10,000 women worked as registered prostitutes, and just as many clandestinely, in a city of less than 400,000 inhabitants. He found this number "truly scandalous" as Paris, a city five times larger than Mexico City, counted only 4,000.[22] An unofficial "red light district" existed just south of the Alameda and National Theater, housing brothels where women stood in doors and windows "displaying their wares."[23] North of the Alameda, the neighborhood Santa María la Redonda was notorious for prostitution.[24] But men could find prostitutes in all classes of neighborhoods in the commonest of cantinas and tenement apartments that served as *casas de cita* (rooms rented by the hour for sex).[25] Officials noted that outside of registered brothels, and indeed as a justification for their expansion, prostitutes and their johns caused scenes of moral depravity around the city as people had sex on "public streets as well as in some secluded locations, availed by the lack of light and police presence."[26] For the city's residents, prostitution was a ubiquitous part of everyday life. Men and women, even the most chaste according to Lara y Pardo, knew where to find bordellos. Young boys looked with "sick curiosity" toward those balconies and windows from where "whirlwinds of laughter, cries, and sensual music escaped."[27]

While prostitution, to social reformers and government officials, represented the most extreme sexual danger, a sense of moral crisis pervaded the era. Obscene literature found its way into schools and barracks, pornographic pictures were scrawled on the walls of buildings, and bawdy songs emanated from apartment patios.[28] Officials posted notices around the city warning residents that certain cigarette packages contained images "of the most repugnant obscenities"[29] and shut down theater shows that made too many *albures* (double entendre, often of a sexual nature).[30] The poorest residents bared their flesh too easily. Men and women exposed their genitals relieving themselves in public, and mothers sat on the streets visibly breastfeeding children.[31] Foreign travelers commented on the scantily clad indigenous women whose tattered shirts exposed their breasts.[32] Everywhere, it seemed, to bourgeois residents and visitors alike, the city offered too liberal a sexual license.

The city offered sundry social spaces where men and women gathered. The streets gave refuge from the crowded, smoke-filled viviendas where most people lived and, outside of work and the cantina, was where most spent their time. Loitering in the streets, though, meant possible harassment by beat cops who too willingly threw *pelados* (a derogatory term for lower-class, mixed-race, urban men) in the city jail.[33] Couples met and forged relationships while working in markets and on street corners as well as in the factories built in and around poor neighborhoods. In the working-class districts of the city, visitors were struck by the throngs of people buying, selling, and bartering around market stalls.[34] Peddlers, beggars, carters, and domestics, men and women, old and young, navigated crowded streets of impromptu market stands and food vendors and the din of organ-grinders, street musicians, and the shouts of paperboys. The streets served as a place to eat, chat, sleep, fight, get drunk, and, with no other option, have sex.

Many other amusements, traditional and new, sinister and civilized, continued in and around the city. While kept outside the city to the neighboring municipalities, well-established pastimes such as cockfighting and bullfighting (the latter of which returned in 1888 after a brief ban) drew crowds of all classes.[35] At the same time, a new consumer culture emerged, most notably demonstrated in the rise of department store shopping. While the poor continued to patronize the market stalls of Merced and Tepito, they nevertheless could also be found among more affluent crowds in new shopping centers such as the Palacio de Hierro opened in 1891.[36] Over a dozen religious holidays—such as Tuesday Carnival—as well as civic holidays commemorating independence, the constitution, and national heroes offered plenty of opportunities for drunkenness and ribaldry.[37] In an effort to combat public drunkenness, city officials passed several ordinances to close drinking establishments early on holidays.[38]

Puppet theater represented the "most popular and genuinely national" diversion, delighting audiences with well-recognized characters that dramatized shared everyday experience.[39] Picaresque comedic musicals—zarzuelas—were performed within one-act plays known as *tandas* that, from the 1870s onward, became increasingly popular among the middle and lower classes. These spectacles offered viewers obscene language (though often veiled in the double entendre of the *albur*), scantily clad dancers, and depictions of well-known national types such as beggars, carters, and dandies.[40] The cinematograph began to displace the opera and, for the working class, made inroads against popular theater. By 1900, just a few years after the first moving pictures were shown at the Cine Lumiere, cinematographs could be found all over the city in venues ranging from elegant and properly lit establishments that charged five pesos to ramshackle wood buildings that played short films alongside tandas and puppet theater at a much more affordable fifty centavos.[41]

Vecindades

Romantic relationships were formed in the tenement buildings where people lived or in the streets and factories where they worked. The cramped quarters of vecindades provided young people with ample opportunity to meet potential love interests. Drinking, fighting, carousing, and seduction all took place in the common patios. While the sanctity of domestic privacy emerged as a central tenet of middle-class values, the crowded tenement blurred the lines between public and private space.[42] Some vecindad occupants ran food stalls out of the street-facing *accesorias* or converted the open-air patios into makeshift eateries, creating opportunities for workers on their lunchbreaks to socialize with the women who lived there.[43] Anselmo Orajudo, for example, met his future lover while eating lunch at the vecindad where she lived.[44]

Despite the lack of domestic privacy, tenement living allowed young couples the opportunity to mask their relationships—because the interactions might not raise suspicion among family—as well as to take advantage of the absence of household members to initiate romantic and physical relationships in empty viviendas.[45] Melesio Ramírez, seventeen, and Pomposa Saucedo, fourteen, began an amorous relationship as they both lived in the same building, meeting for sexual trysts in one of their viviendas (it is unclear which) while their families were out. When discovered, the relationship was totally unknown to Pomposa's father.[46] In other cases, parents followed their suspicions when daughters disappeared. The mother of Luz Pineda suspected that a vecindad neighbor had taken interest in the thirteen-year-old girl. That he failed to return to his vivienda that night was enough evidence for the mother to report him to the authorities. The couple was eventually found weeks later, proving the mother's instinct correct.[47]

In a similar example, fifteen-year-old Cayetana López, late one night, left her vivienda to use the vecindad's common bathroom, or at least so she told her sister, Concepción. Instead, Cayetana sat weeping on the patio steps after a fight with her older sibling. It was there that her *novio* (boyfriend) Bernardo Rodríguez found her. Trying to console her, he proposed they run away together. When Cayetana failed to return home, the sister immediately suspected Bernardo who lived in the same vecindad. Concepción recalled how, earlier that day, she had witnessed the couple strolling down their street. Although not suspicious at the time, the fact that he did not return to his vivienda that night confirmed her fears that he had absconded with Cayetana. Two nights later, when she saw him return to his apartment, she called on a police officer stationed at a nearby corner to arrest him.[48] The social interactions within vecindades that blurred the public and private realms, in the imaginations of the elite, confirmed the promiscuity that existed in the close quarters of tiny apartments and common patios. The eroticization of the interiors of tenements became a fascination of the era's urban reportage.[49]

Social gatherings such as dances were popular community events that put residents in conflict with police and the city council. Especially on Sundays, loud music and bawdy lyrics could be heard emanating from build-

Figure 1. Penny press depiction of a neighborhood dance. *El Diablito Bromista,* May 17, 1908.

ing patios or cantinas as dances celebrated births, deaths, or saints' days.[50] Popular dances stood in stark contrast to those organized by the elite on the west side of town in grand ballrooms or elegant theaters that advertised as alcohol-free (although beer was often sold) and kept undesirables out with an entrance fee for men.[51] Popular dances, where the working class and poor went to *tirar el hilo* ("let the thread fly"), drew the ire of polite society critics who reproved cantinas that ignored city ordinances, staying open all night and allowing "the most dirty . . . scandalous orgies."[52] José Juan Tablada, renowned author of the era, recalled the "tawdriness" of neighborhood dances, their "vulgarity" and "infamous concupiscence."[53] The working-class penny presses portrayed popular dances in a similar vein, yet without the moral remonstrations. A humorous tale published in *El Diablito Bromista* described an example of vecindad revelry with couples "pressing hard up against each other to the sound of the dance," fueled by an array of available alcohol including "six buckets of pulque" and "a vat of punch laced with cheap whiskey and water."[54]

Vecindad festivities, especially dances, offered further opportunities for young couples to meet. Events were held in the common patios of tenement buildings, and bands played while residents danced and drank into the early hours of the morning. Dances allowed neighborhood youths to

Figure 2. Penny press depiction of a dance. *La Guacamaya,* April 6, 1903.

meet and court, usually under family surveillance, although that did not always deter romantic dramas as the case of Catalina González demonstrates. One afternoon, in a tenement building just south of the Alameda, a woman claiming to be the *amasia* (nonmarried partner) of Francisco Rivera, a local musician, approached Agustina Guzmán, a fifty-year-old widow. The mysterious woman protested that Agustina's daughter had been carrying on a sexual relationship with Francisco. In response, the shocked mother threatened Francisco that "things would not end well for him" if he continued to see her fifteen-year-old daughter, Catalina. Francisco Rivera, faced with the mother's accusation, denied any wrongdoing. Two weeks later Francisco found himself playing music at a dance held in the patio of the vecindad where the mother and daughter lived. Young Catarina took advantage of her mother's being ill in bed to abscond with the musician after a night of revelry.[55]

The vecindad's lack of privacy made romantic lives public knowledge. The one-room dwellings that housed the city's poor sometimes forced them to have sex surreptitiously while family, friends, and boarders were in the same room sleeping. Moral reformers often noted that cramped confines bred promiscuity and sexual license in children. Indeed, criminological studies of the period identify young people's early introduction to sex— whether that involved witnessing parents having sex in the same room or early sexual experiences with prostitutes—as a portent of criminal behavior.[56] Bárbara Torres told interrogators that while she slept on the floor, her half-sister's novio Ignacio Bejarano entered the room at 1 a.m. and the couple had sex while she pretended to sleep. The fact that her half-sister had not put up any resistance convinced Bárbara that it was done willingly.[57] In another example, José Jesús Martínez, as proof that he did not rape his own half-sister Juana, told officials that they had had sex in their one-room vivienda where, had she resisted, it would have surely awoken her father.[58] Yet, despite the concerns of moral reformers, such instances were rare. The city offered plenty of private spaces to make love. Empty streets, vacant fields, secluded woods, after-hours workplaces, and cheap lodgings, among other places, provided the poorest residents opportunities to seek erotic pleasure away from potentially prying eyes.

Labor and Love

Domestic labor represented, by far, the most common occupation of the girls and young women who appear in the court records. These women, popularly referred to as *garbanceras*, occupied a precarious social position. They came from poor families who placed them in the houses of the upper, middle, and, at times, even respectable working classes as a means to gain income.[59] Domestics were a common sight in the streets and markets of the city, buying their daily *mandado*, the foodstuffs for their employers' family meals as well as household goods (soap, candles, pots, etc.). Their time in public meant that they received considerable attention from men, attention that ranged from "love talk," flirting, and cat-calling to sexual assault.[60] Indeed, many domestics often ran away with men with whom they had begun relationships on the street. Especially in the homes of the elite, which could have a throng of servants, domestics developed amorous relationships with coworkers. At the same time, serving in the homes of others could be a brutalizing experience. Many young women complained of experiencing *mala vida* (the bad life) while serving. City newspapers often ran stories about thieving maids who abused their employer's trust, pilfering what they could or absconding in the middle of the night with the family's possessions. Newspaper ads for domestics consistently stressed "honesty" as the central requirement for employment. This negative popular attitude toward domestics meant that they endured verbal and physical abuse.[61] Many also suffered sexual abuse at the hands of their male employers.[62] Indeed, the cases adjudicated in Mexico City reveal exploited girls whose courtships allowed them to run away from abusive employers or use the courts to hold their abusers legally accountable.

Fourteen-year-old Joba Arenas had served for over a month at the house of an upper-class family who lived east of the Zócalo. One night as the girl slept, she awoke to find her employer, Don Jacinto Mejía, on top of her, covering her mouth with a rag. He threatened to kill her if she made a sound. After the assault, the girl reported what took place to Don Jacinto's wife who shoved her husband into the home's interior courtyard, locking the door and leaving him there for the night. "This was not the first time he had abused the maids," the furious wife told Joba. The next morning, the girl went to her mother and urged that she file a complaint against Don Jacinto.[63]

Another girl, originally from the State of Mexico, fifteen-year-old María Garduño, had been sent by her family to Mexico City to work for a prominent doctor. The young woman ran away from her service with a twenty-three-year-old silversmith, claiming that she had suffered repeated sexual abuse at the hands of the doctor. She told authorities that he had conducted three medical exams to verify her virginity: "the first time laying me down on his exam table, introducing his finger, and the second time while I was standing, causing me to bleed." When the young woman had insisted that the exams, at least, take place in the presence of the doctor's wife, he rebuffed the suggestion claiming it would make her "jealous."[64]

But it was not only employers who felt entitled to take liberties with their domestic staff. Twelve-year-old Josefa González was sexually assaulted by a houseguest while she slept in her quarters. A man visiting from Tlalpan entered the quarters and put his "finger in her parts," threatening to beat her if she screamed. The next day, Josefina's aunt noticed the girl was in a great deal of discomfort with hives covering her legs. Josefina divulged to her aunt what had taken place, blaming her condition on the assault. When the information reached Josefina's mother, she immediately reported it to a local police precinct. A week later, Tlalpan officials interrogated Bernabé Garibay who denied everything. He questioned why the young girl had not reported the crime to the owners of the house and had waited several days to alert her family. When a medical exam determined that the girl's hymen was intact, the case ended with the judge citing a lack of evidence.[65]

The sexual danger posed by domestic work was well known and assumed by most members of the working class. The mother of Joba Arenas, for instance, specifically noted in her testimony that she had been assured by the woman of the house that her daughter would be safe "as there were no men there other than her husband."[66] In their courtship romance, Dolores Sánchez admitted to her novio, Manuel Olivares, rather matter-of-factly, that she was not a virgin, having had a sexual relationship with a man at whose house she had served the previous year.[67] The penny press likewise assumed that sexual relations with household members were commonplace in domestic work. The poem "La Garbancera," published in *El Diablito Bromista*, offered a sanguine account of a pretty, young servant who buys her mandado at the Merced market while being disparaged by the female vendors jealous of her sexual relationship with the boss's handsome son who protects and respects her.[68]

The brutality, exploitation, and poor pay of domestic work caused many girls to abandon their positions without notice. In one such case, a Xochimilco judge initiated a rapto investigation when eight-year-old Modesta Martínez disappeared from the house where she served. The case ended days later when officials discovered that the girl, homesick, had simply returned to her family in San Francisco Tlatenco, fifteen kilometers away.[69] Similarly, while working at a home on Calle San Francisco, a wealthy area located between the Alameda and Zócalo, seventeen-year-old Ángela Villafuerte met Lino Pérez, a bricklayer who had found work at the same house. After two years of service, it appears that Ángela sought to escape, leaving the very next day after Lino promised marriage.[70] As with the case of Lino and Ángela, many domestic servants took advantage of their positions to assert command over their own lives. Domestic service put girls and young women in contact with a wide range of male workers outside the constrictions of paternal, or, in most cases, maternal authority. They forged relationships with boys and young men with whom they worked as well as with those they met in the streets while running errands.

Domestic service also brought young men and women together, especially in the homes of the well-to-do who employed large staffs to attend their families and, thereby, provided opportunities for young workers to start romantic relations or run away. Indeed, the conditions and poor pay received by domestics made their turnover high.[71] Opportunities to flee with newfound lovers offered an attractive alternative to domestic work. Manuel García and Felisa Sánchez met while working in the house of Víctor de Grande, a large manor in the historic center of the city. Manuel, one of the cooks, courted Felisa for four of the nine months the fourteen-year-old girl worked at the home. She eventually relented to his desires after he promised marriage and to "take her very far away where no one would see her again."

The young couple's romance was assisted by another cook, a woman named Luz Becerra, who would unlock the kitchen door to allow Manuel into the hallway where Felisa slept on the floor. Manuel and Felisa would have sex not far from where Luz slept. At around 4 a.m., Luz would again open and then lock the door behind Manuel as he returned to his quarters. When the family learned of the young couple's relationship, as well as of the woman who facilitated their encounters, they fired both Manuel and Luz, keeping the youngster Felisa on as the *criada* (domestic servant).[72]

Feliciana Concha Jiménez and Paula Valencia both worked as domestic servants at the house of the Buenrostro family. Each had run away with a *peón* (day laborer) working at the same house. The large staff at the house proved a source of confusion in the legal case where erroneous testimony landed the wrong peón in prison for the rapto of Feliciana. As witnesses had mixed-up the two ongoing romantic relationships among the staff, the rapto of Paula was discovered only *through* the investigation of Feliciana's whereabouts.[73]

Sisters Petronila and Guadalupe Villegas served at the same house in the south of the city. Petronila noted that her sister left to run an errand at the behest of the *ama* (patron) and failed to return. Petronila immediately suspected a neighborhood gendarme who had been "chasing [Guadalupe] for some time." Indeed, according to the testimony, while she was out on her errand, Guadalupe was approached by the gendarme, Cristóbal Buendía, who offered to take her to his home on Campo Florido with a promise of marriage.[74]

Just as domestic labor threw young men and women together, the presence of the unskilled working poor in the streets of the city provided ample opportunity for couples to meet, court, and, usually, drink alcohol. Young women who hawked wares in the street or sold food in markets or out of vecindad *accesorias* (street-facing rooms) met their future lovers while eking out a living. On a Sunday afternoon, fifteen-year-old Adelaida Lozano was selling lottery tickets in the Zócalo. Her novio of two months, fourteen-year-old Eusebio Díaz, invited her to drink pulque at a nearby cantina. The couple then decided to live together as a justification, it seems, to initiate sexual relations. Eusebio "rented a room for a week," paying fifty centavos, but did not get his money's worth. Adelaida's mother apprehended them the next day near La Merced market.[75] The city's cheap and easily accessible alcohol served to ease inhibitions between couples, but not just to have sex. It could also spur more drastic actions such as commitment to a domestic partnership that declared adult independence. In other cases, though, the use of alcohol laid bare its hazards for women. Merced Garfias sold tortillas on the west side of the Alameda. There, Juan Molina approached her and invited her to "drink a cup." Because he had been courting her, she agreed. After several drinks and feeling drunk, as she told the judge, she lost all recollection and awoke at Juan's home, realizing that "he had made use of her."[76]

The rise of factory work dramatically remade the lives and lifestyles of the urban poor. Industrial job opportunities lured migrants from across the country to Mexico City in search of work and wages. As a result, the number of factory workers rose 355 percent between 1895 and 1910, especially in the booming sectors of tobacco and textile production. One-third of those workers were women.[77] The rise of mechanization undercut the traditional craft economy, pushing artisans toward proletarianization, albeit in small workshop settings geared toward new urban infrastructure and services.[78] Yet, despite the growing industrialization of the city, the majority of the workforce toiled as unskilled and casual labor. The 1910 census estimated that 65 percent of women were employed in unskilled positions such as domestic service, laundry, and the food and clothing sectors.[79]

Factory work provided a common setting for forming new romantic relationships. Parents and guardians were aware of the dangers and temptations that such work offered young women. The mixed-sex environment made the factory floor a "sexualized space" that could jeopardize the sexual honor of women.[80] For example, Francisco Nájera embarrassedly admitted that he had—with great reluctance—allowed his daughter to work at the match factory in Colonia Valle Gómez, in the far north of the city, as he was in desperate need of funds. It did not take long for his fears to come true when his daughter failed to return home one night. The next morning, he walked to the factory and found his daughter working her usual shift. He interrogated her to learn that one of her coworkers had taken her to a hotel in the center of the city where they had had sex and returned to work the following morning.[81]

Josefina Cárdenas, for eight months, had worked at a match factory in Colonia Morelos, south of Tepito market. During that time, twenty-one-year-old Manuel Aguirre began to court her. Manuel was new to the city. A recent migrant from the State of Mexico and a saddler by trade, he found work selling tickets at a theater to make ends meet. Like so many poor migrants to the city, he made his home in the squatter settlement that would become Colonia de la Bolsa. He told officials that, while courting Josefina, she had complained about her "mala vida." She suffered beatings from her mother and sexual abuse from her stepfather. On October 29, 1889, Manuel went to visit his *novia* (girlfriend) and encountered a scandal at their vecindad apartment. Josefina's mother, apparently drunk, was beating her daughter, which forced Manuel to intervene. He reprimanded the mother who responded, "if you are a man, then take her." And so he did. But, after more than two weeks, Josefina's family seemed to regret their decision and had Manuel arrested for rapto. Providing his testimony, Manuel maintained that he planned to marry Josefina. When asked specifically about the status of Josefina's virginity, he told officials that she had already had sexual relations with another man who worked at the match factory. Placated by the promise of marriage, Josefina's mother dropped the charges.[82]

Opportunities to meet love interests while working at a factory, when coupled with the diversions and anonymity the city could provide, allowed for secret romances hidden away from the prying eyes of parents and, as in the following example, a man's wife. Twenty-two-year-old Vicente Guerrero and fourteen-year-old Guadalupe Salcedo met on the factory floor of the Cigarrera Mexicana. After her first day at work, Vicente approached her, asking if she wanted to go for a stroll. The two hit it off and continued to meet after work most days. They spent hours talking and walking around colonia Hidalgo. Afterward, they would canoodle under a tree in an empty field near the cigarette factory where they worked. Guadalupe, who started work at 6:30 a.m. and finished at 2:30 p.m., would then stroll with Vicente until 7:30 p.m. She always made sure to return to her vecindad accompanied by a female friend so as not to arouse her mother's suspicions. On Sundays, the couple would amble through Chapultepec Park, Tacubaya, and the Jardín Porfirio Díaz. Vicente would also take her to dances at the popular locale known as La Granja. To go out, especially late at night, Guadalupe would lie and tell her mother she was meeting girlfriends. One day, while dropping off her lunch at the factory, Guadalupe's younger brother saw something that exposed their relationship, but he kept it secret.

On the Tuesday of Carnival, 1906, Guadalupe and Vicente, after hours walking the streets of Tacubaya, returned to the empty field where they often spent time after work. According to Guadalupe, "after much begging" and "because he promised marriage" she consented to having sex with Vicente. Afterward, lamenting her decision and loss of virginity, Guadalupe began to cry. Vicente, to console her, swore "by the ashes of his father" that they would marry. Convinced of his good will, she had sex with him again. That night, when she returned home, Guadalupe's mother angrily reported that a woman claiming to be Vicente's wife had appeared at their house demanding that Guadalupe stop "strolling" with her husband. Immediately Guadalupe and her mother went to the local police precinct and reported Vicente for the crime of rapto.

When brought before authorities, Vicente offered an account almost identical to Guadalupe's until he reached the topics of sex and marriage. He had never made a promise of marriage, he insisted, as Guadalupe "knew perfectly" that he was married ecclesiastically and had three children. Vicente then accused Guadalupe of having had a relationship with another factory worker named Juan Quintanar. Upset at being rejected by Guadalupe, Juan had angrily revealed to her that Vicente was already married, to which Guadalupe allegedly replied, "I don't mind being his second woman." Guadalupe acknowledged her relationship with Juan Quintanar but stayed mute on the other allegation.

The judge, seemingly confounded by the apparent lack of parental supervision, called Guadalupe's mother in for questioning. To his interrogation the mother insisted that she had not had any idea about the relationship, as both Guadalupe and her brother had kept it secret. Guadalupe was always accompanied by one of her two friends, Concha and Sara, and so never appeared suspicious. Even when she found blood on her daughter's underskirt the night of Carnival, she assumed it was menstruation. When the medical exam concluded that Guadalupe was indeed recently deflowered, the judge decided to continue the investigation, which led Vicente to hire a lawyer.

The defense attorney put forward a scathing attack on Guadalupe's honor, and especially that of her family. He argued that Vicente had not stolen her away using deceit or seduction, but that Guadalupe had willingly gone with him to dances, secluded locations, and outside of the city of her own free will. She had repeatedly lied to her parents about going out with her girlfriends, which showed her dishonesty but also her agency in the matter. She returned home "at all hours of the night" and was "never reprimanded for her excursions." The defense attorney's argument hinged on Guadalupe's inability to resist the allure of the city, both its amusements and the anonymity it offered, as well as her parents' failure to protect their child from its corrupting influence. The case file ends with the judge ordering the imprisonment of Vicente in preparation for a trial.[83]

By 1900, although most women continued to work as unskilled laborers, those working in factories outnumbered women found in domestic service.[84] New opportunities for wage work, as demonstrated in the case of Guadalupe, allowed young women earnings and independence that eroded family control over their leisure time and sexual choices. As has been suggested for turn-of-the-century New York City, independent working girls helped foster a new sexual and commercial culture freer of domestic obligations and family supervision than was possible before opportunities for wage work emerged.[85] Industrialization, in particular, as demonstrated in the European context, served to shift daughters' balance of power within the family and promoted their personal freedom and sexual openness.[86]

Strolling and Sexual Possibility

Once couples had started amorous relations, their strolling the city together (*pasear*) represented one of the principal pastimes of courtship as well as the most common way that romantically involved men and women used the streets. City expansion and the development of transportation infrastructure in the late nineteenth century opened up popular new spaces. The municipalities of Tacuba, Tacubaya, and Guadalupe Hidalgo (home to the Villa de Guadalupe) became highly frequented destinations accessible in mere hours rather than a in day's walk. Because strolling encompassed urban mobility, social space, and the public gaze, many young couples took advantage of new technologies (for example, trams or cinematographs) to publicly avow their romance while, at the same time, doing so away from the scrutiny of neighbors and family.[87] The Zócalo and Alameda remained common strolling locations, as they had been since the colonial era, especially for the middle and upper class for whom the ritual was meant to publicly affirm one's relationship with a family-approved suitor.[88] Especially on Sundays, couples also strolled around the Viga Canal and Chapultepec Park.[89] Yet during the Porfiriato, public space became increasingly democratized as the urban poor pushed into territory that had once more exclusively belonged to the well-to-do. *La Patria* newspaper, in 1897, lamented that the Alameda's usual crowd of respectable strolling couples had been overrun by "social zeros" and "tenement lotharios."[90] The author clearly described a shifting spatial and social mobility that gave the city street its allure, danger, and democracy.

Couples' practice of wandering together, since colonial times, had been pervaded with a sense of sexual possibility.[91] In Porfirian Mexico City, couples' strolls often led them to one of the many *pulquerías* (businesses selling pulque, an alcoholic beverage made from the fermented sap of the maguey) that dotted working-class neighborhoods and, after that, to the cheap hotels, *casas de huéspedes* (boarding houses), and *mesones* (flophouses) strategically located near those very same drinking establishments. The financially strained bohemians who frequented less expensive boarding houses brought to these places an atmosphere and lifestyle associated with *plena fiesta* (an outright party).[92] *Casas de cita*, which rented rooms by the hour specifically for sex, were interspersed among vecindad apartments. One young woman, after a stroll with her intended, was disappointed to learn that the apartment to which he took her was not "the house where they would live," but a casa de cita.[93] Testimony makes clear that a couples' wandering together was a public and personal declaration of romantic commitment. One witness, for example, doubted the relationship between the couple in question as he "had seen them talking, but never saw them strolling."[94] For working-class couples, strolling assumed a certain expectation, or at least the possibility, of sex. One defendant specified that he had invited his novia for a stroll "but without any bad intentions."[95] Another noted that although he and his novia had gone on several strolls "he never touched her."[96] When a young woman insisted that he take her for a stroll, one man saw this as a clear invitation to sex, immediately taking her to a "casa de cita."[97]

Strolling, while nevertheless a public statement for couples, took place with or without parental approval and commonly led to the initiation of sex, both consensual and not. Most commonly in cases of consensual sex, wandering the city until late often led couples to return home to find vecindad doors shut for the night. Often involving the consumption of pulque or other alcoholic beverages at cantinas or cafés, it also led to inebriated youngsters arriving home to angry parents. To avoid such confrontations, couples frequently agreed to spend the night at inexpensive hotels or, worse yet, at mesones, the city's cheapest form of temporary lodging.[98] The middle-class merchant, Manuel Navarro, found himself arrested for a rapto he did not commit when a stroll to Tacubaya with his novia ran late. After taking Elena Maldonado for a stroll, something he did regularly with her parents' approval, he failed to get his novia home before 10 p.m., having missed the last train from Tacubaya. With the vecindad doors shut for the night, the couple decided to walk the city until morning. Manuel, who returned Elena home early the next day, was promptly arrested by a nearby gendarme on the mother's orders.[99]

Numerous cases followed a similar pattern: young couples having sex after a stroll. Eighteen-year-old Belén Millares went out to run an errand for her mother. She encountered her novio, thirty-one-year-old mechanic Jesús Salazar and, "seduced by her affection for him," agreed to go on a stroll. From San Antonio de Abad in the south of the city, the couple walked to the Santo Domingo Church, the Zócalo, the Alameda, and Paseo la Reforma. Arriving back at the Santo Domingo Church at 8:30 p.m. and still far from home, Jesús suggested they stay for the night at the Hotel Vienna, a well-regarded establishment near the Zócalo. The couple had sex that night, a decision that instigated a rapto investigation to determine whether the mechanic had used a false promise of marriage to convince Belén to sleep with him.[100] In another example, Alberto Cortés convinced his girlfriend, Juliana Zamorano, to meet him in the Alameda by making a promise of marriage and vowing to make arrangements with her mother. Trusting his word, she met him and they "drank several cups of sherry" at a nearby establishment. The couple then strolled the Alameda until midnight when Alberto took her to a house with an "empty room . . . where only an old man lived." Juliana appears here to describe a casa de cita as the location where she "had the carnal act."[101]

Some strolls were less complicated. Alejo Ramos visited the home of his novia Vicenta García who lived in the Tacuba neighborhood of Santa Julia. Offering to take her for a stroll, they ended up in one of the many secluded fields located between Tacuba and the city where they had sex.[102]

Cantinas and Alcohol

The many cantinas and pulquerías found across the city offered romantic couples a setting to let inhibitions slide in the often-raucous atmosphere that characterized popular drinking establishments.[103] The penny press acknowledged pulquerías as the universally accepted place of socialization for the popular classes. Far from male-only spaces, the penny presses portrayed them as frequented as much by women as by men, whether they went with male partners or female friends.[104] Not simply the fancy of penny press writers, the social world evidenced in the testimony of couples confirms the primacy of pulquerías, at least in the courtship process.[105] Cantinas and pulquerías served as important venues where the poor gathered to eat, drink, and talk, forging social connections among the people of the street, market, workshop, and factory.[106]

In 1901, the city registered 1,253 pulquerías, one for every 307 inhabitants (by contrast the city counted thirty-four bakeries),[107] and its residents consumed 500,000 liters of pulque a day.[108] Additionally, hundreds of taverns and *fondas* (inns) with pulque licenses could be found throughout the city.[109] Officials waged an endless war against the popular class's predilection for pulque, seeing alcohol as the root cause of subaltern criminality.[110]

From the 1880s onward, strict regulations aimed to lessen threats to social order by requiring pulquerías to open only during normal working hours (6 a.m. to 6 p.m.), to keep their front doors shut, to remove tables and musical venues, and to ensure that patrons consumed alcohol with food and only inside establishments.[111] Treating these places central to working-class culture, the penny press regularly proffered fictional, humorous dialogues between men and women at, on their way to, or just leaving pulquerías.[112]

The easy availability of alcohol and the popularity of drinking establishments shaped a courtship culture where intoxication served to loosen sexual inhibition. A night of drunken sex could lead to marital commitments made in the morning. For example, María Burgos told officials that her novio Simón Peralta had gotten her drunk with three cups of tequila before taking her to a hotel where she lost her virginity. The next day, Simón went to visit her mother in Colonia Guerrero, seeking approval to marry María, to which the mother agreed.[113] Similarly, one afternoon, Magdalena Galicia passed by the San Juan Plaza, several blocks south of the Alameda. She encountered her novio of almost one year, Alberto Sierra, who pulled her into a cantina and invited her to drinks. The couple then agreed to walk to his vecindad on Salto de Agua where he "made use of her . . . with her full will."[114]

Some cases make known the bohemian lifestyle of working-class youths who roamed the city in raucous revelry, patronizing several drinking establishments in one day. In the prefecture of Azcapoltzalco, Carlos Morales and Benita Pineda walked arm-in-arm down the street and came across their friend Petra Martínez who invited them to a pulquería. The trio, after several hours, left the establishment inebriated (*trastornados*). Carlos was so inebriated that, when he walked onto the street, he stumbled and fell into an enchilada stand, causing enough of a scandal that police arrested all three of them. When Benita failed to return home that night, her family initiated a rapto investigation against Carlos, a crime he did not commit.[115]

Sixteen-year-old Luisa Ramírez sold tortillas at the Plazuela de Aguilitas, a few blocks from the Merced market. According to two witnesses who worked at the barber shop across the street, Luisa often left her tortilla basket (*chiquihuite*) for the barbers to keep safe while she went to a local pulquería. On the afternoon of February 2, 1898, she again stopped by the barber shop, asking to leave her basket. The barbers agreed and Luisa went to the pulquería. When Luisa failed to return to pick up her basket by 9:30 p.m., one of the barbers, Darío Arteaga, knowing her address, brought it back to her family. Luisa's sister, suspecting that another barber was her abductor, headed to the shop the next day with a police officer to have twenty-seven-year-old Emilio Socio arrested. As it turned out, Emilio was not Luisa's love interest, and she had instead gone to the pulquería, and then a hotel, with an unnamed man who was courting her (la pretendía).[116] Like those of Benita in the previous example, Luisa's actions show the kinds of freedom and diversion the city afforded young women, who openly frequented pulquerías with their lovers seemingly unconcerned that it would affect their public reputations.

Young women often blamed drunkenness for their decision to have sex, described in some cases as an assault or, in other cases, as a loss of inhibition. Fifteen-year-old Juana Canchola claimed that her novio Marciano Magos had invited her to a cantina to drink with some friends in Colonia Guerrero. He made her imbibe a "green liquid" (perhaps absinthe) that made her lose her senses and inhibition, which allowed him to take her virginity.[117] Authorities and litigants alike accepted the connection between the loss of one's will and alcohol. For example, to convince a judge that she had had consensual sex with her novio, Luz Saucedo stated specifically that he "did not force her or give her alcohol."[118] Legal authorities also treated alcohol and drunkenness as a mitigating factor for men. Judges routinely recorded whether or not the male defendants hauled into police precincts for sexual crimes (rapto, estupro, violación) appeared inebriated.

Drinking and drunkenness, although common to both sexes, nevertheless had more severe consequences for women. In a night of intoxicated revelry, lowered inhibition might later lead women to face venereal disease, unwanted pregnancy, or dangerous childbirth alone. Inebriation could put young women in dangerous situations where they were vulnerable to sexual assault. Poor and working-class women and girls felt it was acceptable to publicly carouse with men but did not think that their interactions should be interpreted as invitations to sex. The 1908 case of fourteen-year-old Isabel Beltrán shows that while young women might expect clear boundaries between merrymaking and sex, alcohol provided opportunities to overstep those limits. Brothers Felipe Hernández, nineteen years old, and Salvador Hernández, sixteen, sat in their one-room vecindad apartment drinking jars of pulque on a Monday morning. Both identified as bricklayers but were only erratically employed and lived in the rough-and-tumble neighborhood of La Bolsa. At some point in the afternoon, Isabel—who lived two buildings over—visited to return a pot her family had borrowed. The brothers claimed they had invited her to drink pulque and she agreed. Isabel drank five jugs and found herself, like the brothers, heavily intoxicated. As the trio drank, Isabel's older sister appeared and began reprimanding her for not returning home. When she hit Isabel in the back with a brick, Felipe decided to hide her until her sister left. The incident persuaded the brothers to walk to the Tepito neighborhood and find their aunt who had more pulque as well as access to a storage shed where they could sleep.

Marina Hernández heard a noise outside her apartment door and found her nephews there, "scandalously drunk" and accompanied by a girl. Felipe beseeched his aunt to let them sleep in her building's storage shed, for which she had a key. When his aunt worried about leaving a young girl alone with him, Felipe assuaged her concerns by telling her that he and Isabel planned to marry. Marina agreed, reluctantly, to let them use the shed. Sometime later, she returned to find all three of them asleep, and she covered Felipe and Isabel—who were lying together—with a serape before locking the door. Hours later a gendarme arrived, demanding that Marina open the storage shed as there were youngsters inside making a racket. The officer then ordered Marina, as well as the three youths, to the police precinct. After spending the night in jail, all four were released.

But, later that day, Isabel and her mother appeared at the precinct accompanied by a police officer who had Marina and Felipe in his custody. The mother explained that while Felipe and Isabel were drunk, Felipe had deflowered her daughter with the help of Marina. She accused Felipe of estupro and Marina of being an accomplice. She further demanded an immediate medical examination of her daughter to show that she had been deflowered. Isabel recounted the previous day's events. She explained that even though she had agreed to drink some pulque with the brothers, she had later tried to leave. Her egress was prevented by Felipe who "tackled" her and forced her to accompany the brothers to Marina's house, where she drank more pulque. By this time, Isabel explained, she had "lost her senses." After Marina locked them in the storage shed, Felipe "laid [Isabel] on the floor . . . opened her legs and introduced his member." This caused her "much pain" and, as a result, she "let out strong screams, which is surely why Marina" was forced to unlock the door. She insisted that she had no romantic relationship with Felipe whatsoever and wanted him punished by the law.

The brothers gave nearly identical accounts of the day. Both claimed that Isabel had willingly joined their revelry. They also agreed that they had gone to Marina's house after Isabel's sister had arrived and hit her with a brick. So that her sister "wouldn't fuck her up" (*no la chingara*), Isabel had agreed to go to Marina's house. Salvador testified that, once locked in the shed, he immediately fell asleep. Felipe claimed he had asked Isabel to have sex. She agreed, and Felipe "without losing time . . . made use of her." He found her to be "like any woman of the world." When pressed by the judge, Felipe acknowledged having made a *verbal* promise of marriage because he did not know how to read or write.

Because of conflicting testimonies from the Hernández family members (Felipe, Salvador, Marina) on the one hand and Isabel on the other, the judge performed several *careos* to attempt to clear up matters. Marina and Salvador both maintained that Isabel willingly accompanied and drank with the brothers, a claim Isabel challenged. Felipe and Isabel, when brought face-to-face and shown the discrepancies in their testimonies, produced a longer back-and-forth. Felipe insisted that they had been in an amorous relationship for three years and that, weeks earlier, he had even asked Isabel's mother for permission to marry. Isabel denied a relationship but conceded that Felipe had asked her to marry, a proposal she had flatly rejected. Again, she insisted that Felipe be punished for his crime. In response, Felipe contended that Isabel was not a *doncella* (virgin) as "no blood came out." Though Felipe confirmed that Isabel "did cry or scream," he claimed that this occurred when she realized she was locked inside the shed, not because of sexual pain. Isabel insisted she was a "girl" until that day. A medical exam corroborated Isabel's assertions, concluding that she had been recently deflowered. Then, abruptly, Isabel and her mother appeared before the judge to desist from their accusation because Isabel was now "disposed to marry."[119]

Isabel's sudden about-face demonstrates how cheap amusements and revelry could easily yield serious, even life-altering, consequences. Facing the potential costs of unplanned sexual initiation—pregnancy and single motherhood or a tarnished public reputation that *might* hinder future conjugal prospects—Isabel and her mother likely agreed that marriage, and the financial commitment it offered, provided the best possible outcome. Indeed, Isabel's sister so aggressively reprimanding her—beating her for drinking with the brothers— and Marina's worries about letting a young woman occupy the shed with her nephews suggest that while the city's drinking culture included both sexes, women were acutely aware of the potentially serious repercussions of drinking alone with men.

Manuela González learned a similar lesson and was forced to rely on the often-unsupportive legal system to seek justice. Refugio Sánchez, a seventeen-year-old day laborer (*jornalero*), found Manuela on the streets while she was running an errand. Refugio claimed Manuela was his *novia* although, when asked by officials, he could not recall her last name. He accompanied her to drop off some clothes at a tenement in the south of the city. When she emerged from the building, Refugio, who waited outside, suggested they go to a pulquería. As it turned out, the couple visited three different establishments before taking a long walk to the isolated Calzada de la Piedad—the city's southern edge where it blended into countryside. There, the couple had sex "three times," Manuela "not resisting because of her state of drunkenness" as she later told officials. Afterward, the pair walked back to the city, stopping at the cemetery Panteón de Campo Florido. Saying he would be right back, Refugio deserted Manuela who, after an hour, found somewhere to sleep until morning. The next day Manuela ran into her cousin on the street and, after telling her the story, the two agreed to go to a local police precinct and make a complaint against Refugio. Both the judge and, eventually, a jury viewed Refugio's actions as so flagrant that he was found guilty of rapto and sentenced, as a minor, to a reduced sentence of two years and eight months in a juvenile prison.[120] While young women surely found freedom and amusement in the bohemian lifestyle that the city availed, especially considering the reprieve it offered from the daily drudgery suffered by the poor, it was always tempered by the risk of sexual danger or abandonment.

Because the city's working classes chose cantinas and pulquerías as places to socialize and unwind, as more women entered the factories, they, too, visited the same locales for after-work gatherings. As the next three examples demonstrate, the sense of independence and adulthood that accompanied entering the workforce led young women to patronize alcohol-serving venues after their shifts, sometimes with male coworkers and sometimes with novios who worked elsewhere. Eighteen-year-old Valeriana Cadena and fourteen-year-old Ángela del Villar became friends while working at a factory located several blocks north of the Alameda. One night, after work, they went to a cantina with their two would-be suitors and, following several drinks, each departed with their beau to different locations to have sex.[121] Likewise, Beatriz Gutiérrez, at the end of the day, prepared to leave the box factory on San Antonio de Abad where she worked. Her coworker José Aguilar approached her and offered to walk her home. She agreed. Along the way, they stopped at a cantina to have some drinks (*tomar unas copas*). Drunk, she lost consciousness. When she sobered up by midnight, she could not recall whether the "act of coitus was verified" although she had found herself inside a casa de cita.[122] María Guadalupe Rodríguez similarly left the cigarette factory where she worked, taking her usual route[123] and passing the vecindad of José Méndez. María had shown much interest in the young man. So much so, that José's mother had twice reprimanded her for seeking him out. That day, José and María agreed to go to a cantina for a drink. The pair, apparently out for a night of revelry, patronized three different establishments, drinking "twelve cups of *rompope*" (eggnog) and then sherry. Feeling intoxicated (*trastornada*), María agreed to have sex with José at a hotel. Noting that she had much "affection" for José, a sentiment he shared as well, the couple agreed to marry, a demand made by María's family.[124] The claim to adult independence that wage labor offered women allowed them to participate in the same after-work pastimes—especially the culture of after-work drinking—as their male counterparts. These working-class venues brimmed with sexual possibility and the allure of asserting adulthood. Yet, as demonstrated by the example of José and María, a rapto arrest could easily dampen such youthful adventures.

The Streets at Night

As a safety precaution vecindad doors usually closed for the night by 10 p.m. Young couples used this routine as a ready excuse to wander the streets of the city and its surrounding municipalities and rural areas into the wee hours. Natalia Cosio told her novio, after a night spent at the Teatro Arbeu and various cantinas, that her building's doors would be closed and that they would have to find a hotel.[125] Young women, especially, noted in their testimonies that they failed to return home because the vecindad door had been shut for the night. Some feared angry reactions from their parents or guardians who might scold or beat them for arriving late. Sisters Rosario and Consuela Verdi had spent much of the day strolling the streets and drinking at cafés with the brothers Ignacio and José Cosio. By 9 p.m., the brothers offered to accompany the girls home but were told that their mother would beat them and lock them up for several days if they returned late. Ignacio proposed that the group stay at a casa de huéspedes north of the Zócalo.[126] In a dramatic example, when María Alcántara failed to return home one night, her mother had her novio Alejandro Alvarado arrested the next day. As he testified and María later confirmed, they had strolled the city streets so late that María feared being reprimanded by her mother. Alejandro took her to his aunt's house to spend the night while he went back home. The case was concluded immediately as sex had not taken place.[127] Similarly, Manuel Pérez and Ángela García had spent the day strolling around the center of the city. They stopped at a cantina for refreshments, where Manuel had two beers and Ángela a rompope. As it was getting late, the couple rushed to Ángela's vecindad only to find the front door locked. Manuel contemplated taking Ángela to his home, but his middle-class family would have found it "an inappropriate hour." Instead, the couple rented a room at the Hotel Juárez, one block west of the city's main cathedral.[128]

In some instances, staying out too late to return home spurred young women to leave their families altogether. When María Rodríguez stayed out beyond door-locking time with her novio, she "determined to leave her home" and agreed to his long-offered marriage proposal.[129] Because she feared her father would reprimand her for returning late, María Gutiérrez also decided to run away with her beau after they lost track of time talking on the street.[130] Fourteen-year-old Delfina Pérez told officials that Albino Hernández forced her to walk down Guerrero street until 7 p.m., pulling her along by her shawl. Afraid that it was too late to return home, Albino took Delfina to stay at the house of a friend where they had sex. The couple made marital life for the next month until Delfina's family discovered them.[131] As these examples suggest, the decision to emancipate from parental authority appears to have been a drastic, even a desperate, action. The extremity of this choice highlights the gravity with which parents regarded a daughter's failure to return home at an appropriate hour. In the tenement buildings where gossip so freely flowed, appearing in front of one's neighbors to lack parental control over children caused shame and diminished public standing.[132] Children were well aware of this dynamic, too, repeatedly noting in the judicial record examples of corporal punishment for arriving home after hours. When a daughter did not return home, sexual activity was assumed, an assumption that readily led to rumors and attacks on family reputation.[133]

Community Knowledge and Personal Secrets

Porfirian Mexico City offered, at once, both anonymity and a lack of privacy. On the one hand, young couples could run away from parental restrictions and prying neighbors by hiding in one of the dozen working-class eastside neighborhoods or the newly emerging barrios at the edges of the city. On the other hand, the cramped quarters of vecindades, with their thin walls and notoriously nosey *porteras* (housekeepers) who collected rents and controlled access to buildings, made protecting intimate information nearly impossible.[134] The vecindad's lack of privacy made some relationships common knowledge to neighbors and, eventually, family. Indeed, the initiation of rapto proceedings within these settings demonstrates how parents and guardians tapped into a network of information based on neighborhood gossip to locate runaway youths and bring young men to account before authorities. Several cases reveal that while parents might be ignorant of their children's relationships, building tenants, housekeepers, neighbors, and siblings often knew a great deal about such amorous goings-on and acted as informants when pressed. Indeed, it was community gossip and the everyday politics of the vecindad—imbued with its own social and cultural expectations and values—that determined status and influence at the community level and helps explain why parents so often sought legal arbitration in the face of well-known knowledge that deflowered daughters rarely received justice. Gossip worked in working-class communities as a self-policing mechanism where sexuality and morality were concerned.[135] The very act of reporting a crime could salvage the parents' public reputation.[136] As has been shown for Paris's urban poor, community standing could be a matter of economic survival when hard times forced people to rely on mutual aid in matters of credit, food, and housing.[137]

The parents and guardians who searched for runaway couples most often managed to locate them. They were usually found in the same neighborhood or another one of the city's working-class barrios. In some cases, parents succeeded in finding runaway couples who had eloped to another municipality or state. For example, María Enríquez, an intrepid mother, learned that her daughter had run away with a man to Oaxaca. A letter provided by an "unknown woman" from the vecindad offered enough information for the mother to have authorities bring her daughter back to the capital and for the man to be charged.[138] Those looking for their missing children relied on a network of local information, mainly gossip, that circulated through the vecindad or wider barrio. Information flowed through neighborhoods in a variety of ways. Jilted wives and cuckolded men often learned of their partners' betrayal through the loose lips of neighbors. Couples used friends as go-betweens but also paid neighbors or carters to pass along messages, a practice essential to youngsters coordinating elopements. Domestic servants often held vast repositories of knowledge about private family affairs gathered by overhearing conversations.

Parents often told officials that after "making investigations," "learning from a neighbor," or, simply, being "given information" that they had located runaway couples. For example, Petra Carrión, mother of a runaway fourteen-year-old daughter, told officials that "despite making investigations, I could not find her whereabouts until eight days later when I found her on a street in Colonia Santa Julia. I went looking for her after receiving [new] information."[139] One mother, searching for her missing fourteen-year-old daughter, Gregoria Carrizales, received valuable information from the occupants of the building. The doorman informed her that he saw Arnulfo Lara, a man he knew from the neighborhood, escort her from the cigarette factory across the street where Gregoria worked. They then took the *rumbo* (route) to Plaza de San Pablo in the south of the city. Continuing her investigation, Petra learned from a vecindad neighbor that on the previous Sunday Arnulfo had visited Gregoria, bringing her *obsequios* (gifts) of fruit. The neighbor proved even more useful, providing an address that allowed Gregoria's mother to have Arnulfo arrested.[140]

Jilted wives also tapped into information networks to learn about their adulterous husbands. Luis Morales, a married merchant from San Luis Tlatilco in the State of Mexico, came to the municipality of Tacuba regularly on business. In June 1905, he began an extramarital sexual relationship with Guadalupe Vilchis. His wife "learned from loose voices" that her husband had "another woman." She planned to travel to the city and confront Guadalupe with the fact that "she was legally married to Luis Morales and moreover had a family." Luis, at another point in the investigation, told officials that after the relationship with Guadalupe ended, he learned from a muleteer that the girl was back with her family and planning to marry.[141]

Guadalupe Rodríguez, who earned a living making and selling tortillas on the streets not far from the Viga Canal, returned home one night to find her fifteen-year-old daughter missing. As she told officials, she had no idea why she had left or where she had gone. An investigation of the vecindad brought to her attention that a neighbor, José Hernández, had not returned to his apartment. She recalled that he had been "stirring up" her daughter (*la andaba inquietando*), but Guadalupe had not suspected a relationship. The mother gathered useful information from neighbors that allowed her to locate the couple on the street San Antonio de Abad, several kilometers away. The networks of neighborhood information and gossip that allowed Guadalupe to locate her daughter also served as her justification in opposing José's intentions toward her. She opposed the relationship because José was known among neighbors as a thief (*ratero*) and hung around a woman of bad living, more than likely a prostitute.[142] Indeed, neighborhood gossip played a critical role in how litigants, defendants, and witnesses tried to establish the public reputation of an individual. One father, an innkeeper, rejected his daughter's suitor because he was well known among the establishment's regulars as a "marijuana smoker."[143] Jesús Salazar called into question the reputation of Belén Millares when her family accused him of rapto and estupro. He stated that Belén and her sisters, who had "dedicated themselves to coitus," had earned "a bad reputation among the people in her vecindad."[144]

Deeply personal information about relationships flowed through the community as when Ignacio Jiménez initiated an investigation telling officials, "it has come to my attention that my niece was deflowered by José Félix Pacheco in a room in the vecindad on the Zacate street," several blocks away.[145] Alejandra Martínez learned about her domestic servant's relationship when she overheard "some señoras from the vecindad" gossiping about the sexual relationship with a neighborhood man.[146] Local rumors about a pork butcher's possible sexual relationship with a young client led him to stop making intimate jokes (chanzas). He began "treating her with great seriousness."[147]

The public reputation of men, especially their relationship status, proved a crucial component in whether or not parents and guardians accepted their children's relationships and whether or not they decided to seek the help of legal authorities. That a man was already married, whether civilly (officially according to the state) or canonically, or that he was living with a woman in amasiato (nonmarried, consensual union), shaped how family and the broader community viewed the moral legitimacy of relationship with him. Likewise, the reputations of men pertained to their capacities for fidelity, violence (especially against women), and trustworthiness (especially their ability to financially support a family). In short, a man's reputation was important to the character of his public persona. Concepción Parra, for example, disapproved of her daughter's relationship with José Estrada "because he is in amasiato with a woman and I've been told she gets the mala vida from him." Furthermore, the resolute mother, who lived on the north side of the city, succeeded in tracking down her daughter in the municipality of Tacubaya, eight kilometers away, using the information provided from vecindad neighbors, some of whom were dragged into the police precinct to testify.[148]

The passing along of messages—both written and verbal—represented one common way information flowed across the city. Friends and acquaintances passed messages between couples about, for example, meeting times and locations. Messages might be written, but most often they were simply relayed verbally through a go-between. One penny press offered a humorous dialogue between women, one passing love letters between vecindad novios (romantic couples) as a way to earn extra money.[149] Guadalupe

Romero, after arguing with her father, slipped out of her house around midnight, walked several blocks to Calle de Rayón, and sent her novio a message to come stay with her that night, not specifying to officials whether that message was written or verbal.[150] In another instance according to the testimony of Luis Rubín, the thirty-year-old owner of a corner store, he had been having occasional sex with fourteen-year-old Josefa Herrera. Expelled from her home, she sent him multiple messages through her friends that she wanted to live with him, all of which he ignored.[151]

In middle-class (and occasionally respectable working-class) families, the *criada* (maid) was commonly the keeper of many secrets, especially about the love affairs of the sons and daughters of the families they served.[152] When Petra Torres ran away, her mother quickly gained a great deal of information when she questioned her criada. The domestic knew the abductor's name and the promises he had made to Petra, having overheard them at the public baths talking about their plans to run away.[153] Another pair of middle-class youths used the girl's domestic servant to pass love letters and messages back and forth.[154]

The disappearance of nineteen-year-old Xóchitl Pérez is worth examining in detail as it reveals how gossip flowed in the vecindad setting—in this case transmitted by the building's porteras, figures notorious for their knowledge of the goings-on within a building or throughout a neighborhood. One September afternoon in 1904, Xóchitl feigned illness in her vecindad apartment on Calle San Miguel, about eight blocks southeast of the Alameda. A wet rag on her abdomen, she begged her stepmother to buy stomach medicine from the druggist. The stepmother obliged and left Xóchitl's younger sister Lila to look after her. Moments later, Ángela Mejía appeared at their door with a copy of the morning newspaper—*El Imparcial*—to lend the family. Ángela was the daughter of the building's housekeeper and friend to both Lila and Xóchitl. When the stepmother returned with medicine, she found Ángela Mejía and Lila "entertaining themselves" looking at stamps. Then, walking into the room where Xóchitl had been sick, she found her missing. Questioning Ángela and Lila immediately, the stepmother discovered that neither knew anything of Xóchitl's whereabouts. Furious, the stepmother beat Lila, calling her a "whore" and accusing her of having "sold" her sister into prostitution. Running to the vecindad patio, a neighbor informed her that she had seen Xóchitl pass the threshold (*umbral*) of the building onto the street. Finding that unusual, the neighbor had followed Xóchitl and saw her accompanied by an unknown man.

This episode triggered a four-month investigation that brought forward five different neighbors living in the vecindad to provide testimony about Xóchitl's possible whereabouts. Manuel Pérez, her father, reported the crime to the local police precinct claiming that Xóchitl had also stolen a silk dress and a new pair of shoes before running away. He further accused the building's housekeeper, Luz Sánchez, and her daughter, Ángela Mejía, of being accomplices in his daughter's flight. He claimed that both women were of doubtful conduct who trafficked "in the commerce of Spanish women." Manuel repeated this accusation at a later deposition, telling the judge that he knew a member of the "secret police" who had confirmed that these two "have business with women and a Spanish woman." While both women were formally accused in the file, the judge did not place either in prison during the investigation. An anonymous letter received just two days earlier had raised the father's suspicions about the porteras' relationship with his daughter. It read:

> My dear and respected friend . . . I tell you that you need to take much care with your youngster because in this vecindad there are four women who are helping her to escape (*sonsacando*). . . . They tell her to not be stupid and to not be afraid to leave home. Although the girl is scared to leave, Luz has obtained money from a man and with it is trying to get the youngster to leave. Three times they have departed in a coach which is parked outside the door. Friend, I tell you this because I know it all because I have gone on a stroll with one of these women and she has told me everything. They go to wash [their clothes] with doña Luz and she keeps and gives the letters for [Xóchitl] to read. . . . The day that she leaves the house, bring in those women [for questioning] for they are the ones seducing the youngster . . . this is what your friend has to say because he cares about you.

In scouring his house for possible clues, the father found a love letter from a man named Fernando written to Xóchitl. It confirmed the involvement of the building's housekeeper in their love affair:

> Girl (*Nena*) of my soul: A week has passed since you received a message from me, which I still now believe is the cause of your anger. And I, in a moment of violence, thought everything had ended, but with the experience of these days, I know that I cannot survive without your affection. Last night I sent a message to Luz for her to

tell you to have compassion for my suffering. If you have a smidgeon of love for me, you would let go of so much bitterness.

I have wanted to drown my sorrows at the theater, cantinas, and wandering the city, and your image doesn't leave me, following me everywhere, telling me that it is untrue that you scorn me. As Luz will tell you, I have taken a temporary furnished room. I don't know what I would have done without your letter from today that shows that I haven't died in your heart.

I wish to speak with you, even if for a moment. Tell Luz how and when. I see her every day at 8 a.m. I need to voice an explanation that you shouldn't be afraid that *they* will bother us [my emphasis]. I need to know from your own lips that you love me as before and that you will abandon your life of sadness and work, where no one appreciates you, and that you accept my proposal and the happiness I offer you with my entire soul . . .

Do not give credit to Luz for what I write to you in letters. I believe she likes to [claim to] compose the messages [*componer los recados*] of my love. Xóchitl, idolized one, I desire to see you. I cannot wait any longer. Have compassion for my suffering. I adore you with an immense love and I want you to know that I would give my life for what I propose. Tell me whether you are resolved to do it and nothing more. . . . Have pity on me as I have a bitter life when far from you, when not seeing you, when not adoring you in person. I beg that you tell me your thoughts.

Your passionate slave who sends you kisses, Fernando.

The building's housekeeper appeared before a judge immediately after the father's opening deposition. Luz Sánchez admitted that she has aided correspondence between Fernando and Xóchitl, although she denied helping the couple run away. She detailed her close relationship with Xóchitl who would come to the building's wash basins to do her family's laundry every week, which gave the two women opportunity to chat. Luz noted that Xóchitl had told her about "several novios, the last being a man named Fernando . . . with whom [Xóchitl] was recently in love." Although Fernando's love letter suggested that the housekeeper agreed to play messenger, Luz denied it. This was the only time she had involved herself with the couple, she insisted. It was only when she encountered Lila, sobbing in the building's patio after the beating inflicted by her stepmother, that she learned about Xóchitl's disappearance. Luz appeared perplexed by the accusation, noting that she had recently thwarted an attempt by Xóchitl to run away, exposing the plan to the stepmother.[155]

The case of Xóchitl's disappearance makes clear the role that tenement building housekeepers played as the keepers and purveyors of community knowledge and secrets. The information exchanged in the common patio while women and girls performed domestic chores blurred the lines of public and private knowledge. Furthermore, as the mysterious informant's letter shows, neighbors were better informed about the romantic escapades of young people than were their parents. Community knowledge of intimate matters shaped the everyday politics of social standing, prompting parents to call on the law to protect their family reputation.[156] The initiation of a rapto or estupro complaint allowed for public denunciation of a deceitful suitor that, at least to some extent, shielded a daughter's moral reputation and, thus, the family honor, even in the face of scandalous rumor.

Conclusion

Mexico's rapid modernization and urbanization fostered new social and living conditions that accompanied capitalist development. Respectable Porfirians, moral reformers, and social hygienists, interpreting those changes, viewed Mexico City as an incubator of vice and sexual degeneracy. For the lower classes, though, the city streets offered reprieve from the crowded tenement apartments, made more oppressive because of heat, humidity, and poor ventilation. The character of the city, the spaces and opportunities it offered its residents, shaped the romantic lives and courtship practices of the poor while defining the contours of sexuality and desire. The crowded confines of tenement slums, the availability of cheap amusements, the growing independence of working women, and the expanding and modernizing city, coupled with an increasingly liberal view that diminished the value of virginity (which will come into sharper focus in succeeding chapters), injected lives beleaguered by the monotony of work and grinding poverty with moments of immediate gratification, both emotional and physical.

Yet the ways that urban life liberalized sexual mores, especially among the young, sparked intergenerational and community conflict. The dread of returning home late at night to locked building doors—after strolling the streets, attending theaters, or drinking alcohol—stirred young women to run away or initiate sexual relations, both proclamations of adult independence. Seemingly minor child–parent disputes erupted into legal battles of serious consequence that ended in promises of betrothal, acts of abandonment, or time spent in jail (at least for the young men involved). While the city offered many locales for young couples to form secret romantic unions, family quarrels over how the young entertained themselves, how they comported themselves in public, and how and when they chose to begin sexual relations played out in the crowded confines of tenement buildings before the curious or prying eyes of neighbors. Rumors and secrets about wayward daughters or about elders incapable of asserting paternal control pushed parents to call on legal authorities as a public declaration that their daughters were deceived or that they opposed acts of youthful indiscretion. It is these interactions between working-class families and the state's legal apparatus—police, judges, lawyers—that are the focus of the next chapter. The Porfirian regime's consolidation of administrative power and the development of a medico-legal infrastructure—whose bureaucratic epicenter was the capital city—shaped everyday sex and sexuality.

2

Love, Sex, and Vigilance

The increasing stability of the Díaz regime allowed the state to emerge as ever-present in people's lives. Parents quickly and readily called on the authorities when they believed their daughters were in danger or that their paternal power was threatened. The growing presence of police forces on the streets of Mexico City allowed parents to immediately call on locally stationed gendarmes or file complaints at one of the city's eight police precincts.[1] As a result, state agents and state power became intimately involved in the personal lives of some of the city's poorest residents. The interactions of judicial officials and the police—as the face of the Porfirian state—with ordinary citizens demonstrate the diffuse workings of power that instill themselves within the social space.[2] This chapter argues that rather than emanating from a privileged focal point of authority, the state's capacity to surveil, detain, and adjudicate manifested itself in the instances when residents called on legal authorities to arbitrate matters of courtship and intergenerational conflict. The state's arbitrational functions demonstrated, on one hand, the diffuse nature of state power wielded by ordinary citizens against one another through their involving the state in the intimate lives of the most marginalized while, on the other hand, legitimizing and bolstering the authority of the Porfirian regime in its access to all citizens' personal lives.

Starting in 1878 and 1879, the Porfirian government overhauled its policing of the capital as well as its system of police precincts (*comisarías*). The regime worked to gradually modernize and professionalize the city's law enforcement, which had been notoriously unreliable since the nation's independence.[3] The city police (known as gendarmes) were provided standard uniforms and regular pay while the police precinct became the epicenter of Mexico City's law enforcement.[4] Nevertheless, pay remained low and turnover high, factors that undermined the police as agents of the regime's "order and progress" mantra.[5] Similarly, the city's police precincts suffered from overcrowding and unhealthy and dangerous conditions. Precincts

were established in rented tenement buildings ill-equipped to serve as police stations. They often lacked cells to hold prisoners, sanitary facilities,
medical equipment, and ventilation, making them vulnerable to typhus
epidemics. In 1905, the first and only adequate and modern station was
built during the Porfiriato—the 6th Precinct—located just southeast of the
Alameda.[6]

The city tripled the number of police officers who patrolled the streets to
over 3,000 by the final years of the regime. Yet most were concentrated in the
central district between the Zócalo and Alameda as well as the newer, well-
to-do neighborhoods west of Reforma Boulevard. The city's working-class
and tenement districts suffered a lack of law enforcement despite repeated
petitions from neighborhoods such as Colonia Morelos for police service.[7]
The readiness of poor families to call on police to investigate cases of runaways or deceived daughters indicates the tenacity of parents and guardians
who most often lived in areas devoid of police presence. In neighborhoods
such as Tepito or La Bolsa, for example, families wanting to lodge a legal
complaint were forced to walk long distances in search of a stationed officer
(known as the *punto*) or a police precinct. As the judicial record often states,
most rapto and estupro case files began with a parent or guardian hauling
a suspect to a precinct "with help from the police." Gendarmes were forced
either to use their clubs or, sometimes, guns to force uncooperative suspects
to the station. In other instances, a gendarme would walk the suspect to a
punto who, in turn, would take the suspect to the next stationed gendarme
until they reached the precinct.[8]

Arriving at the precinct, the *comisario* (precinct official) would write an
affidavit in which the accuser (the parent or guardian of the young woman
or girl), the victim, and the suspect would provide statements about the
events in question. In rare instances, the arresting officer and additional
witnesses also made declarations. The comisario would then determine
whether the accusation merited the suspect's being handed over to the
courts for investigation and possible prosecution. If so, the comisario
handed the case over to the Ministerio Público (public prosecutor) and
the suspect to jail. In the days, weeks, and even months that followed, an
investigating judge would summon witnesses and, at times, deploy court
officials and police to search for evidence. When suspects, victims, and witnesses disagreed on the events in question or put forward contradictory
claims, the investigating judge would order a careo where two individuals
were brought together to present their conflicting testimonies in the rarely
met hope that one would change his or her account. The court would take

anatomical descriptions of the accused and, starting around 1900, submitted accompanying mugshots into the record. Judges also routinely ordered medical examination to determine the state of the victim's hymen, signs of sexual violence, and the victim's age. If the accusers did not withdraw their accusation, once all the evidence was gathered, the prosecution and defense would write brief arguments and conclusions. The judge would then summarize the case and determine guilt or innocence. When the accused was found guilty, the judge would pronounce the length of sentence and fine amount.[9] Very rarely was a jury summoned to decide guilt or innocence (only 2.7 percent of the 234 cases examined in this study).

As the outward face of the Porfirian legal system, gendarmes, comisarios, and judges came from different social sectors and classes. Police were plucked from the ranks of the poor, reluctantly serving as gendarmes and deserting when better job prospects arose.[10] Comisarios lived more comfortable lives as salaried officials who represented the state as judicial and administrative authorities.[11] Porfirian judges were members of the respectable middle class and were most often well-educated lawyers who began their tenure between the ages of twenty-five and thirty.[12] Champions of staunchly middle-class values that emphasized sobriety, domesticity, and work ethic,[13] judges more severely punished members of the popular classes whom they considered naturally disposed to crime because of the misery and vice of their environment.[14]

Crimes such as rapto and estupro—in the minds of judicial authorities and government officials and as defined in the 1871 Penal Code—represented crimes that offended individuals more than society. Such crimes were nevertheless seen as attacks on morality that, although not necessarily assailing society broadly or taking place in the public sphere, warranted punishment. This relational perspective evinces an inheritance from colonial law that castigated sinful acts committed in the private realm and condemned by the Church.[15] Yet, by the Porfiriato, judicial officials linked crimes of morality to the regime's broader civilizing mission where a citizenry defined by a set of proper behaviors—morality, domesticity, sobriety, work ethic—formed the foundation upon which a modern nation was predicated.[16]

Medical and legal theorists connected lower-class sexual mores to the degeneration of the family and society. Ending concubinage, illegitimate births, and sexual vice would reinforce the family as the basis of society and, by so doing, promote hygiene, work, and sobriety to uplift the laboring class and poor.[17] Francisco Flores's 1885 doctoral dissertation "El hímen en México," later published by the Secretaría de Fomento (Ministry of Development), identified the work of medical-legal experts seeking to protect nonmarried women's virginity as central to the state's civilizing mission. "Today," Flores wrote, "virginity is one of the jewels sought so much by man. All civilized nations protect it, establishing severe penalties for crimes committed against it."[18] For what he identified as the "vices of lust" and "orgies of crime" undermining the civilizing hopes of the government, Porfirian criminologist Julio Guerrero, in his 1901 *El génesis del crimen en México*, blamed the liberal separation of church and state, arguing that secularization had failed to replace institutions that uphold Catholic morality. Guerrero viewed the bourgeois family—the bedrock of civilization—as threatened by the wantonness of the lower classes.[19] Guerrero argued that the lower-class preference for amasiato privileged pleasure over love and, as a result, weakened the family unit. He proposed that the "regulating aspects of the law" needed to teach the difference between love and pleasure and to firmly establish the idea that, by upholding family honor, marriage is the basis for Christian civilization.[20] And, indeed, the investigation, adjudication, and punishment of sexual crimes and sexual practice sought, as a moralizing campaign, to give the liberal state greater control over the lives of its citizenry.[21]

Even so, the laws related to rapto and estupro enshrined in the 1871 Penal Code proved an ineffectual tool for reforming lower-class sexual life. The colonial origins of the laws protected the racial purity, lineage, and inheritance of the elite by punishing acts that jeopardized female chastity and legitimate births.[22] For the urban working class, who represented the vast majority of the population in seduction and sex crimes, matters of inheritance and property played no role whatsoever in the economic structures that defined daily life.[23] In practice, the law—despite its efforts to uphold a formal pact that linked the initiation of sexual relations to marriage—failed to protect women by providing men ample opportunities to shirk domestic and financial obligations after sex.[24] Lax enforcement of the hermeneutic legal code and a presumption of female guilt severely undermined the options available for women to seek legal redress.[25] And, as a result, the laws did little to curb illegitimate births and illicit unions, the primary concerns for social reformers. Indeed, the law and social reformers placed the onus on women's chastity as the ultimate backstop in protecting a moral and hygienic civilized nation.[26] Yet, as will be shown, in the face of considerable odds, poor young women succeeded in bending the legal system to their benefit in a variety of ways.

The Scope of State Power

One striking aspect of the rapto and estupro investigations treated here is the considerable amount of official attention such cases garnered. City and municipal authorities invested significant time, resources, and labor in investigating and adjudicating cases focused on the sexual lives of the city's most marginalized groups. While the working class—or, at least, the working class as represented in the penny press—viewed city police as untrustworthy and arbitrary in their harassment,[27] the city's poorest residents, nevertheless, readily called upon city officials. This reliance on officialdom manifested itself, for instance, in several cases where overly eager parents called on authorities when no crime or elopement had taken place. The law could be wielded arbitrarily by the people in power in ways that upheld racist, sexist, and classist assumptions about marginalized groups. Nevertheless, the rise of an increasingly technocratic and centralized state that oversaw crime and punishment was not impulsively resisted by subaltern groups as they, too, and perhaps most often, were the victims of crime.[28]

Federal District authorities gave city police considerable discretion to impose order through surveillance, intervention, and punishment. By using their newfound powers as a modernizing force to impose upon all citizens the civilizing vision of the elite through social order, hygiene, and sanitation, city police became an everyday presence in the lives of the working class.[29] Court officials repeatedly called upon city gendarmes to search apartments and tenements for runaway lovers. When Hilaria Martínez refused to return home after running away, the Jefe Político (political boss) of Tacuba had police forcibly enter the house of her novio to whom she had fled.[30] Similarly, an investigating judge ordered the 1st Precinct police to search an entire vecindad for a runaway couple.[31] One well-to-do family enlisted the help of local police to find their runaway domestic, seventeen-year-old María Juárez. Another servant at the house informed the family that María and her novio could be found in the forests near the municipality of Guadalupe Hidalgo, presumably consummating their relationship there. The informant and the officer successfully located the runaway couple in the woods and hauled them to the local precinct.[32]

Investigations that had started in the police precincts of Mexico City were coordinated with authorities in municipalities across the country when young couples crossed state lines. One couple who ran away to Toluca in the State of Mexico planned to start a new life there and found work at a cigarette factory. Just nine days later, they learned that police in Toluca were looking for them after the girl's mother made a complaint at the 1st Precinct near Tepito market. The couple returned on foot to Mexico City to turn themselves in.[33] In a similar example, Mexico City authorities located a runaway couple in Ocoyucan, Puebla, and had them apprehended by local officials.[34] When one father located his runaway daughter in Toluca, Mexico City officials coordinated with the Jefe Político in that city to have the couple returned. But rather than use police to escort them back to the city, a Toluca gendarme paid a friend who was traveling to Mexico City to accompany the couple. On arriving, the runaway couple—knowing the city better than their escort—duped him into letting the accused abductor "visit a friend's home to get some money." The home turned out to be a hotel with three backdoor exits that allowed the young man to escape.[35] Even at the start of the twentieth century, the continued underfunding of police forces and their sometimes-dubious professionalism revealed the considerable gaps that existed in the disciplinary mechanism of state power.[36]

Although the scope and scale of the police's reach expanded considerably during the Porfiriato, gendarmes were scarcely a source of civic pride or security. Residents viewed police as objects of scorn associated with violence, corruption, and the *leva* (forced conscription into the army). A lack of professionalism among police and their often rude and rough demeanor—a result of their generally low wages—led most citizens, no matter their class, to question their trustworthiness.[37] The appearance of city police at the homes of middle- and upper-class families caused them public shame. Gendarmes searching houses or stationed outside waiting for a runaway to appear could draw neighborhood attention, leading to the gossip and rumor that jeopardized families' public honor. Indeed, the legal record shows that honor crimes were seldom reported to police by middle- and upper-class families, reflecting their reticence. Newspapers, when reporting rapto and estupro cases among the elite, omitted names to circumvent public scandal. One newspaper even noted that well-to-do families came to agreements with local police and court investigators to not record depositions or testimony in order to keep their family dramas secret.[38] Central to middle-class respectability lay an adherence to moral reform and morality that served as markers of citizenship and work ethic. Police presence at a family home or news of sexual indiscretion leaked through the media or gossip threatened middle-class parents' ability to differentiate themselves from the iniquitous hoi polloi.[39]

When fourteen-year-old Ramona Paredes caused a protracted investigation by lying about her abduction, she inadvertently brought scandal to the middle-class home where she had briefly worked as a domestic. After running away from home, Ramona went to serve the Valades family on Calle del Carmen, a few blocks north of the Zócalo. After only three days of work, she returned home to her mother and, when asked about her absence, claimed that her novio had abducted and raped her. In front of the judge, though, Ramona presented a story quite different from the one she had told her mother, admitting instead that she had run away and worked for the Valades family. In response, authorities sent police officers to the Valades residence to verify Ramona's altered testimony. The family, horrified by the sight of police at their door, refused them entrance and declined to answer any questions. The next day, another of the family's domestic servants appeared before the judge, asking that the officer stationed outside the Valades house be removed because they were a family of "good manners and honor." She also confirmed that Ramona had indeed served briefly at their house, which prompted the judge to close the case.[40] The Valades family's refusal to interact with the police or to answer questions before a judge reveals weak points or gaps in the machinery of state power, especially where upper- and middle-class reputation was concerned.

Seemingly minor episodes could bring to bear the full power of the court, spurring it to deploy its resources to search the city and adjacent municipalities for runaways and to take depositions from numerous individuals, even those only loosely related to events in question. When Concepción Parra accused José Estrada of seducing her fifteen-year-old daughter, Teresa Cordero, she instigated a drawn-out investigation that, despite considerable time spent and multiple depositions taken, never located the runaway girl. The case is worth examining in detail because it shows the lengths to which judicial officials were willing to go in investigating rapto claims as well as how these investigations pulled neighbors and residents into the orbit of the state's legal apparatus. When the mother entered the 5th Precinct police station to denounce José, she noted that her daughter had "taken advantage" of being asked to run an errand and used it as an opportunity to flee with her sweetheart. José, the mother added, already had an amasia who received the mala vida (bad life) from him. Living in the same building as José, the mother knew much about him, including the pulquería where he worked and from where she had him dragged to the police precinct for questioning.

José testified that, the previous morning, he had encountered Teresa on the street bemoaning the poor treatment she received at the hands of her mother. Because José and Teresa planned to marry and thereby emancipate Teresa, she had asked José to go ahead and "deposit" her at the home of her cousin. Although José could not recall the cousin's name or address, he offered to take a court representative to a building in the municipality of Tacubaya where Teresa hid. The mother, at first, doubted this claim because José's amasia, a woman named Matilde Espinosa, had convinced her that Teresa was hiding elsewhere. The jilted amasia, during her questioning, insisted that José had taken Teresa to a friend's home in the Guerrero neighborhood. Matilde, also wanting to get her hands on the young seductress, had unsuccessfully searched for her several times.

Wherever her whereabouts, it was clear that Teresa did not want to be found. The desperate mother called on neighbors to help look for her daughter, several of whom testified. A month into the investigation, one neighbor claimed to have seen the missing Teresa at a park in San Ángel (near Tacubaya) accompanied by her cousin. Another neighbor noted that, before the rapto, she had seen Teresa with José in the vivienda of Matilde Espinosa (presumably while she was not there). She had also seen the couple drinking together at a pulquería. Recently, while in Tacubaya, she had again seen Teresa with her cousins in the main plaza and, another time, at the Portal de Cartagena, a popular market. Both neighbors, though, failed to find out where she was living.

By this point, José received a state-appointed defense lawyer who provided the court with a specific address in Tacubaya where Teresa was hiding. He also provided the names of two individuals who lived in the building—one of whom was Teresa's cousin (as José originally claimed)—that the court should summon for questioning. José's amasia Matilde had gone so far as to go to the building and call on police stationed nearby to search it, but they refused without a formal request from their superior. When the court finally summoned two residents from the vecindad in Tacubaya where Teresa was purportedly living, it again failed to locate her. The first individual denied knowing Teresa and insisted that no one by that name was living in the building. Teresa's cousin then testified that she had not seen her in the building and that Teresa's mother, as well as Matilde, had appeared on various occasions asking about the missing girl. In the end, authorities never located Teresa who seemed to have run away while José languished in prison. José—five months after the ordeal began—was released from jail as the case could not proceed without the missing girl's testimony.[41]

The time, manpower, and resources invested in finding Teresa Cordero reveal a striking example of how ordinary individuals with differing goals used judicial and police apparatus. A wide net pulled neighbors and residents into the orbit of state authority, transmitting it as a mechanism for surveillance, regulation, and discipline. Each function operated in its own way, shaping people as both subjects and objects of the law. Overlapping neighborhood and state surveillance, although failing to find the missing girl, incorporated neighbors as active agents of the state to regulate sexual behavior and courtship practice, part of a broader state welfare project that also included the regulation of hygiene and prostitution at the barrio level.[42] Presumably, José's long stint in prison forced him to internalize some notion of state power and its efforts to promote morality by enforcing legitimate marriage and childrearing, although how profound or resonant that internalization may have been is impossible to know. The case offers an example of how power operated not as an attribute of the state but, rather, as a modality exercised by subalterns as much as by the dominant classes.[43] The everyday workings of Porfirian state power emerged in the most minor episodes and among the most marginalized people; it invested in them and they in it. State authority worked through ordinary people, relying on them to exert it and thereby cement its legitimacy.

Revenge and Fear

The increasingly panoptic state did not afford the poor autonomy or privacy. The prime targets of its disciplinary mechanisms, the lives of the poor, were delivered to the public by the state as lessons of what constituted improper behavior and the government's capacity to curb it. The readiness of local police to arrest lower-class men at the behest of concerned parents led, in some cases, to wrongful detentions where suspects languished in the Belén prison for days and weeks. Authorities arrested the former novio of Matilde López, for example, accused of her abduction by the girl's mother. He sat in a prison cell for a week until authorities determined his innocence. Matilde, it turned out, had run away from the poor treatment inflicted by her mother and had stayed with a priest's family at the Church of Santa Ana.[44] Román Guerrero, a twenty-two-year-old bricklayer, spent ten days in Tlapam's municipal jail wrongly accused of rapto. The mother of the missing girl claimed she had "seen her daughter speaking with Roman, for which reason she believed he had stolen her."[45]

The police's readiness to arrest on allegations of rapto allowed some people to exact revenge on their neighbors. While a case that lacked merit would be eventually thrown out, those accused would nevertheless be dragged in front of authorities and spend time in jail, losing workdays and creating bureaucratic entanglements for their families. For example, in 1893, local police brought Eriverta Chavarría to the 4th Precinct on the south side of the city. A neighbor accused her of involvement in the rapto of his domestic servant, an eight-year-old girl who was missing. Indignant at the accusation, Eriverta charged that her neighbor was "spiting" her because she had refused to have sex with him. The next day, her accuser retracted his claim, noting that his domestic servant had, in fact, simply returned to her pueblo.[46] In a 1908 case, two witnesses testified that María Felipa threatened Arturo Guevara, vowing that if he failed to marry her, she would have him arrested so that authorities could "grind" him. They claimed that she had publicly boasted about her plans to lie to authorities with the tale that Arturo had abducted her at knifepoint.[47]

The growing capacity of the Porfirian state to police and discipline the poor also allowed parents to wield state authority, through its agents, in arbitrary and vindictive ways. One mother, in 1894, after a physical altercation with her daughter's amasio, used a rapto denunciation to have him arrested. Although the couple had lived in common law for a year, she had a police officer haul him to the precinct where he spent eight days in jail.[48] In a similar example from 1904, Modesta Trejo called on authorities to arrest her daughter's amasio as an act of vengeance against the girl. Aurelia Oviedo and Santos Banda had lived in common law for over a year and, at one point, Modesta had even resided with them. The mother wore out her welcome with drunken antics, insulting and abusing her daughter Aurelia. Nevertheless, Santos paid the mother-in-law's rent when she found a new apartment and periodically provided money when she was ill. A serious altercation between mother and daughter led Aurelia to threaten that Santos would no longer offer financial support. The next day Modesta falsely charged Santos with rapto. To bolster her accusation, the mother enlisted the help of the well-to-do family for whom she worked as a domestic servant. She lied to her employers, telling them that Santos Banda had stolen Aurelia, "abusing her confidence as the girl had little experience." Both employers testified that Santos had absconded with the girl, which led to his arrest. Santos would spend the next two months in prison seeking to clear his name.[49]

Because judicial intervention always loomed, the capacity of the state to intercede shaped the love lives of couples. In this way, the legal system itself shaped the contours of courtship culture,[50] especially for the poor and working class. Legal cases make clear that young men feared official intervention in their courtships and sought to protect themselves from the possibility of arrest. Ignacio Montaño, after having sex, threatened his lover that he would renege on his marriage proposal if her parents got the authorities involved.[51] Similarly, before going to a cheap hotel with his novia, José Méndez beseeched her to not "harm him" with a rapto denunciation.[52] When fifteen-year-old María Calderón disappeared from home, rumors swirled around the neighborhood that a local butcher, Teófilo Fuentes, was the culprit. He immediately presented himself to the mother protesting his innocence and imploring that she not have him arrested.[53] Men's fears about arrest were well justified. Belén prison, the national jail that housed men while investigations proceeded, was crowded, squalid, and lacked ventilation. More fearsome, it contained dangerous hardened criminals and could be a recruiting ground for the leva.[54]

Parents and the State

The state's role as arbiter and, sometimes, adjudicator of family conflicts over spousal choice provided both parents and children with a powerful tool to challenge or uphold the latter's emancipatory hopes. The cases examined here reveal intergenerational conflicts over patriarchal and paternal rights, especially parents' authority over children in meting out physical violence, making demands of their labor (in or outside the home), and approving romantic relationships. The colonial notion of *patria potestad* (patriarchal authority), legally, had been eroded considerably by the late eighteenth century.[55] Nevertheless, the nineteenth-century legal code, with its inheritance from colonial law, continued to grant patriarchal control over wives and children.[56] On the matter of spousal choice, scholarship has demonstrated that, over the colonial period, the absolute freedom to choose marriage partners, guaranteed by the Catholic Church, was eroded by the increasing power of the Crown. Most notably, the 1776 Pragmática Sanción, for the first time, mandated parental consent for minor children's marriages.[57] Parental oversight on matters of marriage continued into the national period and was legally enshrined in the civil and criminal codes. Yet, in its everyday practice, the law and social and cultural convention provided children ample opportunity to exert their own wills. Indeed, the same social and cultural mores that shaped patriarchal rights also served to challenge them. At times, gendered expectations about the appropriate behavior of daughters *or* fathers could be wielded as legal stratagems for achieving a child's emancipation, causing severe reactions among parents who fought desperately to retain their authority.[58] Furthermore, patria potestad extended beyond paternal privilege. The 1871 Civil Code had granted single mothers and widows authority over their children, and within the considerable number of female-headed households throughout the city many women sought to exercise patria potestad over their children.[59]

Parents' decisions to involve authorities in domestic matters reflected their dual desire to protect family status within the community as well as to safeguard their children from the hardships that could result from bad life choices.[60] In some cases, parents succeeded in getting their daughters back within the constraints of family authority. Because rapto law assumed male use of seduction or deceit when girls under the age of sixteen were abducted, parents' legal leverage vis-à-vis suitors could be significant. While they initiated an investigation, parents could hold a suitor in jail, pressuring him to make a marriage promise or pledge financial recompense, even if an underage daughter admitted to willingly running away. In contrast, when a daughter older than sixteen years admitted to willingly running away with a lover, judges were forced to end rapto investigations as no crime had been committed. In tenement neighborhoods, parents' calling on authorities after the elopement or deflowering of a daughter represented an important moment for them to make known their moral values to the wider community as part of the everyday struggles for standing and influence. As has been argued in the context of turn-of-the-century Rio de Janeiro, the lack of privacy in working-class housing easily exposed parent–child conflicts over sexual life to neighbors, forcing parents to report crimes to protect their reputations in the face of community gossip.[61] Rapto and estupro denunciations, therefore, might be considered a "neighborhood ritual."[62]

Once a male suitor was arrested, parents might refuse a daughter's ongoing relationship with him for a range of reasons. Sometimes it was simply the parents' personal dislike of the man. More often, though, parents showed concern over a man's financial prospects, his social reputation (for example as lazy, violent, a drunkard, or a marijuana user), or a couple's young ages. In cases such as these, families demonstrated concern for a daughter's social standing and economic security. Many of the mothers who brought criminal cases to authorities were poor, unwed themselves, and often had started having children out of wedlock between the ages of twelve and sixteen.[63] They believed that marriage could improve a daughter's lot in life. Other times, parents and guardians needed a daughter's financial contributions to family income. When fourteen-year-old Jacinta Uribe ran away from her job as a domestic servant, her mother did not seem to care about her sexual relations with a day laborer. She dropped the charge against him as soon as she had Jacinta back in custody and had put her back to work.[64] Family dependency on daughters' work exposed tensions between the increased freedom wages offered young women and the parental right to claim their labor. It also highlights the insecurity that working-class families faced as their daughters spent more time away from home and in public places that allowed them opportunities to form romantic unions. The risk of a runaway daughter—made more likely by her working outside the home—always loomed as a potential disaster that could further strain family finances.

The securing of financial agreements with abductors represented another important means by which parents sought security for their daughters and for the family generally. The increasing economic precariousness that lower-class families endured during the Porfiriato made forging financial commitments all the more necessary, especially for young women's mothers, many of whom similarly suffered economic hardship compounded by raising children out of wedlock.[65] Not infrequently, the penny press published poems and stories about parents who used the law to interfere in young women's relationships largely for financial benefit, especially when suitors lacked social status and money.[66] Although parents most often called on the law to compel marriage proposals from suitors (perhaps the safest way to secure long-term support for their daughters), suitor pledges of monetary compensation provided another, more limited, form of economic security.[67] As the specifics of financial restitution were seldom entered into case records, parents simply stated that they had "made arrangements" and desisted from their accusations.

Promises of marriage, often cited by parents as the reason for dropping charges against a suitor, nevertheless could make for murky outcomes. A majority of parents were in common-law relationships themselves. This fact has led one scholar to argue that, in a culture of amasiato, parents often demanded marriage to "cover the honor" of a daughter.[68] One tenacious father, a seventy-two-year-old day laborer from Tenango in the State of Mexico, went to great lengths to ensure his twenty-four-year-old daughter, Carmen Cabello, received a promise of marriage from her suitor. As the father recounted, when his daughter failed to return home, he suspected that Juan Torres had taken her to Mexico City. The next morning, the father searched the Tenango station and then boarded a train. Despite making inquiries at the next major station, he learned nothing about the couple's whereabouts. Frustrated, but knowing the address of Juan's mother, he enlisted the help of a friend to go to the city and search for the couple. The friend reported that he had seen Juan "looking for a room [to rent] for a girl he had brought from Tenango." The father then reported Juan to the authorities who promptly arrested him. Juan, during questioning, denied knowing anything about Carmen, saying they had not been in a relationship for three years. The father then took a train to the city and found his daughter staying at the home of Juan's mother. Juan confessed. He promised to marry Carmen "as soon as possible," and the resolute father dropped his accusation.[69]

Parents quickly enlisted the help of police when they believed that men had failed to marry their daughters in a timely manner. One father could not have been too optimistic about the financial prospects of his daughter's suitor when he took her to live in an abandoned house. Nevertheless, the father had the young man arrested, forcing him to make a marriage proposal. He told the judge he would have him arrested again if the marriage was not celebrated in a timely manner.[70] In another example, Jorge Santillán had already had his daughter's lover thrown into prison once for failing to marry the young woman. When the suitor again failed to follow through, the irate father had him arrested less than three weeks later. In what must have been a disappointing blow, Jorge Santillán learned that the suitor already had an amasia and a son. He determined that his daughter was better off alone and dropped the charge.[71]

Mexico City's high illegitimacy rates and its prevailing culture of common-law union[72] suggest that the securing of marriage promises did not always, or even usually, end in civil matrimony. Instead, parents' use of legal authorities to apprehend young men mainly provided families with time to make arrangements: matrimonial, financial, or otherwise.[73] The cryptic nature and time-buying benefit of the agreements reached between parents and suitors are revealed in the testimony of the widow Mariana Espinal. She filed a complaint against Emilio Martínez who, eight days after deflowering her daughter, had yet to "cover her honor." A short stint in municipal jail was enough for Emilio to make "a particular arrangement" that soothed the mother's concerns.[74]

Calling on state authorities provided an opportunity for the city's families, from the most marginalized neighborhoods, to get money from male suitors who had skirted the legal boundaries of sex and courtship. Casimires Vélez, a market vendor who lived in Colonia de la Bolsa, had tried for six weeks to apprehend her runaway daughter and her novio Miguel Meléndez. She had seen the couple on several occasions at the Tepito market as well as around the neighborhood. The couple had not gone far, living on the city fringes in one of the many ramshackle *jacales* (huts) that housed new arrivals like Miguel, who had recently migrated from Querétaro. Yet each time she approached the youngsters, they ran. Miguel told officials that he had been unable to work because of being constantly followed by Casimires and one of her other daughters. When the mother finally succeeded in having the couple apprehended by an officer, it was not a promise of marriage she demanded. She instead reached an undisclosed financial agreement with Miguel before dropping the charge.[75]

Access to state agents to mediate matters of marriage and economic obligation revolved around a language of honor, yet in ways that showed its context-specific and performative aspects. Delfina Pérez had been missing for a month when she returned home to her mother. She told of her abduction by Albino Hernández and complained that he had only provided her one *real* a day as her *diario* (daily provision of money for domestic expenses). Immediately, the mother went to the local police precinct and lodged a complaint against Albino. She claimed that he was already in a relationship, suggesting that her daughter had been kept as a so-called *casa chica* (mistress; literally, "small house," a second residence where a married man keeps a mistress or second wife).[76] As the judge filed paperwork calling for the apprehension of Albino, Delfina's mother reappeared asking that the case be dropped. She had made arrangements with Albino's family that the couple would marry within four months "to cover the honor" of her daughter.[77] While Delfina's mother had told the judge she sought to protect her daughter's honor, it was Albino's lack of financial support—not his other conjugal relationship—that led her to force a marriage promise from him. Through a civil marriage, Delfina traded the likelihood of marital infidelity for her daughter's greater economic security as Albino's primary spouse.

One fourteen-year-old girl told officials she "loved" her novio and had had sex with him at a hotel after he made a promise of marriage—a promise he immediately affirmed for court officials. Nevertheless, the father, Feliciano Nava, a poor soap-maker living in the tenement district near Tepito market, quickly ended the case stating that he did not want to "harm" the fifteen-year-old suitor and did not want his daughter to marry him.[78] Rather than show concern for his daughter's deflowering, Feliciano—legally married himself—called upon state authorities to stop the young couple's rush to married life and the possibility of even greater economic instability. Because his daughter was under the age of legal consent, the father used the law—which assumed seduction on the suitor's part—to ensure her return.

The father, by making the suitor languish in prison while the rapto case slowly proceeded, convinced his daughter to return home, more than likely using the young man's suffering as leverage.

Young Couples and the State

Young couples successfully used the legal system to emancipate themselves from parental authority. They employed strategies that indicate their firm grasp of the law despite obvious barriers to formal legal knowledge such as illiteracy. Their strategies reveal that legal knowledge floated around lower-class communities by word of mouth. While such information was more than likely shared by literate members of the community who read newspapers, it is just as likely that popular legal knowledge developed through citizens' everyday interactions with the law as families, neighbors, and coworkers brushed up against it for minor or serious infractions. Moreover, young women used legal formalities—such as a parent's requirement to submit a birth certificate to prove paternity and a child's age—or judicial practices—such as the medical examination—to undermine the legal standing of those opposed to their courtship. Young women often clashed with parents and guardians about their official age and demanded they deliver a birth certificate to the court. Such demands were often made with full knowledge that parents did not have official birth or baptism records and that acquiring them would be costly and time-consuming. As noted, because the 1871 Penal Code reserved presumptions of male seduction or deceit only for girls under the age of sixteen, proving one's age could quickly end an investigation.[79] When women over the age of sixteen admitted to eloping with a lover willingly—without his use of trickery or violence—judges had little recourse but to end court proceedings. Parents then faced a dilemma: either keep a deflowered daughter at home against her will (though she might very well try to run away again) or accede to her choice of partner.

Likewise, young women sometimes demanded a medical exam to prove that they had been recently deflowered. This proof could force disapproving parents to reluctantly accept a suitor, especially when they were concerned about the public impact of a daughter's virginity loss on family honor, although such concern was by no means universal. Many cases reveal that young couples consciously engaged in premarital (and nonmarital) sex as a strategem to force parents to accept their decision-making.[80] Especially for young women, the choice to begin sexual relations—while fraught with potentially serious consequences such as disease, pregnancy, single motherhood, and social stigma—also offered opportunities to make independent decisions about life partners or to set out as autonomous adults.

Most young women and girls who ran away did so voluntarily, often masterminding rapto dramas as a means to emancipation.[81] To this end, many played strategically upon their elders' cultural values and social reputations. Though some working-class parents showed concern about female sexual purity and its relation to family, especially male, honor, most did not ape the more conservative values of their middle- and upper-class counterparts. Yet, when they did, young women and girls could gain formidable leverage in asserting their independence. Because the law defined rapto and estupro as assaults on family honor and assumed that male honor hinged on the sexual purity of female family members, it allowed young women to use an oppressive legal system that sought to control their sexual lives to subvert patriarchal authority. Laws written to protect family honor by limiting female sexuality, instead, created openings for women to initiate sexual relations as a means to gaining greater autonomy, demonstrating how in the innumerable points of confrontation—between youths and families, youths and the state—possibilities for the inversion of power relations emerged.[82]

Young women who ran away could expect family members either to accept their decisions or to call on legal authorities to intervene before sex took place (something that parents rarely achieved). The more immediately that young women engaged in the sex act, the greater leverage they gained if their parents took the latter course. Three cases serve to illustrate this dynamic. Orphaned at a young age, Ángela Villafuerte was raised by her uncle who put her to work as a domestic servant by the age of fifteen. In 1889, while working at the home of a prominent family located on Avenida San Francisco, between the Alameda and Zócalo, she ran off with her "lover" (*amante*)—as she called him in the court record—living with him and losing her virginity. Although he opposed the union, her uncle appeared defeated in the face of a young couple determined to marry. He ended the investigation stating that after "long and serious thought about the matter . . . it was the only way that the honor lost [could] be regained."[83]

In 1905, tired of the mistreatment inflicted by her mother, Cenorina Miranda used sex and the state to emancipate herself, leveraging her family's concern over honor. Cenorina's mother had started beating her regularly after learning of her relationship with Jesús Gutiérrez. For Cenorina, this was the final straw. She simply went to live with Jesús and began sexual relations. After having Jesús apprehended at a local pulquería, her father quickly desisted when he learned of his daughter's deflowering and that

Jesús was willing to "cover her honor."[84] Similarly, in 1905, Luisa Orozco was furious when Jesús González asked for permission to marry her daughter, María Quintana. Not only did she reject the proposition, according to María, her mother began beating her, "even on the streets." María's declaration about the public nature of the abuse she was suffering suggests her awareness of a concern for her reputation within the community, a concern related not to her sexual behavior but rather to her pride. María responded by running away with her lover. After initially filing a complaint at the local precinct, Luisa grudgingly accepted the suitor's offer to "fix" the situation after learning that her daughter had been deflowered.[85] In these last two cases, parents' concern over honor and social reputation prompted their use of physical violence to confine daughters to the family home. Yet, both daughters used their deflowering to force their parents to accede to their choice of partner and decision to marry. Such strategies, though, did not necessarily mean that young women subjugated themselves to a new man's authority. Using sex offered opportunities—even if symbolic—to assert adulthood by breaking the bonds of dependence and family control.[86]

Even in cases where parents demonstrated little concern over honor and its impact on public reputation, a daughter's initiation of sexual relations still proved a powerful motivator for them to accept a suitor. By calling on the state to arrest men who had stolen their daughters, parents initiated a process that most often ended with young couples getting their way. Looking at Porfirian Oaxaca, Kathryn Sloan argues that such decisions reflect state sanction of love and reason while simultaneously undermining the paternal authority of working-class parents.[87] In Mexico City, though, judges rarely had the opportunity to side with young couples as it was parents who, realizing they had run out of legal options, most often withdrew accusations. In only eighteen cases (7.7 percent) did judges end criminal complaints when young couples acknowledged a marriage promise. Furthermore, in cases where young women left home voluntarily with a suitor, the Penal Code assumed male seduction only when the women were under age sixteen, leaving little legal recourse for parents. Because the father of sixteen-year-old Josefa Ramos repeatedly rebuffed the marriage offers from her sweetheart Alberto Pinzón, the young couple took matters into their own hands. Josefa, one afternoon, left her vecindad on the pretext that she wanted to listen to an organ grinder performing on the street. Instead, she ran away with Alberto. The couple lived together for three days before being discovered, with Alberto "making use of [Josefa] several times." Josefa insisted before a judge that she "no longer wanted to live at home." Faced with her daughter's steadfast refusal to return to the family and her admission of having had sex, her mother immediately closed the case. She told the judge that "knowing her interests . . . she had celebrated an arrangement with Alberto who promised to marry her daughter."[88]

Parents often found themselves frustrated when their daughters began sexual relations with men the family viewed as having doubtful economic prospects and social standing. Arrested for the rapto of his sweetheart, Antonio Chávez told the judge that he "resolved to take Sara Hernández because [her father] refused to give consent." The father, after learning the couple had already made love twice, agreed to their marriage.[89] As Sara was only fourteen, the father could have pushed authorities to further pursue a rapto conviction and seek a four-year prison term, yet he chose to accede. José Martínez, the adopted guardian of sixteen-year-old Vicenta Rodríguez, forbade her relationship with Alberto Monseváis because he "did not earn enough money." Vicenta, one Sunday night in March 1907, slipped out of the vecindad and went to a hotel with Alberto where the couple made love. The next morning, she returned home and confessed her actions. José Martínez had Alberto arrested, during which time José made marriage arrangements with the suitor's mother.[90] In both cases, the fathers preferred to reluctantly accept a son-in-law with limited economic means rather than have an unwed, deflowered daughter. The fathers may also have considered the rarity of guilty verdicts in rapto and estupro cases. Indeed, of the 234 cases examined in this study, in only eight were the accused convicted (3.4 percent or 4.1 percent of the 196 complete case files) to suffer jail time and a fine.

Young women and girls used nonmarital sex to escape parental authority as well as family abuse.[91] Behaving as wayward daughters, they spurred family members to rely on state intervention, creating opportunities to cement independence by having parents officially acknowledge their daughters' decisions before legal authorities. María Jesús Vega, fourteen years old in 1904, explained her decision to leave home to a judge. Paying attention to María's choice of words is worthwhile. In ranking her motives for leaving home, María made clear that it was her parents' meting out of physical and verbal abuse that drove her decision and that José's proposal provided the opportunity to escape her family's punishments. María predicated her actions "first" on the poor treatment inflicted by her siblings and "second" on José's promise of marriage. She decided to go to his house where "he made use of her—being a virgin—with her full will." This decision allowed María to emancipate herself, and her mother withdrew the charge given that "José offered marriage and her daughter left by her own will."[92]

While the administration of the law promoted liberal principles of choice and freedom by so often allowing youths to get their way in the face of parental opposition,[93] young women reinforced these principles by effectively manipulating state apparatus to accomplish their emancipation goals. In so doing, they demonstrated individually oriented decision-making that often eroded parental control over their lives and sexuality. Cándido Estrada, in 1907, admitted to the rapto of his sweetheart, having had sex with her at his home in the Tacuba neighborhood of Colonia Santa Julia because "her mother did not consent to the marriage." The tactic worked. Her mother agreed to the marriage, claiming that she no longer "doubted his good intentions."[94] In other examples, youngsters were even more explicit with judges when explaining their motivations. In 1906, Merced González's lover, Cosme Villa, was arrested at the behest of her uncle who explained that he had initiated the investigation because Cosme had shown "bad behavior" and "not acted like a gentleman" when he deflowered his sixteen-year-old niece. Merced made her plan perfectly clear, testifying that "despite the opposition of my family, no one is opposed to the marriage now because of what happened and because there is no other remedy." Her uncle acknowledged Merced's determination and that his hands were tied. He agreed to a marriage because "she is very much in love with her novio and insists on marrying him, or to leave if she is not permitted."[95] Carlota Melchor, that same year, lamented to an investigating judge that although she had managed to bring her daughter back home by calling on city officials to arrest her suitor, she was forced to accept their marriage. "Since [my daughter] said that she went willingly and gave her body willingly," Carlota stated regretfully, "and since she insists on marrying him or again running away, I have come to desist."[96]

Young women wielded the power of the legal system not only against parents but also against men reluctant to marry. The case of Columba Jiménez is worth a detailed examination as it highlights how women could use the state's legal and medical apparatus to gain desired outcomes. In January 1893, fourteen-year-old Columba disappeared. Her mother, Julia Cardeña, suspected that a neighbor, a woman named Rosa Lozano Vargas, had convinced her daughter to run away to Pachuca. While it is unclear why Julia Cardeña thought her neighbor sought to abscond with her daughter, she went to Rosa Lozano's house demanding to know the whereabouts of young

Columba. Rosa Lozano denied that she was hiding Columba and told the concerned mother that Columba had been seen staying with two other neighborhood women: Ángela Solano and her daughter Leonor Malda. Immediately, the mother went to their residence and, not finding them home, began asking neighbors whether they had seen a youngster of Columba's description in the area. When neighbors confirmed that they had, the angry mother returned to Rosa Lozano and, with the help of a police officer, had her escorted to a precinct to pry further information from the unwilling informant. And, indeed, in front of a judge, Rosa Lozano provided more detail about the possible whereabouts of young Columba. She told officials that the girl was staying with two other women but that she was unaware whether they had "seduced" her or whether Columba had run off with a man. She elaborated that she had often seen Columba speaking with a neighborhood pork butcher (*tocinero*) near a milk stand he often worked.

The next day authorities caught up with Ángela Solano and Leonor Malda, bringing them to the police station for questioning. Both women gave similar accounts. Days earlier, Columba appeared in their building looking for Rosa Lozano who was not home at the time. Rather than leave, Columba decided to wait. Ángela and Leonor began chatting with the girl who, after some time, began divulging intimate details about her relationship with a neighborhood pork butcher. Lovestruck, Columba planned to leave home and marry him. Hours after the two women provided testimony, Columba appeared at the police station. She told officials that Rosa Lozano, Ángela Solano, and Leonor Malda had been apprehended because her mother mistakenly believed they had "seduced" her to go away with a pork butcher named Jesús Gudiño. Insisting this was untrue, she asked officials to release the three women. She had left her home, she continued, because Jesús Gudiño invited her to come live with him. She agreed and "lent herself to him out of affection."

When brought before investigating officials, the butcher's testimony differed considerably. He told authorities that he had only met Columba a few days earlier when she came to buy meat. The teenager had been hanging around his shop for several days, showing him signs of affection. So much so, that one night as he closed the shop, he falsely claimed to be married so that she would leave. Nevertheless, according to Jesús, the youngster persisted, continuing to come in and even ask him for money. Unable to tell her no, he had given Columba four pesos. The following night, the girl returned, again stayed until his shop closed, and then refused to leave. She insisted on staying at the shop and, seeing that Columba behaved "as a woman," he allowed her to spend the night. Seeing this as an invitation to sexual intercourse, he told officials that he "made use of her . . . not finding her to be a doncella." The butcher's claims appeared to dispel any notions that he had seduced the teenager. With two different accounts provided by Columba and Jesús, the judge ordered a careo. When both individuals confronted each other, Columba agreed with the majority of Jesús's testimony but maintained that he had given her far less money than he claimed and that she was indeed a virgin until the moment "he made use of her." Jesús countered that neighborhood chatter had told him that Columba was known for "playing" in the streets with many men. Columba denied the accusation, clarifying that her brother-in-law was the only man she "played" with on the streets.

Testimony taken afterward from the neighbors noted that Columba was boastful about her relationship with the pork butcher. During a second questioning, Rosa Lozano, for example, recalled how Columba bragged about losing her virginity to the butcher "don Jesús." Leonor Malda also added that she had seen Columba around the neighborhood riding with Rosa Lozano in coaches "with various men," a claim that placed Columba's chastity in question. By this point in the investigation, the court provided Jesús with a defense attorney who immediately asked the judge to inquire into Columba's sexual past, accusing her of having lost her virginity to her brother-in-law, a secret she allegedly divulged to Jesús. The lawyer also provided the names of two individuals who later attested to the honorable behavior, good conduct, and work ethic of the butcher. Yet, as court officials and Jesús prepared themselves for legal battle, the medical experts' report seems to have already brought the case to a sudden end. The report determined that the fourteen-year-old indeed had been recently deflowered and thus undermined any questions about her sexual past. Columba's mother, Julia Cardeña, then appeared before the judge to inform the court that Jesús Gudiño had agreed to marriage arrangements.[97]

The case of Columba and Jesús proves mysterious; it remains difficult to fully understand the circumstances that moved the drama forward. If we accept the testimony of Jesús and at least one neighbor, perhaps a risky presumption, Columba can appear as a precocious teenager seeking to use her virginity as leverage to leave her parental home and live as a legal adult, a maneuver which prompted the butcher's attempt to undermine Columba's credibility by questioning her sexual past and purity. His strategy was one commonly marshalled by men, who held greater sexual freedom in society and before the law than did women. Men were rarely sanctioned for their behavior, while women's sexual conduct came under considerable scrutiny.[98] Yet Columba's actions show how young women could bend the law to their benefit and suggest their understanding of legal precepts related to the interconnections among honor, virginity, and marriage. Moreover, while Jesús appeared reluctant to acknowledge that his relations with the teenager were motivated by affection or a desire to marry, the state's medical exam of Columba—confirming that she had been recently deflowered— forced the butcher's admission that the couple had indeed had sex and prompted him to offer Columba's mother a promise to marry her daughter, at least as an attempt to make his legal troubles disappear. The question of Columba's virginity emerged as a "form of capital," as defined by Sloan, wielded by different individuals in this case.[99] How each party used virginity as a mitigating factor in the ordeal reveals how personal court strategies channeled themselves through medical-legal processes intended to protect public honor and family reputation.

Hymens

Medical exams to verify deflowering were important and common components of rapto and estupro investigations. No other aspect of the legal process revealed the intrusive power of the state more emphatically. While the examination could be humiliating and horrifying, some young women, as well as their parents, demanded that medical experts undertake the *reconocimiento* (medical exam) as a necessary legal strategy. When called upon by the investigating judge, doctors performed examinations to determine: (1) whether the girl had reached puberty; (2) whether she had been deflowered; (3) whether her deflowering was recent or old; (4) whether her body showed signs of violence; and (5) her age. When determining deflowering through an examination of the state of the hymen, doctors used the terms *reciente* (recent), *no es reciente* (not recent), or *antigua* (old). While the terms "not recent" and "antigua" appear to have been interchangeable, both marked an important distinction from "recent," which was used to validate women's claims that their partners had indeed taken their virginity. The medical exam ascended as the incontrovertible scientific truth in determining female sexual behavior, replacing public reputation and witness testimony as the most reliable indicator of a woman's "moral condition."[100] Medical-legal experts venerated the presence of the hymen as the decisive symbol and evidence of virginity, regarding both—along with scientific study dedicated to the hymen's protection—as values and practices that distinguished civilized from primitive peoples.[101]

Doctors touted—dubiously—their precision when examining a "recent" deflowering, going so far as to estimate that one patient's hymen had been ruptured within the previous thirty to forty hours.[102] Yet those very experts admitted that the accuracy of such exams was limited. In one case, the medical official clarified that after ten days it was difficult to differentiate between a "recent" and "not recent" deflowering.[103] In the eyes of judges, such determinations mattered greatly as only a "recent" deflowering meant that a case could continue to be litigated. In many instances, though, runaway couples were not apprehended until weeks or months after starting sexual relations. While the Porfiriato's most renowned specialist in hymen study, Francisco Flores, claimed that examples of women rupturing their hymens before sex were rare,[104] it is doubtful that most people of the time would have agreed with his conclusion or viewed the findings of bodily exams irrefutable. In a society where horseback riding remained an important form of transportation, litigants and defendants surely considered a broader range of non-sexual activities that could tear a hymen.[105]

When young women and girls refused a medical exam, it often brought investigations to a speedy end. Because the law defined estupro as copulating with a "chaste and honest woman, using seduction or deceit,"[106] a positive determination of a recent deflowering by medics was often a legal case's lynchpin. And even though the crime of rapto was not necessarily based on the act of deflowering—but rather on a man's "taking power" over a woman "to satisfy a carnal desire or marry"[107] —a woman's refusal to be examined likewise brought cases to an end. Refusal created doubt among judges, and often parents, about the morality and virtue of the victim.[108] Similarly, rapto cases where a medical exam concluded that a deflowering was "not recent" were—universally—ended quickly by parents or judges.

Parents demanded medical exams when young men reneged on their marriage promises or to punish suitors they believed had deceived their daughters. Ysidro Morán swore that he had not touched his novia Dolores Villagrán after her father had him arrested when she failed to return home one night. Dolores contradicted Ysidro's claim emphatically, insisting they had had sex although "there was no hemorrhage of blood." Ysidro confidently requested that Dolores be examined to prove his claim. Dolores's father, believing her, also asked the judge to order a medical exam. The doctor's report concluded that Dolores had been recently deflowered. It appears that legal authorities took umbrage at Ysidro's falsehood as his was one of the few arrests that went to a trial. The jury found him not guilty.[109] Ysidro, clearly, interpreted the lack of blood during sex as an exculpating factor that would help him avoid a marriage obligation. And while he was forced to serve weeks in prison during the investigation and trial, the jurors believed fifteen-year-old Dolores had demonstrated poor judgment by agreeing to have sex, a finding that allowed Ysidro to avoid more serious jail time.

In a similar case, Manuel Galván repeatedly denied having deflowered his novia Simona Jiménez. In fact, he denied that they had had sex at all. Simona and her parents claimed that Manuel had already asked for her hand in marriage to "cover her honor," a clear indication that they had already begun having sex. Her father, insisting on a medical exam, was proven right when it showed that Simona had been "recently" deflowered. Again, the defendant's lies and his failure to proffer a marriage proposal led to the rare occurrence of a trial. And, as in the previous case, the defendant was found not guilty.[110] In both cases, the juries unanimously agreed that the young women had "followed their abductor willingly." These two cases exemplify the difficulty women faced, not in seeking, but in getting justice, as their very presence in an investigation undermined their virtue and credibility at the outset. In most instances, without a written promise of marriage, women and girls—of any age—had little recourse to prove male deceit.

In one instance, a parent demanded a medical examination for his daughter in order to show a would-be suitor that she *was not* a doncella. This strategy aimed to undercut a wooer's interest by "proving" a young women had a sexual past. With the help of an officer, on December 3, 1905, Guadalupe Rodríguez brought two neighbors into the 4th Precinct accusing them of the rapto of her daughter, fifteen-year-old Carmen Flores. The mother accused José González of absconding with her daughter and Josefa Hernández of corrupting the youngster, facilitating her flight. Guadalupe told authorities that two days earlier she had left her daughter at home while she went out to sell tortillas. When she returned in the evening, she noticed her daughter missing and immediately suspected José González: first because he had also disappeared from the vecindad, having moved out of his vivienda and, second, because he had been unsettling her (*la andaba inquietando*). The irate mother stated that she would never allow her daughter to marry José González as he was known for his thievery (*raterías*). After asking about among the neighbors, the mother located the couple at a nearby vecindad on San Antonio de Abad where they were staying with a woman, she claimed, of "immoral living" (*mal vivir*).

When brought before authorities, Carmen recounted that, days earlier, she had been standing in the *zaguan* (breezeway) of the building when she received a message that José wanted to talk. Carmen went to his vivienda where he proposed that they run away, promising to buy her new clothes and get married. Having affection for him, as she told the judge, she agreed. Carmen insisted, though, that she had protected her virginity because José wanted her mother's permission to marry.

Before the judge could interrogate the accused, Guadalupe Rodríguez requested that the judge undertake a medical exam of her daughter to show that she had already been deflowered two years earlier by another young man, Agustín Ponce, who had lived in the vecindad. And, indeed, the medical exam confirmed that Carmen's hymen had hemorrhages and tears that were not recent and were consistent with her having already undertaken the act of coitus. The mother's decision to demand the medical exam suggests not that she wanted the case thrown out—she had not needed to bring it to authorities in the first place—but that she wanted to dissuade José from courting her daughter. When sixteen-year-old José González provided his brief testimony before the judge, he confirmed Carmen's claim that the couple had not yet consummated their relationship as he wanted the mother's permission to marry. The case file does not disclose whether the mother's strategy discouraged José from courting Carmen. The judge closed the investigation on a technicality when Guadalupe Rodríguez failed to provide documentation proving parentage.[111]

A woman's refusal to undertake a medical exam jeopardized her family's case against a sexual crime and ensured that legal authorities would assume a past sexual history on her part. That the invasive medical exam could be humiliating or further traumatizing to a young woman did not matter in the eyes of the law. Even if she rejected examination to avoid the indignity, a young woman's refusal could leave a family with no other alternative than to accept an unwanted marriage proposal. For example, when Pomposa Zarco's sister rejected an examination, Pomposa concluded she had no choice but to agree to the suitor's marriage offer.[112] In other instances, a young woman's refusal to be medically examined led families to desist from their accusations because, for judges, physical proof of a recent deflowering provided the most compelling scientific support of the woman's account. In 1910, Guadalupe Chávez, who worked at the Salon Ideal cinematograph in the city center just north of the Zócalo, accused the middle-class businessman Ramón Valdés of drugging her with an "unknown brew" that left her "inebriated" (*trastornada*). Ramón's call for a medical exam brought Guadalupe's case to an end. Ramón insisted that when the couple had sex she was "already deflowered," so he did not "enjoy her virginity." Guadalupe's refusal to be examined led her father to write the court: "not wanting to make this matter more public regarding my daughter's dishonor . . . we manifest that the offended is unwilling to undergo the medical exam that is part of the criminal process as it would offend her modesty."[113] The case suggests two potential scenarios. On one hand, for Guadalupe, raised in an aspiring middle-class family in the working-class Morelos neighborhood, having her body examined by medics may have seemed too great a humiliation to endure, an affront to her modesty that warranted rejection. On the other, Guadalupe's job provided her ample opportunities to meet men, often of higher social status, and to make dates with them as she had with Ramón. It is possible, then, that Guadalupe may have feared a medical exam would expose an already sexually active social life.

Conclusion

Criminal investigations surrounding seduction and sex provided the state and its agents considerable opportunity to surveil and discipline the city's population and promote practices that reflected the moral and hygienic values of a modern metropolis. Because men were rarely punished for seduction beyond temporary prison stays while cases were being adjudicated—though, surely, these were harrowing for many—the onus of premarital and nonmarital sex fell heavily on women. Court officials routinely scrutinized the sexual lives of women while ignoring those of men. Furthermore, the law's failure to protect poor women from the dangerous consequences of male abandonment—pregnancy, disease, and destitution—may well have served as the disciplining mechanism that aimed to both civilize and marginalize them.[114] In this regard, the laws did little to discipline what reformers and social critics identified as the primary culprits of lower-class licentiousness: illegitimacy and illicit union. While attempts to promote male-headed families and female domesticity were limited and unsuccessful, the investigation and adjudication of sexual crimes allowed the state to insinuate itself into working-class tenements and the lives within. Despite its failures to reform sexual practice, the Porfirian state nevertheless bolstered its presence in people's everyday lives, propping up power structures that served simultaneously to promote a vision of the policed city—even in the lower-class neighborhoods where it was notoriously absent—and to force among the populace an internalization of the surveilling capacity of the state.

In the face of these challenges before the law, poor women did well to adapt state power, its agents, and its apparatus to their advantage. Girls and young women succeeded in initiating rapto and estupro investigations with the goals of seeking emancipation from parents, demanding adult independence, or securing a promise of marriage through the exercise of sexual freedom. We should not romanticize the lives of lower-class women whose limited options made sex a tool for emancipation or who sought independence in a society where such a choice could mean severe financial insecurity, hunger, and death, especially for unwed mothers. This chapter has sought to highlight how women exercised agency—through the state's increasing power to surveil, discipline, and adjudicate the lives of the poor—in ways that challenged and reformulated patriarchal pacts both at the neighborhood and national levels, both in ideology and lived life. The state's legal structures played a critical role in establishing the ideological and existential context in which people forged relationships, found romance, and made love. The tensions between the law, on the one hand, and custom and moral economy, on the other, were revealed in the diverse ways that working-class couples came together in illicit and licit unions. It is to that topic we now turn.

3

Consent, Coercion, and True Romance

This chapter considers how young couples defined their expectations of what constituted acceptable behavior in matters of courtship, romance, seduction, and sex. It begins with an exploration of the concept of *voluntad* (will) that demarcated the boundaries between force and consent in relationships, sexual or otherwise. As William French notes, "will" was often a contested term in legal proceedings: for judges, it helped determine criminal intent while, for couples, it often represented the clearest statement of their commitment to a romantic relationship.[1] Young women used the term "will" when explaining to authorities their decision to run away, have sex, or accept marriage. Because the invocation of will, in the judicial file, could be clouded by romantic disagreements, parental coercion, retracted testimony, and, more generally, contested versions of events, the articulation of individual will and agency demonstrated different levels of enthusiasm and commitment. Because of these differences, this chapter considers the two extremes of women's expressions of will: on one end, accounts of coercion, violence, and rape where women denied possessing or exercising any will in unwanted sexual encounters or forced abductions; on the other end, clear, vociferous claims of willful intent, referred to here as examples of "true romance." This approach serves to highlight that the emotional, bodily, and legal stakes that coalesced around statements of will were high because they were foundational to what a relationship meant in the eyes of the individual, the couple, the community, and the law.

This chapter argues that, for women, the articulation of one's will was as likely to perpetuate patriarchal norms as to challenge them. Although the liberal legal code's emphasis on female consent and will represented an important shift away from colonial tradition that interpreted sexual crimes against women as an attack on family—primarily male—honor, its humanization of women was not enough to overcome patriarchal bias in law and social relations.[2] Colonial legal legacies continued to influence how the law was applied and interpreted by judges, litigants, and defendants, especially in its gendered double standard.[3] These conditions reflected the broader nineteenth-century development where liberal reforms began to offer women new rights, legal status, and educational opportunities while continuing to discriminate against them through sexual repression, limits on property ownership, and their subjugation to husbands' control.[4] Notably, nineteenth-century liberal legal codes no longer specified, as had the colonial Siete Partidas, that sexual crimes could only be committed against women of "good repute" (*buena fama*).[5] The language of liberal law in defining the crimes of rapto, estupro, and violación, furthermore, emphasized the absence of female will and consent.[6] These changes in the law help explain, at least partially, the dramatic shift away from the reporting of passion crimes as a primarily elite practice to one, by the end of the nineteenth century, universally undertaken by the poor.[7]

The cases of sexual assault explored in this chapter provide examples of the tensions between colonial legacies and liberal law. While the state's use of its disciplinary apparatus and the law might have intended to promote male-headed families and civic domesticity—an early example of what scholars have referred to as the modernization of patriarchy—its reach was shallow and had contradictory effects. The goal, here, is not to establish the kind or quantity of sexual assault that existed in Porfirian Mexico City but to determine how women and couples used the legal apparatus and available social norms to push their own self-determination. As a counterpoint, the chapter also considers the importance of couples' trust in forming companionate unions by exploring examples of women who made clear statements of their will before judges to affirm consensual relationships with men. Such positive articulations reveal how the will was wielded to undercut the patriarchal and paternal power of the family through acts of self-determination fueled by romantic desire. Yet, at the same time, economic precarity, gendered divisions of household labor, and the ever-looming threat of violence that was seen as a legitimate aspect of the courtship process, laid bare the limits of female self-determination under social conditions of misogyny and patriarchy.[8]

Will

Men emphasized women's will and consent to convince authorities that they had not committed male acts of seduction, deception, or rape. For women, expressly stating their own exercise of will was fraught with peril.

Authorities—judges, lawyers, and, occasionally, juries—interpreted such willful decision-making as behavior that invited male violence and sexual assault. When a woman clearly invoked her will to elope or have sex, it most often mitigated a man's legal accountability in rapto and estupro cases. Yet strong statements by women that they willingly engaged in premarital sex also expressed a belief in their entitlement to seduction and pleasure. A clear statement of will also served as a powerful tool with which young women could undermine elders' attempts to reassert familial or patriarchal authority. Because of their colonial origins, tied, as noted, to attacks on family honor, rapto laws assumed that parents had the exclusive right to express the will of a daughter in matters related to courtship, sex, consent, and marriage. While parents might bestow this decision-making power upon underage daughters, giving them agency over their own romantic lives, the ways that girls and young women asserted will in relationships, and admitted so before judges, reveal moments where they wrestled that authority away from parents.[9] When daughters unequivocally declared their willing agreement to sexual intercourse, parents faced a range of possible choices: they accepted a suitor's marriage proposal; they insisted on a marriage proposal (when a suitor appeared disinclined); they demanded financial indemnification; or they simply dropped the charge, ending any chance of legal recompense.

Considering the contradictory ways that assertion of will could shape the outcome of a criminal investigation, women took considerable risk when they admitted to consensual sex. That risk was heightened for women because, while a verbal promise of marriage might give them the confidence to start sexual relations, a written promise was the strongest evidence to prove male wrongdoing.[10] But written promises were extremely rare. Indeed, of the 234 cases explored in this study, not a single written promise of marriage was ever entered into the judicial register. Strong assertions of will by women, as documented in case files, often suggest intimacy and trust between couples. In such cases, women appear to have had enough confidence in their suitors' good intentions to admit to willing sexual activity in order to begin a conjugal relationship, proclaim adulthood, and sever familial ties. Less frequently, the judicial record shows that some women admitted to consensual sex only to be deceived by a roguish man who, once in front of a judge, denied having promised marriage, knowing that a female's admission of having sex considerably lessened the chance he would face legal punishment. It is not surprising, then, that women often accused

men of violently stealing them away or of using physical coercion to force
the sexual act even when such alleged behaviors were accompanied by a
verbal marriage proposal.

This is not to suggest that rape and sexual violence did not occur frequently. But because society's prevailing gender norms defined men as
inherently sexually aggressive and women as sexually passive, for many
people of the time, such acts were assumed as a normal part of the courtship process.[11] Nevertheless, the gendered scripts women invoked before
the law when claiming that their first sexual experience had been a rape
could support a twofold strategy. First, by invoking gender norms, women
catered to judges' expectations about proper female behavior, including
the assumption that women would resist sexual intercourse. By reinforc-
ing such assumptions, a woman could strengthen judicial opinion about
her moral character and thereby improve her legal position within a criminal investigation. Second, by denying that she willingly engaged in sex, a
woman protected herself legally, as much as possible, from a man's potential
denial of having made a promise of marriage. The accusation of forced,
nonconsensual sex placed men in legally defensive positions where they
had to prove their good intentions before a judge by making known that
they intended to marry, an offer women most often accepted despite their
original declarations of coerced sexual violence.

Shifting Narratives and Steadfast Claims

It is not surprising that women changed their testimonies during an investigation. Different and interlocking patriarchal behaviors, norms, and
assumptions—among lovers, parents, and authorities—created considerable legal leeway for men to shirk financial or conjugal commitments.
Confronting such bias, women often shifted their narratives to appear as
sympathetic victims before the authorities and a society that did not afford them equal access to the law. The 1889 case of José Buendía and Petra
Jolalpa highlights how changing and conflicting testimonies clouded attempts to determine who possessed agency and exercised will where case
facts were highly disputed. At the same time, the litigants' shifting accounts
reveal how individuals strategically crafted their testimonies to explain
their actions before a judge. These statements were often highly gendered
accounts of how one articulated will.

On a rainy June night in the municipality of Guadalupe Hidalgo, northeast of the city, Florentino González and his wife María Loperena heard

a knock at their door. María opened it to find her husband's friend, José, accompanied by a young woman she did not recognize. José explained that they were on their way to the city, but that heavy rain forced them to seek shelter. José convinced his friend to let them stay. The next morning, José divulged that he had taken eighteen-year-old Petra from her parental home in order to marry her. José then asked Florentino whether Petra could stay at his home while he went to make marriage arrangements with her parents. After several days, José had not returned. Florentino, worried that Petra had been abandoned, located her father who lived in the nearby town of San Juan de Aragón. Learning what had happened spurred Petra's parents to search for José. They convinced him to meet on several occasions to organize marriage plans. But then, suddenly, José disappeared again, leading Petra's mother to go to authorities and demand his apprehension.

Petra's mother described José's appearance as "tall, thin, and brown-skinned (*trigueño*)." She described his clothes as "muslin pants and a straw sombrero" and specified that "he wears shoes," suggesting that he was an agricultural worker, more than likely of indigenous ethnicity. After the mother initiated the investigation, Petra delivered scant testimony to the presiding judge. She claimed to have had a year-long amorous relationship with José. Late one evening, meeting under the stars, he convinced her to run away and they ended up at Florentino González's home. She offered none of the usual information recorded from rapto victims' statements: whether she had started sexual relations; whether she was a virgin; or whether she thought herself "deceived." And, although she never mentioned that a promise of marriage had convinced her to run away, she did note that José had met her parents multiple times at Florentino González's home to make marriage arrangements.

José was the last person to provide testimony because it took authorities several days to find him "hiding" in the Villa de Guadalupe. His testimony contradicted everyone else's accounts. He stated that one night he stopped by Petra's house and "gave a whistle." When she came out, he offered her ten pesos to spend fifteen days with him in the city. She agreed, but on their way, they found the rain too intense and stopped at Florentino's house. The next day, José left Petra there; he stated that he had returned several times to visit but insisted he had never offered marriage. Seemingly incensed by José's story, Petra provided another deposition that gave an account of events much different from her first account. She explained that "she hid information" in her original testimony believing that José was "true and of his word" (*leal y cumplido*). But "because of his slanderous imputations" she promised now to tell the truth. Petra stated that one night, while she was sewing clothes, José appeared at her window asking her to come outside. When she refused, José's pleas turned into threats. Worried that "something bad might happen between him and her father," she left the house to speak with her novio. Threatening her to stay quiet with a "piece of iron," José and another man wrapped Petra in a shawl and carried her outside of town. After the other man left, José raped Petra in a cornfield, "threatening her the entire time." He then promised marriage and took her to Florentino's house to stay while he made arrangements with her family. Petra vehemently denied taking any money from José.

José, when presented with Petra's new account during a careo, ratcheted up his testimony. He explained that he was hiding in the Villa de Guadalupe because he could not prove to Petra's father that he had paid her ten pesos to come with him (and, ergo, have sex). It was not because he was reneging on a marriage promise. He further insisted that Petra was not a doncella and that she had already had "illicit relations" with a man named Juan Islas. He denied the crime of rapto specifically, contending that Petra could have left Florentino's home at any time and returned to her family. The judge agreed. He ended the investigation, deciding that, as Petra was older than sixteen, no crime had taken place and that seduction could not be assumed. He cited the testimony of Florentino and his wife María—that Petra's parents had visited on several occasions to arrange a marriage—to conclude that José had not used physical or moral violence to steal her from her family.[12]

If some of the testimonies in this case are either clearly or partly untruthful, the way that José and Petra each discuss will is noteworthy. After José denied making a marriage proposal, Petra renounced her original story that he had convinced her to run away, a story that emphasizes mutual agreement and influence rather than force. On the other hand, Petra's new story is about force, violent abduction, and rape and, therein, about a complete loss of her own will. Even if her second version is true, Petra nevertheless found her situation acceptable enough to stay at Florentino's home while her parents made marriage arrangements. In contrast, hoping to tarnish Petra's character before the judge, José portrayed her allegedly willing decision to have sex as driven by financial self-interest rather than love. Moments of breakdown and crisis within romantic partnerships could push the individuals involved to make accusations based on broader societal and gendered assumptions about what factors motivated women to have sex. Despite the testimonies of friend Florentino and his wife María that José had publicly acknowledged making a promise of marriage, the judge considered only the crime of rapto, and not estupro, to determine that an *abduction* had not taken place. Such judicial decision-making, as well as José's behavior in abandoning Petra and questioning her sexual purity, highlights the numerous challenges women faced in seeking legal redress. That women could expect to encounter before the law a bulwark of gender bias helps explain how a change of testimony could serve strategically in a woman's search for a beneficial outcome such as marriage or financial restitution. Nonetheless, when pitted against the obstinance of a recalcitrant man and his legal advantages, such outcomes were rare.

In contrast to the Buendía and Jolalpa investigation, there are cases where women clearly and vociferously proclaimed their wills. By so doing, they may have evinced affection and love for their partners and paramours. The true motivations for such claims are impossible to know with certainty, though, at the very least, they indicate women's confidence and trust that their suitors would not renege on promises and suitors' confidence and trust that their novias would not place them in legal jeopardy. María Dolores Rodríguez testified that she had left with her boyfriend Vincente Guadarrama, having "carnal relations" and "living matrimonially" with him after the two spent a romantic day at the Viga Canal. He did not use "force or deceit," she told the judge. "I willingly went with him because of the affection he has for me."[13] Petra Torres confessed that Manuel Mora "in his sweettalk told me he would marry me and speak with my father, so I willingly gave my virginity." She continued: "by no means did he deceive me. . . . I did everything spontaneously because of the affection I have for him."[14] When sisters Reymunda and Toribia Velásquez ran away to Tacubaya with their carpenter boyfriends, older sister Reymunda spoke for both she and her sister: "we slept in the company of [Jesús] and Tito and they made use of us, making us lose our virginity for we were girls and never had anything to do with men." She ended her declaration: "we consented to go and live with them due to the affection we have for them and because they offered marriage."[15] Because both the physical and reputational risks of intimacy were far greater for women than for men, and because of the multiple obstacles and biases poor women faced, such declarations before judges highlight the considerable trust and affection that some couples cultivated.[16] They provide examples of lower-class courtship as a deliberate search for partnership, pleasure, and romance.

Illicit relationships, in particular, provide examples of strong articulations of will based on feelings of affection that could invite social stigma or undermine family peace. Women who willingly entered taboo unions that transgressed community norms offer striking examples of individuals choosing partners for deeply personal motivations of pleasure, affection, or comfort. When explaining to authorities why she slept with her half-sister's husband, losing her virginity to him, Guadalupe Rangel simply said, "I did so because I love him and it was with my full will."[17] In another such example, Catalina González did not care that her lover, Francisco Rivera, was already in amasiato with another woman. The two had kept a secret romance for six months. She told officials that "I went with him out of my own free will and Francisco is going to leave his amasia and marry me."[18] Simona Jiménez likewise told officials, "I am willing to marry Manuel Galván, not caring that he has a woman or children, because we love each other mutually."[19] There are numerous examples in the judicial record of women who made known their wills, citing affection as their principal consideration in leaving with a lover. Because such action could put women greatly at risk, their will to move forward anyway demonstrates a decision-making process that was authentic, deeply personal, and driven by individual choice—even where family and community viewed that choice as abhorrent. The substantial social risks couples took on to pursue illicit relationships reflect the poor's modern sensibility that prioritized personal choice over obligations related to the reproduction of kinship networks.[20]

Asserting Female Independence

When women openly exercised personal will, judges most often viewed them as accomplices in their own abductions. Regarded as such, many women avowed their will to independence from familial authority, an avowal backed by the power of the law and state. Family squabbles were a common reason why young women willingly left home with their lovers to have sex. Legally, this was an emancipatory act that could sever familial bonds that women, in many cases, found oppressive, if not abusive. For example, orphaned at a young age, Guadalupe Chávez yearned to escape from her grandmother's house where she suffered repeated beatings by her uncles. "I wanted to leave that fate," she told investigators. And, indeed, she immediately did so when her novio Luis Pérez promised to marry her. After her grandmother had Luis arrested eight days later after discovering the couple living together, the judge quickly ended the case because Guadalupe was sixteen and had left willingly.[21] In another case, because her mother "hit, reprimanded, and chased her from home," eighteen-year-old Eglantina Gómez demanded that her novio José Aguilar steal her away, or so he claimed.

Despite "his fear" of possible arrest, he eventually agreed, taking her to a room (*casa de cita*) where they had sex. Both testified that the sexual encounter occurred with Eglantina's full will. Although Eglantina's testimony made no mention of marriage, José ended his deposition by telling the judge, "I don't have any bad intentions with Eglantina Gómez, my aim is to marry her."[22] Sixteen-year-old Concepción Cerón, after a six-month courtship, went to the house of her novio to have sex and lost her virginity. "This was done with my full will and consent," she said, "without him making any promise of marriage nor taking me with deceit or seduction." Concepción had hoped to assert her adulthood by living in amasiato with her novio, only to learn, after the sex, that he was unwilling to make that commitment. Rather than return home after losing her virginity and face her mother's violent reprimand, Concepción entered a *casa de asignación* (brothel) to sever her family ties once and for all.[23] The young women and girls in these examples asserted agency in ways that wrested paternal control away from their romantic decision-making, albeit within a limited range of choices that exposed fissures in patriarchal pacts between family authority and the law. Such cases reveal how the law eroded the paternal authority of lower-class parents by sanctioning the independent decision-making of youths.[24] In the broader context of a legal system that provided young women little protection when men refused or reneged on marriage promises, the decision to admit the exercise of will in beginning sexual relations was a risky one. Even considering the possible perils, though, a woman's urgency to leave home could outweigh the bleak prospect of a lover's abandonment.

Lack of a marriage proposal—either explicitly stated in suitors' testimonies or implicit by its absence from the judicial record—highlights young women's unwavering resolution to leave home with or without a committed conjugal partner. Eighteen-year-old María Santos Yepes used her relationship with José González, a Spanish butcher, to separate from her sister with whom she often quarreled. Things came to a head one night when the sister "threatened [María] with a knife." Making no mention of a marriage proposal, María declared, "I went with José spontaneously and out of pure will." He did not "use any force to have the carnal act."[25] Neither María nor José made any mention of marriage or of plans to live in amasiato after spending the night at the Hotel Vienna (behind the city's main cathedral). In another case, the lack of a marriage proposal likewise makes known a young woman's desire for adult independence and sexual freedom. When the family of Felipa Salas had her novio, Tiburcio Navarro, arrested for her rapto, the sixteen-year-old girl quickly put an end to the case. She admitted that "last January I lost my virginity to a muchacho named J. Portilla with my full will." She added that "eight days ago, with my full will, I went with Tiburcio, so he has no fault at all."[26] Her claim, verified by the medical exam on which she insisted, left her father with no legal standing. Instead, by publicly avowing her sexual history, Felipa declared adult independence, undercutting her father's assertion of patriarchal authority as the right to determine his daughter's conjugal future or to gain financial restitution from her suitor. In cases that describe extremely tormented homelife or ardent desire for emancipation, some young women calculated that adult independence offered better prospects than reliance on family. But women's exertions of agency to this end were often legally precarious. While the law offered avenues to escape oppressive conditions—however they were defined by daughters—those avenues included the risks of economic hardship and social stigma.

Precarious Declarations

The particularities of family dynamics, including how much authority parents wielded over a child, at times limited a daughter's ability to make decisions on her own behalf. As a result, a girl's or young woman's exercise of consent and personal will to achieve independence could backfire because of tenacious parents or an unscrupulous lover. An 1895 case, originating in the State of Mexico, discloses how one woman's legal admission of willingly following a lover exposed her to family pressures to enter an unwanted marriage. It also lays bare the arduous lives of poor women and what could be men's callous cruelty. María Vidal Martínez, originally from Chalco, was working as a domestic in the capital city where her family had recently moved. One night she left on an errand and did not return. As she walked down the street, her novio, Pascual Guevara, accosted her. Pascual, in the past, had made numerous offers for María to run away with him, all of which she had declined. On this occasion, he would not be denied, "grabbing her by the *rebozo* (shawl)" and taking her to the pier at Iztacalco where he cajoled her into having sex. Afterward, he put her in a canoe to return with him to Chalco.[27] Nonetheless, as she later told officials, "I resolved to go with him because he was a good man and he sometimes spoke of marriage." But when they reached Chalco, Pascual proved far from a "good man." He put María to work as a domestic in the house of a family she did not know. For eight days, the couple lived in amasiato. That was until the day Pascual arrived at her workplace with two men to take her away to serve at another house. But "seeing their state of drunkenness, I refused," María recounted. Pascual, angered by his novia's refusal, began to hit her, but "because of my resistance and the defense of the people at the house, I was able to stay put." Now abandoned, María found a new job as a domestic back in Mexico City. Despite the actions of her novio, María later repeated to the court that "from the first to the last carnal act" with Pascual over those eight days, "he did it with my will, not using violence, neither physical nor moral . . . and I willingly followed my abductor." Yet, due to his "inconvenient conduct," she now refused to marry him. María's steadfast position, it appears, was undermined by her parents who had arranged a marriage through Pascual's family.[28] Although parents commonly used the courts to arrest wayward men, either to pressure them or to gain time for behind-the-scenes arrangements, doing so in opposition to a daughter's refusal to marry was less common. By admitting she had willingly left home with Pascual, María undermined any possibility of redress for his violence and temporary abandonment, giving her family few options for an acceptable resolution. The family's insistence on a marriage María did not want reveals the power that loomed within the possibility of destitution some women faced because they had admitted to exercising will in romantic or sexual relationships.

Women's articulation of will before legal authorities could also create opportunities for men to abuse women's trust. Finding themselves before a judge, some men emphasized—in an effort to avoid conjugal, financial, or legal responsibility—a women's agency or will in masterminding an elopement or instigating sexual relations. The relationship between José María Galván and María Martínez demonstrates how contrasting claims of consent and rape, violence and will, made it nearly impossible for women to secure legal recompense, especially before judges who already doubted the morality and respectability of the working class. José's and María's testimonies are starkly at odds in portraying the events in question. The case began with María's mother who, with the help of a policeman, dragged José into the 3rd Precinct, accusing him of abducting her daughter. María had been missing for twenty-two days after not returning home from Mass. Her mother had immediately suspected José as the culprit but failed to locate him until, while out on an errand, she saw him on the street. She followed him to a building and found that María was living there with his family. Although the mother originally declared to the judge that she sought to "make José María Galván marry her daughter . . . as she was a *niña* (virgin) before the incident," María's account of her violent abduction changed her mother's mind. Learning that José had "threatened to kill" María during the kidnapping, her mother demanded a "proper punishment" and that "he have nothing to do" with her daughter.

José, an eighteen-year-old silversmith, unsurprisingly, painted a different picture. He told officials that the day he took María it was "by her will." He countered, contemptuously, that María was not a virgin and that he had no obligation to marry her because she had left with him willingly. Although originally offering a marriage proposal, José concluded his deposition by saying the spurious accusations against him were so shameful that he reneged. María's testimony matched that of her mother. She added, though, that after threatening her, José took her to spend the day wandering the streets (*pasear*) of Tacubaya. When the judge asked why she had not alerted one of the many police officers she would have seen on the street throughout the day, she explained that she was in "terror that he would hit me." Likewise, when asked by the judge why she did not try to escape from José's family home during the twenty-two days she was missing, María explained that she feared "he would kill her." She stated unequivocally that it was *not* her intention to marry José and that "the authorities should know what to do with him." After a careo that failed to offer new information, María's mother appeared before the judge to abruptly withdraw her accusation, more than likely feeling defeated by her daughter's inability to explain why she had failed to alert police at any point over the past three weeks.[29] María's account of abduction, sequestration, and rape, and her failure to notify a gendarme or escape, were interpreted by the judge as her willing desire to be with José. And, indeed, the judge's presumption of María's willingness to live with José—despite her ardent refusal to marry him and her insistence that he be punished for the violence committed against her—undermined her and her mother's attempts at legal redress.

Even if we accept it, the judge's skepticism of María's claims (a difficult proposition considering that both women insisted on José's punishment and rejected the marriage proposal he admitted to offering) again reveals the legal precarity of the situations in which women found themselves when they asserted their wills. If María had, in fact, gone willingly with José, only to insist later, in front of authorities, that a violent abduction had taken place, it is possible that her fear of appearing too willing to leave home and have sex led her to fabricate a story in the face of her mother, the judge, or both. Could it be that the implicit pressure to act out a gendered script of female passivity before authority figures proved so great that María rejected the security of marriage or, at least, amasiato? Although it seems highly unlikely, cases such as this highlight the difficulty of finding the "truth" of events in question. No matter what actually transpired in those days and weeks, the case details an unequal access to justice. Men—whether judges or defendants—assumed that lower-class women were sexually available despite the gendered scripts they so often presented to proclaim their chastity. Similarly, judges placed the onus on women to seek out the authorities, ignoring how violence and fear or a distrust of authorities might undermine a woman's willingness to do so.[30] And, indeed, it was those gendered expectations that drove women to deploy particular scripts in sexual crimes, fashioning self-representations that authorities always doubted.

Gendered Scripts

The line between consent and force was often blurred in women's testimonies. Women "willingly" engaged in sexual relations with men even after claiming a violent, nonconsensual abduction. Whether such accounts reflected the norms of sexual encounter or gendered scripts, they make clear social expectations of aggressive male sexual behavior and female passivity. Martina Verdiguel testified that while out one night with her novio, Juan Martínez, he refused to let her leave. When bidding him farewell, he "grabbed her by the rebozo," keeping her out until far too late to return home. He forced her to accompany him on a walk around Tlapan, "constantly by pulls," before taking her to the house of his aunt. Despite his violence, Martina had sex with Juan twice, stating, "I did these acts with my own will because Juan promised to marry me."[31] Similarly, María Inés Peña said it was "very much her will" to marry Ismael Martínez although he kept her in a house for fifteen days under threat of violence. The housekeeper repeatedly threatened to beat her if she tried to leave or contact anyone.[32] María Guadalupe Contreras explained that her novio had "made use of her" four times. "The first was not with my consent as I was asleep," she clarified, but "the other three times it was with my will."[33]

Beyond the testimonies provided, the ancillary documents that an investigation brought forward (letters, poetry, or, in the following example, a published fictional tale) also revealed the kinds of gendered scripts men and women used before judges and before one another. They reveal how changing patterns of traditional courtship caused anxieties among men that, nevertheless, could be exploited before judges. The freer sexual culture of a modernizing Mexico City created yet another reason for judges to question female chastity when presiding over cases of alleged sexual violence. In 1907, Francisca Salazar walked into the 7th Precinct located in the Santa María la Ribera neighborhood, a mainly middle-class area northwest of the Alameda. She reported her daughter, fourteen-year-old Carmen Carillo, missing and, more than likely, "in the power" of a twenty-six-year-old police agent named Guillermo de J. Escalante. She had asked her daughter the previous evening to go out and buy beer. Carmen did not return. A week later, Francisca Salazar entered the police precinct accompanied by the formerly missing girl. The mother explained that she had enlisted the help of Carmen's previous novio, Ricardo Pérez, to search for her daughter. The young man found Carmen with Guillermo at the train station, headed to the municipality of Iztacalco, southeast of the city. When he approached the couple, Guillermo fled, allowing Ricardo to apprehend Carmen. During her testimony, Carmen recounted that due to her mistreatment at the hands of her stepfather she had resolved to leave home with Guillermo. He took her to a house on the outskirts of town where "she had the carnal act and lost her virginity." She elaborated, noting that "I was obliged by force for I did not have free will to give." Nevertheless, she continued to live with Guillermo until discovered at the train station by her old novio Ricardo.

Guillermo appeared almost two weeks later to respond to the accusation. He was not arrested but provided a brief statement of his own volition. Carmen, on the night in question, came to him with stories of the abuse inflicted by her stepfather. She did not want to return home. "She turned herself over to me," Guillermo touted, "so that I would protect her." He took her to the home of a friend where they stayed for seven days. During that time, they had had sex, and he was willing to marry her.

Two days later, Carmen provided a more detailed report, albeit one that contradicted her previous claim about why she had left home. She began by disavowing having had an amorous relationship with the police agent Guillermo. She only knew him because a woman in her apartment building had introduced them, and it was that same woman who had instigated the rapto, telling Guillermo that "if he didn't take me, he was a coward." The night in question, Carmen claimed, Guillermo had taken her by force while she was out buying beer. She had not screamed "because she feared a scandal." When she sought the help of a stationed gendarme, Guillermo used his police credentials to foil her rescue. Later that night, she resisted sex with Guillermo, which led to a violent struggle that tore her clothes and took her virginity. For the next seven days, Guillermo kept her prisoner, not allowing her to leave or seek help. All of this, she insisted, was enabled by his position as a police agent. Carmen also confessed that her initial testimony of being mistreated by her stepfather was false and that in the seven years she had lived with him "he had always been good." Carmen refused Guillermo's marriage proposal because Ricardo Pérez was already her novio. Instead, she wanted the police agent punished for his abuse.

Due to the conflicting testimonies, the judge ordered a careo and issued a formal order that the police place Guillermo in the city jail while the investigation proceeded. Carmen and Guillermo each kept to their version of events. Carmen argued that, because of his police credentials, any witness he provided would uphold his statements, just as he had used his position to thwart her attempt to find help. Guillermo added that Carmen was not a doncella. She had told him that "one night while dreaming she had introduced her finger and that is how she lost her virginity," an account that Carmen acknowledged as true. The medical exam confirmed that her deflowering "was not recent."

Carmen's mother, Francisca Salazar, then appeared before the judge, holding a bundle of letters. The mother lamented that Guillermo had taken advantage of Carmen's young age and naivete. He must have seduced her, she asserted, because "he is very eloquent" and "words come easy to him." The mother appeared disappointed that Guillermo had failed to live up to his promise and marry Carmen in a timely manner, a promise she believed was made clear in several letters he had written to both her and Carmen. She was also convinced of Guillermo's "bad motives and perversity" when he had Ricardo Pérez arrested on false charges, although Ricardo was eventually released because of his obvious innocence. Along with the bundle of letters, Francisca provided a newspaper clipping of a short story from *El Popular* newspaper. Although the story had been written anonymously, she alleged Guillermo was the author because it mentioned Carmen by name and the street on which she lived. Finally, the mother recounted that an unknown woman had approached her, claiming to be Guillermo's amasia whom he had abandoned during her pregnancy, leaving her "to give birth at the hospital without his help."

The three letters Francisca provided had been written after Guillermo's original declaration to the investigating judge but before he was formally arrested and jailed. In the first letter, dated the day after he provided testimony, Guillermo addressed Carmen's mother, which suggests a familiarity between them. It showed that they had been working out marriage plans despite Carmen's protestations. He lamented that Francisca's actions, in bringing Carmen (whom he called his "intended") to the police precinct, had caused everyone involved embarrassment. He worried that Francisca had gone against the "assurances" she had offered him earlier that day. Guillermo had planned to go on the lam and leave Mexico City until the investigation was ended by a marriage agreement. At the end of the letter, Guillermo addressed Carmen specifically, telling her, "If you are with Ricardo, do not write me and it will be a sign that you have rejected my promises and give me my freedom. But, if your promises are not false and you are as dignified as I believe . . . [write me] and I will return to the capital. Goodbye . . . many kisses." Two days later, Guillermo had not yet left the city. He again wrote Carmen: "Thinking about leaving, but I don't know where. What will I do? Write verses for you while I think. I will dedicate them to you in some newspaper. Maybe *La Guacamaya*, for example, but my poor verses are so bad!" Alongside Carmen's testimony that she loved another, these letters make known a romantic rivalry, at least in Guillermo's mind.

The short story that appeared in *El Popular* accompanied the letters Carmen's mother provided authorities. It was published on March 1, 1908, during the nine-month investigation into Carmen's rapto. Titled "Flirtation: Of Which a Woman is Guilty" (*Coquetismo: De la que una mujer es culpable*), it tells the tale of a young woman named Carmen who lives in a vecindad on Puente de Esquiveles (the street that Carmen gave as her home address in her opening deposition) in a "horrible and infected hovel." The author describes Carmen's "profound stare," "upturned nose," and "a plump and red mouth made only, it seems, to give endless kisses and utter amorous words." Her body is "full of enticing curves made known by her bawdy dresses." Her flirtatiousness has generated a great deal of male interest in the neighborhood. Among her admirers two "charming" young men, Marquel Trovar and Ranulfo Wilchis, have gained her attention. Carmen relishes having these two "docile hearts at her feet" and is "in no hurry" to choose between them. Events take a tragic turn when each admirer learns of his rival. "An uncontrollable passion driven by jealousy" leads to a bloody street fight across from the "filthy window" from which Carmen watches. Trovar falls mortally wounded, a knife plunged into his chest. Wilchis, at the moment of the murder, regrets his actions, "immediately . . . coming to realize the cause of his perdition." With tears in his eyes, Wilchis is taken away by police "without resistance."[34]

Guillermo's story, as well as his letter to Carmen, offered investigating officials an account radically different from the one she had given them. In contending expressions of agency, Carmen and Guillermo each portray the other as the willful mastermind in an ordeal whose dual representations rely on the gendered scripts and expected roles that men and women had traditionally acted out in romantic dramas.[35] For Carmen's part (the passive, wounded female), even in her original declaration where she had reported her determination to leave home because of her stepfather's ill-treatment, she had explained her decision to have sex with Guillermo "as obliged by force" because "she did not have free will to give." In her second declaration, Carmen again denied possessing any will because she had been abducted by force and raped by Guillermo, a man who had used his police credentials to thwart her attempts to escape. Furthermore, she explained, it was a female neighbor's affront to his masculine honor—her calling him a "coward" if he failed to steal Carmen away—that had driven his decision-making. For his part, despite his claim that Carmen had masterminded the elopement in order to leave her abusive family, Guillermo's language couches his position in the gendered trope of the valiant male, protector of women. By reporting that he had honored Carmen's decision to leave home, Guillermo styled himself as a man who had relinquished his own will in a selfless act of chivalry. The letter he had written to Carmen—very likely knowing that a judge would read it—again characterized her as the mastermind pulling all the strings. It was *her* decision to choose between her two lovers, a decision that, according to Guillermo, "would set him free."

The tale of romance gone wrong published in *El Popular* was very likely Guillermo's. It presents an audacious characterization of male victimhood that underscores Guillermo's anxieties related to shifting class and gender roles in the modern city. As a member of the *policía reservada*, the plainclothes officers who served as detectives, Guillermo held a sense of middle-class respectability. He lived in a single-unit townhome and fancied himself a man of letters. In contrast, Carmen and her mother lived in a tenement building in the working-class neighborhood of Morelos that, in his tale, he ridicules as an "infected hovel." The story reproaches Carmen both for accentuating her beauty with bawdy dresses and for her "red mouth." These are likely references to lower-class women's newfound access to makeup and modern clothing styles made possible by a growing consumer culture and the rise of department stores that emerged in turn-of-the-century Mexico City.[36] Expanding urbanization and leisure opportunities increased young women's ability to meet potential suitors and maintain various premarital romantic relationships.[37] For Guillermo, as well as for numerous social critics of the day, modernization and the changing urban landscape had sparked a "social plague" of single women flirting (*coquetismo*) in order to "prostrate" men to their "cruel intention."[38] Carmen's alleged flirtations with the two suitors epitomized for Guillermo and like-minded critics a reckless form of female will that, rather than expressing moral rectitude and genuine commitment, instead expressed a moral flexibility that allowed modern girls the newfound agency to exercise romantic and sexual freedom. Indeed, Guillermo's claim that Carmen had lost her virginity by masturbation is further evidence, at least from a male perspective, of female freedom, a dangerous freedom that jeopardized traditional gender roles and had severe social repercussions, as the deadly fight between the not-so-fictional Marquel Trovar and Ranulfo Wilchis suggests. (It is likely that Marquel and Ranulfo are based on the real-life suitors and rivals, Guillermo and Ricardo.) Of course, the great irony in Guillermo's fictionalized portrait of his own victimization, particularly by a fourteen-year-old girl, is its damning disclosure of the obvious power imbalance between them. A reserve police officer who at one point had used his professional sway to arrest Carmen's other love interest, Guillermo represents a legal establishment that overwhelmingly allowed men to initiate sexual relations with few repercussions while lower-class girls' reputations were easily and, sometimes, seriously or even permanently damaged.

Rape

Women's assertions of will proved a double-edged sword. Such assertions empowered or subjugated them in different contexts and, at times, served to reinforce male-on-female, gender-based violence protected by enduring social, legal, and family beliefs about the inherent character of male and female sexuality. The 1871 Penal Code defined rape (violación) as the use of "physical or moral violence to copulate with a person, no matter their sex" or as "copulation with a person who does not have their faculties."[39] Despite this seemingly straightforward definition, rape accusations were rarely punished and were often reclassified as rapto or estupro during an investigation. Because legal authorities ranked deceit over violence as the defining trait of sexual crimes, the overwhelming majority of rape cases—even when women detailed a sexual assault—were adjudicated as rapto (abduction) or estupro (deflowering) rather than as violación (rape).[40] Furthermore, judges and lawyers viewed sex as inherently consensual and men as sexually aggressive by nature.[41] As a result, legal authorities and even parents often viewed sexual violence and rape as normal features of the courtship process. Within this context, it was extremely difficult for young women and girls to make legally credible accusations of sexual assault. Adding to this difficulty, women often summoned gendered scripts, strategically concocting accounts of violent abduction to gain emancipation while, at the same time, portraying themselves as chaste victims in an effort to bolster their social standing before the law.[42] On one hand, the prevalence of male sexual violence *could* make this a useful legal strategy. On the other, however, the normalization of gender roles identifying males as sexually aggressive and females as sexually passive, along with the repeated manipulation of these roles in the courts, often rendered testimonies unpersuasive.[43] Judges harshly interrogated young women who claimed they had been raped, asking why they had not screamed to alert family, neighbors, or police. In other cases where women claimed to have been taken by force, judges interrogated them as to why they had failed to alert one of the numerous police officers stationed across the city. In short, judges placed the legal and ethical onus on women by focusing on *their* actions rather than on those of the assailants. Given the entrenched nature of the social and legal biases against them, it is little surprise that most women avoided authorities altogether after suffering sexual violence.[44]

Similarly, considering the multiple obstacles women faced in holding men accountable for sexual assault, it is not surprising that some parents quickly capitulated to the status quo despite their daughters' demanding legal or financial indemnification. A parent who decided to end an investigation evinced either disbelief in a daughter's account or a pessimistic outlook on the probability of receiving justice. A case from 1889 highlights the seeming ambivalence parents demonstrated once a rape investigation began. Sitting in her vecindad apartment, Luisa Hernández grew concerned that her daughter had not yet returned from buying cigarettes. Luisa went out to the street where neighbors informed her that they had seen her daughter enter a nearby tenement. Alarmed, the mother ran into the building to find Ángel Cadena hiding her daughter, Regina Carrillo, under a blanket. She recruited a policeman standing at his post for help. The officer later told officials he had found Regina with blood on her *enaguas* (underskirt) and the mother, who had run ahead, struggling with the culprit. Regina testified that on the way back from buying cigarettes, she took a detour to return some borrowed scissors to her novio. As she entered his accesoria apartment, she told the judge, "he attacked me consummating the carnal act, leaving me in a state of de-virginity." "At the moment of consummating the carnal act," she continued, "he gave me a word of marriage." In his statement, Ángel disputed the claims of both the officer and the mother, denying he "had ever touched" Regina. Rather than push the matter further, though, Regina's mother abruptly dropped the accusation against Ángel without having secured a marriage proposal or financial agreement.[45] Although the judicial record does not detail Luisa Hernández's rationale for ending the case, her daughter's admission that she had entered a man's apartment alone may have been enough for the mother to see little hope in securing justice.

Similarly, in 1908, Raquel Ortega and Carmen Murillo, two friends employed at a printshop, left work at the end of the day to meet their boyfriends. That night the foursome went out drinking and then to the Hotel del Semanario near the city's main cathedral where each couple rented a room. Carmen told officials that she reminded her novio about his promise of marriage before he "forced himself and abused me several times." Responding to the judge's queries, she explained that she had not screamed in order to avoid a "scandal." Raquel, in a similar account, said that her novio "held my hands against my head while the next two times he did not have to as I did not resist despite the pain." She, too, did not scream, also, like her friend, trying to avoid a "scandal." Yet before the men could be arraigned for questioning, the mothers of the two girls dropped their accusations and brought their daughters home.[46] In these two cases, we find parents seemingly resigned to a lack of legal justice and ambivalent about the community and social repercussions of non-virgin daughters. Indeed, judges were highly skeptical about rape accusations, viewing women's public presence, alone, as evidence of disreputable behavior that instigated men's sexual violence.[47] Conceivably holding views similar to the judges', parents also may have doubted a daughter's account, though, perhaps, with more sympathy, recognizing the allure of romantic adventure and sexual pleasure.

Tolerating Sexual Violence

As long as a marriage promise had been made and kept, parents tolerated or, even, accepted sexual violence against a daughter as part of the courtship process.[48] The mother of Romana Montaño, for example, demanded that her daughter marry her alleged rapist. According to Romana, as she left her vivienda, Jesús Medina pulled her into his apartment. "After he closed the door," she recounted, "he pulled down my underskirt (*enaguas*) and pushed me face-up on the bed . . . and laid on top of me. I was about to scream but Jesús held my throat and said if I screamed, now or later, he would kill me." Despite Jesús's claim that Romana "loves me very much," Romana insisted that they did not have the kind of relationship that would permit him "to take such liberties." Romana's mother nevertheless sought a marriage, only to learn that Jesús was already ecclesiastically married to another woman in the neighborhood. She ended the investigation telling the judge, "it is better for Romana to stay as she is and not suffer with a man who doesn't know how to deliver on his promises."[49] Parents' demands that daughters marry their rapists reflected two realities: first, the legal system provided men ample opportunity to commit violent sexual acts with little repercussion, whether a marriage promise was upheld or not; second, confronting a set of limited options, parents usually preferred marriage to the economic hardships a daughter would likely face if she became pregnant or the social stigma that could threaten her future marriage or amasiato prospects. Indeed, for the mother in this case, Jesús's commitment to another woman and his inability to "keep promises" suggest that concerns about trustworthiness and economic responsibility weighed more heavily than the violent assault on Romana.

The testimony of some girls and young women also exposes the idea that sexual violence was forgivable as long as men offered marriage and economic security in the form of the diario. Rather than suggest an acceptance of rape as a standard part of courtship, the notion of forgivable rape reflected the realities women faced in a legal system that viewed sex as inherently consensual and denied them free will in the right to refuse it.[50] When twelve-year-old Luz Pineda left her vecindad to do her morning shopping (mandado), she was approached by Félix López who lived in the same building. Luz told the judge that Félix "had never spoken to me about love," so she was surprised when he invited her on a stroll. She declined. Feeling jilted, according to the girl, he threatened "to cut my face if I didn't go with him." They spent the day wandering the streets and ended up in Tacubaya, eight kilometers away from where he had abducted her. While there, Félix tried to have sex with Luz in a cornfield, but she opposed. Later, he took her to a fonda (inn) to eat before they walked back to the city and spent the night at a casa de cita. "It was there I lost my virginity," she told the judge: "Félix made use of my person four times," and "each time I screamed." When the judge pressed her as to why she had not run away or notified a police officer on the street, Luz reiterated that she feared Félix would cut her face. Luz then claimed that she lived with him "against her will" for one month, during which time they "lived a married life" with Félix providing two reales a day as her diario. It was only after Félix had failed to keep his marriage promise that she returned to her mother to have him arrested.[51]

Fifteen-year-old Julia Rojas returned home early one morning in 1907. When pressed by her mother as to why she had not come home the night before, Julia lied, saying she had lost track of time chatting with friends in the *zaguán* (breezeway) of another building. Her mother, incredulous, compelled Julia to confess that she had been "tricked" by Pablo Hernández. He had invited her to go see his aunts but, instead, took her to a room where he "obligated her to have the carnal act." Julia "did not expect anything nefarious," as she later told officials, because Pablo had been courting her "for a long time." She went on to provide a graphic account of Pablo's sexual assault: "He put me in a room where there was only a bed and a table. He grabbed me by the arms and threw me on the bed. I did not want to open my legs, but by sticking his knees between my legs he finally did the carnal act. Throughout the night he did it several more times. Each time it was against my will and I screamed for help."

Pablo's account differed considerably. He claimed to have met Julia on Calle Rebelde as she left her job at a printshop. He invited her to the cinematograph, but she initially declined. Julia, though, according to Pablo, proposed that he pay her four pesos to cover her work shift so that she could accompany him. Pablo and Julia then spent several hours walking around the city while Pablo looked for friends and family to lend him the money. By 10:30 p.m., Julia had missed her shift, and Pablo had given up looking for a lender. It was also too late for either one to go home. Pablo rented a room at the Hotel de la Amargura, an establishment of dubious repute known for its clientele of prostitutes and criminals.[52] "I made use of Julia with her will," he told officials and concluded his testimony saying, "had Julia not come willingly she could have called a gendarme or any other person to make known her opposition." After a failed careo where Pablo and Julia both insisted on their original statements, Julia's mother withdrew the accusation.[53] It appears that Julia's mother saw little benefit in extending the legal proceedings against her daughter's assailant. She more than likely interpreted Julia's willingness to stroll the streets with her novio and to spend the night with him at a hotel—at least in the judge's eyes—as proof of *her* culpability in the assault.

Although Fidoncia Iturralde had been living with her amasio, José García, for eight months and was pregnant, her parents, from the rural municipality Milpa Alta, dragged the couple to court when they located them living in Mexico City. José, the parents alleged, had been married ecclesiastically to Fidoncia's sister before running away with her younger sibling. When questioned, Fidoncia—who spoke Nahuatl and not Spanish—provided contradictory testimonies. She initially claimed that, once José promised marriage, she "agreed to his desires," losing her virginity and moving to the city. Yet, when questioned several days later, she provided a strikingly different account. He had threatened her with a gun, she now claimed, to make her leave her family and have sex. The judge concluded there was no crime because Fidoncia was eighteen and living with José in amasiato.[54] Both this case and the preceding one involving Julia and Pablo demonstrate that judges and parents were skeptical about daughters' claims of male sexual violence when it appeared that they had willingly accompanied their attackers, whether for a night or for a month. Judges were especially suspicious when women altered their original testimonies, retelling events to stress abduction and sexual violence.

Indignation

The preponderance of cases examined here foreground social mores tolerant of male sexual violence, especially as an accepted precursor to marriage or cohabitation. Consequently, case examples of young women who vehemently refused marriage, even in the face of parental pressure, stand out. They reveal moments when women steadfastly rejected patriarchal norms and expectations in spite of the considerable economic and social risks such refusal could entail. Dolores Martínez, a domestic servant, was out buying her employer cigarettes when Apolonio Franco dragged her to a house in Colonia de la Bolsa. There, according to her testimony, "he made use of me, as a result [taking] my virginity." "These acts were without my will," she insisted, "as I have no affection toward Apolonio Franco and want him punished." Although Apolonio swore they had had a three-month relationship and that he planned to marry Dolores, her father ended the case without seeking a marriage because of his daughter's opposition.[55]

Marcelina Zamudio, a domestic working in Colonia Guerrero, reported that, while on her way to night school, she was yanked into the accesoria of a vecindad where José Hernández, with help from his brother, took her virginity, raping her and injuring her arm. When authorities dismissed the case for "lack of merit," she penned an angry letter to the judge. After recounting the events that led to the rape, she wrote:

My abductor did not even use seduction as is commonly used by criminals of this nature, first making promises of marriage and starting amorous relations. Instead, he used no words, kidnapping and threatening me until consummating the crime. The force that was used to put me in the accesoria was witnessed by two people . . . as well as my *patrón* (boss) Don Alfredo and the gendarme who took me from that room where I was sequestered. . . . José Hernández has already confessed to the crime of estupro but seeks to evade responsibility by offering marriage. . . . As I see that he is free and continuing to mock me, I suppose it has been declared that there is no way to proceed against him for these crimes, although I was not notified of this decision. . . . As such, based in article 67 of the Code for Criminal Procedures, I intervene to appeal that resolution.

After composing another letter asking the judge to reconsider his verdict, the case file ends.[56] While her view was surely shared by many women, even though its expression is difficult to find in the judicial record, Marcelina articulated a clear rejection of misogynistic conventions that ignored acts of violence when they were followed by a marriage offer. For Marcelina, José's marriage proposal offered cold comfort in the face of her rape. In her letter, Marcelina not only makes clear her rejection of José's proposal but challenges the categorization of her sexual assault as an "abduction" or "deflowering," a common legal practice. By emphasizing that José "used no words," Marcelina debunks any claim of seduction or deceit—both essential to the legal definitions of rapto and estupro—plainly arguing that his crime constituted the crime of rape (violación). Having witnesses that included her patrón and a police officer whose testimonies supported her claim fortified Marcelina's hope to secure José's punishment. But as a domestic, Marcelina lacked respectability in the eyes of the elite officials whom she admonished. As noted in chapter 1, the middle and upper classes regarded domestics as both dishonest and sexually available. This mindset, coupled with a legal system that viewed sex as inherently consensual, ensured in this case that a violent male's sexual entitlement ultimately prevailed.

True Romance

While it would be easy to conclude that male violence dominated lower-class premarital or nonmarital sexual relationships, as well as gender relations more generally,[57] many cases suggest the possibility of true affection between couples. Let us call these cases "true romance" cases. The dry, legalistic recording of testimony, together with the secrecy and privacy that many young couples protected, fogs the flirtations, passions, and intimacies that surely shaped romantic love. It is also worth noting that by positing a binary relationship between truth and authenticity on one hand and manipulated gender scripts (explored in the previous examination of sexual violence) on the other, we run the risk of oversimplifying judicial testimony and thereby missing its subtleties. Nevertheless, "true romance" cases hint at moments of joy, tenderness, and devotion between men and women. Such cases, where testimonies are straightforward and couples show no disagreement in their accounts of events contrast sharply with the shifting testimonies that characterize cases of sexual violence. Similarly, third-party descriptions of young love and intimate letters between couples found in the judicial record offer glimpses of presumably authentic affection. Even so, the following examples, produced in legal proceedings, show romantic couples who strategically crafted their testimonies to portray themselves in the best possible light. Consequently, it is often impossible to know whether or not the scripts they enacted truly represented the emotions and desires that lay in their hearts. But they do offer us an idea of how the possibility of true romance might be imagined.

The fact that some young couples made clear their desire to be together, despite family opposition, suggests an authentic disposition to base their relationship choices on deeply felt affection and attraction, on self-realization and pleasure, rather than on family, community, and social expectations. While such feelings and aspirations define romance in twentieth- and twenty-first-century modernity,[58] rapto cases provide abundant evidence that the roots of romantic love were well established in turn-of-the-century Mexico City, especially among the working class and poor. Examples of companionate unions highlight women's opportunities to exercise agency in contexts that did not assume male sexual aggression and thereby challenged misogynistic norms of male domination.[59]

The legal risks women took when acknowledging that desire and affection had led them to initiate sexual relations suggest that their declarations were less scripted than authentic. Indeed, when articulated by both the man and the woman, the clear expression before judicial authorities of willing and mutual emotional engagement suggests genuine trust between couples. They show confidence that the other will not renege on a pledge or change testimony in a way that could place the other in legal jeopardy or diminish his or her social standing. Women's positions in cases involving accusations of rape were markedly different from those in cases involving genuine romance. In both, women could express will and agency, but under starkly dissimilar conditions. In the first instance, women often exercised will to achieve emancipation from parental authority. But because of entrenched gender bias in the law, where female consent was often legally evaluated to a woman's disadvantage, the exercise of personal will was always a precarious choice. By contrast, in cases that seem to indicate a couple's genuine romance, women could exercise agency to achieve their desired ends without fear of a partner's abandonment. In its simplest articulation, women told officials about the "affection" they had for their lovers to contradict family claims that men had used deceit or coercion. "[He] did not use force or deceit and I went willingly with him because of the affection I have for him" was a common declaration.[60] Such positive affirmations of personal will suggest that cases involving true romance helped forge a "simultaneous construction of self and couple."[61]

Numerous cases show young couples unequivocal about their love for one another. In 1885, Luis Vásquez courted María Concepción Delahanty despite her family's opposition because he lacked "a career or profession." "I love her a great deal and could not stop seeing her," he professed to her brother, warning that he would be with her "by good or by bad means" (*a la buena ó a la mala*). María Concepción clearly felt the same way. She ran away with Luis after her parents declined his marriage offer. "We decided to run away from my paternal home to freely marry," she recounted.[62] In a similar case, when her lover made a sudden proposal to get married after four months of courtship, María Trinidad Nava eagerly agreed, "being in a position to do so because I love him," she told authorities. They went to the Hotel Merced to consummate their love and their decision. Pablo de la O, her novio, told officials in equally enthusiastic terms that "everything stated by María Trinidad is true. I am willing to cover her honor and marry." María's initially skeptical father, it appears, saw Pablo's claim as sincere and was convinced to support their marriage.[63] In another remarkable, case, an illiterate day laborer paid a scribe to record his unequivocal longing and love. In the letter he addressed his novia as his "adored young lady," telling her, "I love you with all my heart, and it is a pure and true love as the angels' love. If you love me as I love you, if you are the young woman who I love and adore, I will be happy with you as you will be with me."[64]

Most cases, though, proved less dramatic. Women made candid statements of affection for their lovers and exercised highly personal decision-making that typically left parents with little recourse. "Because I have much affection for him I agreed to go to a house on 5a Guerrero and spend the night," Dionicia Esteves explained.[65] Similarly, fifteen-year-old Inés de la Fuente admitted, "I went voluntarily to the Hotel Independencia and had carnal relations with him several times that night. I did this only obligated because of the affection I have for him."[66] Cayetana López brought the investigation against her novio to a speedy end when she insisted that no accusation should have been made against him because "I went with my full will and because of the affection I have for him."[67] Though accused by her mother of having been seduced by a thirty-year-old bricklayer, Macedonia Escobedo countered by telling authorities that "When José made use of my person, he did so with my full will as I love him and it is my will to marry him as he promised."[68]

In the previous cases, sexual desire and pleasure appear as both motivation and basis for fulfillment, romance, and marriage. In other cases, the judicial file shows either no discussion of sex at all or instead documents a couple's decision to postpone sex until after marriage. In cases such as these, emotional bonding outweighs an impulsive drive to sexual gratification, exemplifying what William Reddy calls "longing for association."[69] Because the initiation of sexual relations was often strategically and legally key to a daughter's emancipation, examples of purely companionate unions rarely emerge from the case files. Although they had never consummated their relationship, Franquilina Ramírez went to live with a neighborhood gendarme from Tepito because of the "affection" she had to toward him and his daughters from a previous relationship.[70] In 1898, Tomás Bernal followed his love interest, Hilaria Martínez, from the State of Hidalgo to Tacuba, where her parents had sent her to live with her aunt. He found work there as a jornalero. Not long afterward, the couple ran away and lived in amasiato for six months. With Tomás earning five reales a day, Hilaria told officials, they had saved a little each day in the hope of returning "to their land (*tierra*)" to marry.[71] In a case revealing a couple's similar longing to be together, María Arce made known her desire for a relationship with Luis Guevara and received from him a proposal. When Luis offered to marry her, she told him, "if you keep your word, I will work to sustain us."[72] Case files that show men and women identifying mutual goals and mutual support as central aims in their relationship provide tangible examples of how the exercise of personal will could become a "construction of self and couple." A man's or woman's open declaration of commitment to another individual, the attempt to make real to court and community the facts of personal will and relationship, provided proof of an authentic union.

Mutual confidence and commitment also revealed themselves in the actions of runaway couples who postponed sexual relations in order to demonstrate their strength of will to apprehensive parents and skeptical judges. Twenty-year-old Pedro Balleza and fifteen-year-old María Javier Acedo chose to run away together in the face of their parents' opposition to their relationship. María made clear the couples' mutual fondness and defended their actions by stating, "I ran away from home this afternoon with my novio Pedro because I love him very much and he loves me too." The confidence of her declaration stands out vividly because few women made claims so bold before legal officials. Not only did Pedro agree, he elaborated on their justification in a language of honor and endearment: "We mutually agreed to abandon our homes because our parents do not want us together. . . . I promise on my word of honor that I respected the girl and haven't touched her at all. . . . I wish with all my will and affection that she be my wife under the law of god and under civil law."[73] By *not* initiating sexual relations, young couples had less leverage with parents opposed to their union because, without the shame of her dishonor, parents had the option to bring a daughter back home. But for Pedro, it was that very abnegation that served, in his mind, as irrefutable evidence of his sincere and honest commitment to María. Rather than describe María as having willingly agreed to her abduction, as men most often did, Pedro spoke of their "mutually agreed" decision to run away and *not* have sex.

Young couples' desire to be together was not only demonstrated in their plans to marry or form mutually supportive unions. It was also shown in acts of sacrifice. For example, the words and deeds of Refugio Falcón proved her loving commitment to José Zaynos. When her parents brought her home while José sat in prison, she immediately ran away again. She did so, she told the judge, to prepare him food and bring it to the jail every day while the court investigated. "I did this by my own will and because of the great affection I have for him," she explained. And although she acknowledged having had sex with José and hoping to marry him, she told the judge, "I ask nothing of him." While José sat in jail, Refugio penned a letter to her "Adorado Prietito mio," (my adored little darkskin). In it, she reiterated her view of marriage: "If they want you to, say you will marry me, just say it, even if we don't. All I want is for you to be in liberty." Her admission to the judge, as well as her written pronouncement that marriage did not matter, left her mother with little choice but to end the case.[74] Refugio's actions, writings, and clear articulation of will make known a selfless commitment beyond the bounds of family expectation, a preoccupation with and devotion to the well-being of her romantic partner.

Conclusion

For the judges who investigated and adjudicated sexual crimes and sought to determine legal culpability, personal will was a legal term used to identify who possessed and exerted agency. For the couples involved in rapto and estupro dramas, acknowledging the exercise of will in forming consensual romantic relationships offered proof of commitment before judges, parents, and one another. Yet the notion of will—and whether or not it was truly possessed and exerted—was articulated differently by the various individuals with stakes in a criminal investigation. The law, for example, denied girls under the age of sixteen the capacity to exercise free will, automatically assuming deceit or seduction on the part of males in cases of rapto and estupro. Yet plenty of cases show underaged girls who vociferously avowed their will to be with their partners or paramours. In the face of such avowals of personal will and agency, parents—even though they knew the law entitled them to control their daughters' actions up to age sixteen—were most often left with little recourse. While the law could allow parents to bestow upon daughters their own right to choose a romantic partner, most often daughters in Mexico City simply seized that right.

At the same time, men demonstrated personal will by asserting their commitment to marry and "cover the honor" lost in a daughter's deflowering. Such statements showed they were men of their word.[75] Most often, though, men emphasized the free will of the women with whom a relationship had landed them before authorities. They claimed that the women had *willingly* run away or had *willingly* had sex. In some cases, they claimed that it was the women themselves who had masterminded an abduction to escape parental authority. One police officer went so far as to claim that his fourteen-year-old girlfriend had manipulated and deceived him, spinning a tale of male victimization and self-sacrifice that revealed his anxieties about the ways the modern city and new consumer culture allowed girls greater sexual freedom and the power to exert their wills at men's expense.

Women took the greatest risk when they made unequivocal pronouncements of will after running away or starting sexual relations because, in so doing, they mitigated men's legal responsibility. A woman's decision to privately divulge her willingness to her lover opened the door for him to abuse her trust. Considering the legal risks women faced, they often characterized their willingness to have sex as something decided only after a promise of marriage had been made. Furthermore, it is no surprise that in their testimonies they employed gendered language that stressed their passive role in forming romantic relationships. In the extreme cases of sexual violence and rape, even when women agreed to marry their abuser, they made known before authorities that they had not possessed nor exerted will when men transgressed appropriate boundaries. Women, then, denied their possession of will in cases of sexual assault, while the law, because it viewed sex as inherently consensual, denied women the right to exercise free will in giving consent. And, indeed, as related to sexual violence, it was within the context of competing views of will that the law defined men's criminal behavior as either deceitful abduction (rapto) or deflowering (estupro) but *not* rape. For this reason, a woman's declaration of will proved much more successful in her gaining adult independence from parental authority and opposition than it did in holding men legally or financially accountable for sexual crimes. In contrast, by making firm statements of their personal will to form relationships, women exhibited confidence in the commitment of their lovers. Cases that disclose romantic partners' mutual trust offer clear indications of how expressions of will simultaneously constructed the self and the couple.[76] In the next chapter, we focus on the different forms of domestic partnership and romantic commitment that constituted a couple's "being together."

4

Being Together

This chapter examines the different ways that working-class men and women formed relationships, whether permanent, temporary, or fleeting. The cases show overwhelmingly that endogamy—the formation of unions between individuals born to similar economic circumstances—was the standard practice among the working classes. Judicial records reflect the social statistics gathered by the era's federal agencies, revealing that partners who mutually agreed to run away together most commonly formed consensual informal unions known as amasiato.[1] Couples also formally married through the state-sanctioned civil registry or were married through the Church, though ecclesiastical unions were not state-sanctioned. In rare cases, they did both. Rapto and estupro cases sometimes expose examples of couples engaging in brief sexual encounters unencumbered by expectations of long-term commitment. Such instances tend to appear in cases where parents brought charges against men whom they believed had seduced or deceived their daughters. While these cases sometimes ended with a (seemingly forced) marriage proposal, close examination of the events and actions of romantically involved individuals suggests examples of youths engaging in casual sex. While endogamy and amasiato were common, an exploration of the judicial record shows a diverse array of behaviors, practices, and values related to domestic partnership and sexual life among the lower classes. This heterogeneity sheds light on how government policymaking, legal codes, social tradition, and cultural norms met people's acceptance, resistance, or ambivalence in their everyday interactions with the state and with each other.

The Preference for Illegitimacy

Working-class Mexicans chose amasiato—long-term consensual unions—as the most common form of cohabitation. Whether officiated by Church or state, instances of amasiato significantly exceeded instances of marriage.[2]

Only marriages conducted by the government's civil registry were recognized as legally binding and, as a result, children born to ecclesiastical marriage were considered illegitimate.[3] Amasiato represented a less expensive way to cohabitate than traditional marriage, which often involved costly ceremonies and administrative fees. Amasiato also offered young women significant independence insofar as they were emancipated from parental authority but not under the legal power of a husband.[4] Furthermore, as Ana Lidia García Peña notes, by the late nineteenth century, the hardening divide between the public and private spheres strengthened male domestic authority and control. Married women found themselves disadvantaged by liberal laws that erased colonial era protections and led to increased domestic violence while eroding women's opportunities to exercise freedom of movement and economic independence.[5]

When describing the nature of their relationships in legal cases, couples often stated that they lived "as married." Living "as married" typically meant that men and women in amasiato expected two fundamental commitments: monogamy and the man's provision of a diario or *gasto* to cover daily household expenses in exchange for the woman's domestic labor. The ability to maintain a home through mutual but gender-specific work was an important marker of adulthood.[6] In Mexico City, though, women were not always able to maintain gender specificity in their household labors because many of them also had to work in the city's formal and informal economies. Furthermore, in many cases, young couples moved into the already-crowded tenement apartments of family, typically the man's parents. Judicial files make clear that the parents of romantically involved couples likewise lived in amasiato, often with their children from previous relationships alongside them. Given such economic and social circumstances, amasiato weakened traditional assumptions about marital obligation as defined by the trope of the nuclear-family household.[7]

The ways that men and women defined their relationships before legal authorities reveal that, although informal and sometimes ephemeral, amasiato was understood as a legitimate commitment despite its lack of civil sanction. Let us consider the following examples. Vidal Pérez told a judge that although he did not find his novia to be a doncella, "I did not find this problematic in keeping our relationship, so we moved into a home and I gave her the title of wife."[8] María Guadalupe Rodríguez admitted that her lover had never promised marriage, either verbally or in writing. She abandoned her parental home, she insisted, "because he promised to provide a house and live by my side."[9] One man who was mistakenly arrested for a rapto he did not commit indignantly declared he had a family "although not being married legitimately" and had "never even thought about getting involved with another person."[10] For him, amasiato was not only legitimate, it was solemn.

Even in cases that were resolved by a couple's promise to wed, the realities of working-class life—as well as Mexico City's low rates of civil marriage generally—suggest that couples simply continued to live in amasiato. Parents might withdraw a rapto or estupro accusation after a marriage promise that, in practice, meant a man agreed to provide a woman with a home and financial support. For instance, when authorities arrested Hermenegildo Madrigal for "abducting" María de San Juan for over two weeks, he insisted that he did so at her bidding. Abused by her mother and her mother's amasio, María left home without a marriage proposal. Yet after several days in municipal jail, Hermenegildo gave a reluctant promise to wed that, while ending the ordeal, was not especially convincing given his insistence that he had not planned to marry and that the couple had made no attempt to do so in the weeks prior to his arrest.[11] Another case shows that even when legal marriage was impossible, the promise of financial support while "living as married" could sway a reluctant parent. Police officer Cristóbal Buendía, who lived alone on the south side of Mexico City near Campo Florido, had separated from his wife to whom he was legally married. He began a new relationship with Guadalupe Villegas, a sixteen-year-old domestic who worked in the neighborhood. He needed a woman, he told officials, "to offer her services because life was tough." The couple "lived as married" for several days before Guadalupe's family had him arrested for deceiving her with a promise of marriage he could not legally fulfill. Cristóbal sought to show his commitment to Guadalupe, telling the judge, "when we had sex she wasn't a virgin but I don't care." He then added wishfully, "if I were not already married, I would give her my name." Cristóbal tried to make things right: he promised Guadalupe's father that, if he agreed, he would live with Guadalupe "by his side as before." If the father did not agree, Cristóbal would pay him an "indemnification." It seems that one of these offers pleased the father, who dropped the charges against him immediately.[12]

Amasiato and Economic Instability

Especially in an urban setting such as Mexico City, amasiato did not replicate the financial and domestic expectations associated with traditional marriage. Middle- and upper-class families—despite the disappearance of the dowry expectation—continued to see marriages as financial alliances between families.[13] Because this view of marriage was impractical for the lower class, concubinage or delaying marriage (perhaps indefinitely) allowed couples the chance to obtain economic stability through shared labor and domestic responsibilities.[14] The experience of Leandra González provides an intimate view of how working-class individuals forged and dissolved amasiato unions and how the freedom and flexibility of these relationships suited lives defined by economic instability. On March 26, 1901, Leandra González appeared before the Ministerio Público of Mexico City to make a complaint against her daughter's novio. Ysidro Moreno, she claimed, had taken her nineteen-year-old daughter, Luz Pombo, from home six weeks earlier with a promise of marriage, only to immediately abandon her. This was the second time the irate mother had come to authorities, as she had already forced the couple to a police station once before in an attempt to get a promise of marriage from Ysidro. Unable to provide a description of the abductor because of her poor eyesight, she instead provided authorities with an address where he could be found, having obtained it from his neighbors. Authorities, though, were unable to find him until two months later at a different vecindad on Calle Hidalgo. They brought Ysidro to the nearby 5th Precinct to make a statement.

The twenty-seven-year-old told authorities that while visiting his girlfriend at her home in Tacubaya, he had invited her to come live with him in the city, to which she agreed "immediately." That day they had the "carnal act," but he did not find her to be a doncella. For that reason, he continued, he could not assure her of a promise to marry. Nevertheless, the couple lived for about a month in amasiato before Ysidro decided to separate from Luz to look for work outside the city. He had not seen her since. In the following months, Ysidro traveled to Guanajuato, San Luis Potosí, and Toluca, working as a painter. When he returned to the city, Ysidro told officials, he had learned that Luz now lived in amasiato with a tailor whom she planned to marry. Ysidro then referred officials to a female neighbor who could elaborate on Luz's whereabouts and current relationship. Providing a second statement that same day, Luz's mother admitted that her daughter indeed had been living in "illicit relations" with a tailor named Ángel Pacheco. The tailor, she explained, was currently imprisoned for beating Luz.

Months after the ordeal began, Luz Pomba finally testified to authorities. She explained that she had been briefly the novia of Ysidro who had taken her from Tacubaya to live in the city. After a short time, Ysidro disappeared, forcing her to leave the house where rent was no longer being paid. Not wanting to return to her parents, she moved to another part of the city, though she never stated where. She explained that her mother nevertheless found her and brought her back home, during which time the charges against Ysidro were being adjudicated. She concluded by telling authorities that as Ysidro had not yet been apprehended, she had begun new relations with Ángel Pacheco and now lived with him in amasiato. The investigating judge quickly concluded that no crime had taken place and closed the file.[15]

Young women could use sexual relationships and cohabitation to break free of parental authority, even if that meant exchanging one form of mala vida for another, as it appears Luz did.[16] The booming population of Mexico City and the crowded vecindades that allowed news and gossip about people's relationships to travel quickly also provided opportunities for young people to form fleeting relationships through amasiato, a form of union less formal than legal marriage. Within this context, young men and women entered and exited amorous and sexual relationships unburdened by feelings of public or family shame. Rather, they undertook actions that aligned with their social and sexual needs. Amasiato offered women the opportunity to be emancipated from parental authority *and* avoid subjugation to male power while retaining the option to legally castigate a partner in cases of abuse, which Luz did.[17] Last, it is worth highlighting that the other man in this case, Ángel Pacheco, entered into amasiato with Luz despite public knowledge of her former relationship, thereby revealing a masculinity that did not hinge on the sexual purity of a partner (the central focus of chapter 6).

While amasiato was the norm, cases also show that some parents, especially those who were legally married, demanded that suitors formally wed their daughters. One family had their daughter's intended arrested after only five days of their living in amasiato. Getting him to recommit to his marriage proposal in front of authorities, the girl's mother—who pointedly began her testimony by telling the judge she was legitimately married—warned that she would bring the accusation again if the marriage was not verified.[18] Likewise, Marcelina Velásquez, a forty-eight-year-old widow living in Colonia Indianilla on the south side of the city, had her daughter's amasio arrested on two different occasions for his failure to marry her. The mother, in October 1903, had the couple apprehended and brought to the civil registry where legal marriages were performed. Although it is unclear why, they were unable to marry that day. The couple again continued to live in amasiato until April 1904 when the mother again hauled them to the local police precinct. Enrique Soto, a twenty-year-old electrician, told officials he planned to marry the daughter but presently lacked the necessary resources (*falta de recursos*). This claim apparently assuaged the mother who dropped her charge.[19] In another case, Soledad Rodríguez had run away twice to "make marital life" but had never received a promise of marriage. Although her parents insisted on a marriage proposal from or punishment for Soledad's lover Enrique Bustos, the judge declared that, as there was no proof of a written marriage proposal, and, as Soledad, who was older than sixteen, had joined Enrique willingly, no crime had been committed. And so, the couple returned to making a "marital life."[20] In these two cases, as in most, the men cited their precarious financial situations as the reason for their failure to keep their marriage promises. Challenging this common refrain among men reluctant to marry,[21] parents dragged them before officials in attempts to keep them honest. A man's financial insecurity often proved a barrier to a couple's legitimate, state-sanctioned marriage, a problem that was recognized and reported by some newspaper commentators but rarely by social reformers.

Amasiato and Gendered Inequality

Couples claimed that amasiato allowed them to live as married while they prepared for a civilly sanctioned marriage with its bureaucratic and financial demands. As already noted, men often claimed that penury undermined their ability to marry. As civil marriage was performed at no expense in Mexico City,[22] the costs associated with it probably involved the expensive process of acquiring necessary documents such as birth records, whether from ecclesiastical or civil authorities, and the pricey celebrations expected by family and friends.[23] But amasiato could prove fleeting and, being legally unbinding, it provided men the opportunity to renege on conjugal commitments. The potentially ephemeral nature of amasiato was always more dangerous to women than to men because women could be unceremoniously abandoned, often with children.[24] One mother allowed her daughter to live in amasiato for more than one year before charging the man with rapto, only to learn he was already married.[25] Similarly, after "living matrimonially" for a month, Antonio Sánchez decided to leave his amasia Delfina Pérez, prompting her family to have him arrested. But because Delfina was seventeen and had agreed to go with Antonio willingly, the judge determined no crime had been committed.[26] Simón Peralta convinced the mother of María Burgos that he had planned to marry her daughter after taking her virginity one night at a hotel. The couple planned to live in amasiato while Simón "prepared the needed formalities" at the civil registry. But after eleven days, Simón got cold feet, abandoned María, and left for Toluca, blaming his actions on María's "insufferable jealousy."[27]

In a patriarchal society where de facto and de jure law allowed men greater sexual freedom than women, amasiato gave men the opportunity to philander with far less consequence, legal or otherwise, than would have been permitted within a legitimate, civil marriage. An adultery accusation, though, could land men in jail during investigations and result in one- to two-year prison sentences, depending on the circumstances. Such instances were rare and only enforceable when a couple was legally married.[28] Teresa Rocha found herself embroiled in a rapto case when her amasio of three years, Ysidro Morán, was arrested for the rapto of sixteen-year-old Dolores Villagrán. She testified that she had noticed a young girl hanging around the shoe store where Ysidro worked. Although he claimed the girl was merely buying borax for her ironing, the suspicious Teresa confronted Dolores, demanding she stay away from Ysidro. According to Teresa, Dolores "laughed and mocked" her and continued to do so each time they saw each other at the shoe store. Dolores, it appears, saw Ysidro's amasiato as temporary and expendable. She told authorities she had begun sexual relations with him after his marriage proposal. But when Ysidro refused to leave his amasia, Dolores turned to her parents who promptly had him arrested.[29] Dolores gambled on the promise of a legally binding marriage only to be disillusioned by her paramour.

The Multiple Meanings of *Amasiato*

One case, though shrouded in mystery, shows that some couples considered amasiato binding and solemn while others considered it provisional and frangible, depending on their hopes and desires. Camila Solís, the mother of Juliana Zamorano, was aware of her amorous relationship with twenty-one-year-old Alberto Cortés. Three years earlier, when Juliana was only twelve years old, she had moved in with her aunt who lived in the same vecindad as Alberto, just north of the city's main cathedral. It did not take long for him to start courting Juliana. His overtures worried Juliana's aunt who, "not wanting any responsibility" for the romance, sent the girl back home. Later, when she was older, Juliana was fired from her job as a domestic servant "because there was a man always chasing her." Her employer had found her regularly chatting with Alberto from the balcony. On the night of June 7, 1906, Juliana told her mother she planned to meet Alberto.

Apparently accepting their relationship, Camila Solís did not oppose. But Juliana failed to return home that night. The mother, concerned, went to the stand where Alberto worked as a coach driver and found Juliana sitting on the ground across the street. After a brief discussion with her daughter, Camila called on a nearby gendarme to take the couple to the nearest police precinct for interrogation, and she accused Alberto of rapto.

During her initial deposition, Juliana recounted that she had met Alberto at the Alameda one evening to go for a stroll. They went to a nearby restaurant where Alberto gave her "several large cups of sherry," which made her inebriated (*trastornada*). The couple returned to the Alameda where they walked until midnight. Alberto then "took her to a house . . . only inhabited by an old man" (more than likely a casa de cita). Juliana told the judge that, in a nearly empty room with only a bed, she and Alberto had had sex after he promised to marry her. Early the next morning, he took her to stay at a friend's house and promised to return after work. By 5 p.m., Juliana got tired of waiting and went to find Alberto; she decided to wait for him across the street from his taxi stand where she was discovered by her mother.

In his initial deposition, Alberto denied everything. He claimed that he and Juliana had planned to meet but that she had never shown up. He then went home and to work the next morning. It was there that Juliana and her mother appeared with a police officer to arrest him. In his next deposition, three days later, Alberto dramatically changed his story. He began by acknowledging his long relationship with Juliana, admitting that their relationship had, on two occasions, "forced" her from where she was living. He acknowledged meeting her at the Alameda and taking her to a hotel to have sex. Alberto insisted, though, that she was not a doncella and that he had never made a promise of marriage. When the judge ordered a careo between the two, Juliana changed her original claim, now asserting that Alberto made her have the "carnal act by force." The judge called for a medical exam to settle the disagreement, but Juliana refused it.

Days passed, and the arrival of a Matilde Zamorano complicated the investigation. Through either strange coincidence or scribal error, the woman had the same last name as Juliana, although no mention of a family relationship was made in the case file. Had there been one, it would have surely appeared in someone's recorded testimony. When Matilde testified, she claimed to be Alberto's amasia of only four months. She insisted that Alberto had never spent a night away from their home, including the night of June 7 when he allegedly slept with Juliana. Moreover, Matilde submitted to the judge two letters from Juliana to Alberto. In them, Juliana's request that Alberto meet her offered proof that she had instigated whatever relationship existed between them. Matilde testified that she had even gone to Juliana's vecindad one night to confront her about the letter, only to learn that she was out "without her mother's permission"—an oddly specific detail that characterized Juliana as precocious and dishonest.

In light of the new testimony, the judge called Alberto to respond to "specific questions." Alberto, who, by now, had been in prison for twenty-one days, repudiated his previous testimony. Instead, he returned to his initial account, denying that he had ever taken Juliana to a hotel to have sex. He had lied, he explained, because he believed it would more quickly get him out of prison. For four months, he stated, he had not left the side of Matilde, the woman he planned to soon marry. The housekeeper at their vecindad, he offered, would verify that he had stayed home the night of June 7. In the end though, there was no need for the judge to request further witnesses. Juliana and her mother appeared before the judge that same day to retract their accusation against Alberto, "because of the harm it could cause his family if he spent any more time in prison."[30]

Alberto, it appears, had some type of relationship with Juliana and treated his amasiato as an opportunity to philander with a young woman whom he had long courted. But what exactly happened and why is difficult to gauge. Nevertheless, paying attention to how the involved individuals positioned and presented themselves during the investigation sheds light on what amasiato meant to each of them. Their testimony also demonstrates concerns about how their social superiors adjudicating the matter would view their lifestyles, a view that carried the weight of legal judgment. For example, in his claim—whether honest or strategic—that he planned to marry Matilde, Alberto sought to convince the judge of the seriousness of his relationship with her and thereby undercut the accusations of his infidelity. Matilde, on the other hand, by telling the judge of her attempts to confront the homewrecking Juliana, underscored amasiato as a solemn and legitimate union, one just as binding as an official marriage. Juliana, whether or not she knew of Alberto's amasiato, made no mention of it, either before the judge or in her letters. And, although her mother's testimony made clear the long courtship that had existed between the two, Juliana insisted that Alberto had used both alcohol and a marriage proposal to convince her to have sex. Considering Mexico City's high rate of illegitimacy and concubinage—conditions that made amasiato a likely outcome for couples— women's common refrain that they had been promised marriage, whether true or not, implied their decency and right to legal protection. If Juliana had indeed known about Alberto's relationship with Matilde, then she found herself in a position similar to that of Dolores Villagrán in the Teresa Rocha– Ysidro Morán case discussed earlier. In both cases, we find that women romantically involved with men already in amasiato could view common-law bonds as conveniently breakable.

Networks of Family Support

A similar, yet even more eventful, case exemplifies how amasiato relationships forged family and neighborhood support networks that helped mitigate the economic instability and insecurity of working-class life. It also reveals the fragility of such networks as shifting allegiances of sex and desire—and what constituted socially acceptable romantic couplings—threatened to undermine family reciprocity. Thirty-eight-year-old Margarita González had lived in amasiato with twenty-four-year-old Pedro Flores for almost two years when the couple decided to separate. They had birthed two children, one of whom survived. The baby kept Margarita and Pedro in contact as they were both committed to her well-being. Although separated for almost a year, they had recently agreed to have the little girl live with Pedro's sister in the State of Mexico as it offered a healthier climate than the working-class colonia of Guerrero. It was Margarita who would take her daughter to Pedro's sister, a journey that took several weeks, presumably because she traveled on foot. In the meantime, with at least two older children from a previous relationship, Margarita needed to find a place to board her fifteen-year-old daughter, Juana Encino. Pascuala González, Margarita's sister and Juana's aunt, who also lived in the Guerrero neighborhood, agreed to lodge the girl.

Pedro Flores had moved to the municipality of Guadalupe Hidalgo to live with another of his sisters, Faustina Flores, and her family. He spent his days traveling between Mexico City and the State of Mexico, finding work as a bricklayer. While Pedro worked outside the city, Faustina encountered Juana Encino—the fifteen-year-old daughter of Pedro's former amasia and, during their relationship, his stepdaughter—at the Plaza San Juan. As the two women conversed, Juana lamented that her aunt Pascuala—with whom she was staying while her mother was away—treated her poorly and gave her the "mala vida." Juana pleaded that she be allowed to stay with Faustina at her home in Guadalupe Hidalgo. Faustina agreed reluctantly, hesitant to get involved in the affairs of her brother's former amasia.

When Pedro Flores returned to the city, he was surprised, so it seems, to find his former stepdaughter Juana living in the same apartment. In the following days, according to the testimony of several people who lived with Faustina Flores, Juana began to "go crazy" (*ponerse loca*) over Pedro. For example, when Pedro was working, Juana insisted on taking him food. She also insisted on washing all of his clothes. When Faustina questioned the young woman about her intentions, Juana "would get upset and demand on taking [his food] to him." One night, according to another witness, as several members of the household slept in the open-air patio of the vecindad because the vivienda was too crowded, a "very bright moon" revealed that Juana had gotten up in the middle of the night and "lifted the sheets and laid with Pedro" who was "very asleep, even snoring." The same witness noted that Juana repeatedly "propositioned" Pedro, but "he never paid her any attention."

During his testimony, though, Pedro admitted that he was not so innocent in the ordeal. Several weeks earlier he had spoken to Juana "about love" but had not seen her again until he returned from working abroad to find her living in his sister's apartment. Pedro further admitted that, in response to Juana's precocious behavior, they had begun having sexual relations and now lived in amasiato at his sister's home, although he insisted that Juana was "not a girl" when they first had sex. In her depositions, Juana portrayed herself as a victim of Pedro's deceptions. Despite the claims of three witnesses who noted Juana's persistent attentions to Pedro, she contended that it was Pedro who initiated their reunion through trickery. He lied, Juana testified, sending her a message to meet him on the pretext that he had received a letter from her mother. That day, she claimed, Pedro took her to several cantinas to drink pulque, spoke to her about marriage, and convinced her to live with him in amasiato. She agreed and "allowed him to make use of her person . . . being a doncella before the carnal act."

The relationship forged between Pedro and Juana, no matter its true origin, was accepted by all the members of the extended family who lived in the vivienda of Pedro's sister. Several even went so far as to lie and keep the relationship secret from Margarita González, Juana's mother and Pedro's ex-amasia. At one point, for example, another of Pedro's sisters, Carmen Flores, traveled to Mexico City to visit both her brother and Margarita and her children, revealing the close relationship that continued to exist between the two families despite the separation. When Carmen arrived, she visited Faustina's family. While she was there, no one dared reveal that Juana was living with them. When asked by the judge why the family had hidden this fact from Carmen, Faustina explained her worry that she might "bare responsibility for consenting to have Pedro live in amasiato in her home with his stepdaughter." Another witness testified that Juana had implored members of the household to withhold her whereabouts from Carmen, fearful that she might tell Juana's mother. Carmen, after visiting with her immediate family, went to see Juana, believing that she was living with Pascuala González. When Carmen arrived looking for Juana, Pascuala "began to cry . . . because she did not know where she was." Concerned, Carmen went to her brother Pedro and asked him to look for Juana. Pedro, keeping up the lie, offered to help.

Days later, though, Pedro sat in jail. His ex-amasia, Margarita González, who had finally returned from the State of Mexico, learned that Juana had disappeared. Making her own investigations, although never describing what they were, she discovered Juana's and Pedro's relationship and had him arrested. In her deposition Margarita attacked the sexual morality of both parties. She accused Pedro of already being married ecclesiastically in his home state of Mexico, which was the reason she had decided to leave him. And her daughter, she claimed confidently, was not a virgin before having sex with Pedro.

Although Margarita, at first, wanted Pedro punished, she eventually dropped the complaint against him. Margarita's decision to have Pedro arrested had put her in turmoil with his sister, Josefa, the woman who had recently taken in their one-year-old daughter. Josefa also boarded Margarita's teenage son, Salvador Encino—Juana's younger brother— and had found him work as a domestic servant. Learning that her brother had been arrested, Josefa had stopped giving Salvador his weekly earnings of two pesos. Margarita explained that she was withdrawing the accusation against Pedro so that his sister would "return [her son], even if without the money." She only demanded that Pedro promise to "no longer get involved with her or her daughter."[31] From this complicated ordeal, we learn that even while amasiato might prove ephemeral, the kinship and community networks of mutual support it forged were less so. In a society where amasiato's acceptance as a legitimate form of domestic union allowed men *and* women to have multiple romantic partners over a lifetime, and, even as individuals moved in and out of their relationships, the family networks left behind continued to proffer help in securing food, housing, and work.[32] Arguably, the safety net of family connections—that bolstered the precarious lives of the poor—may have also permitted relative tolerance of less-than-respectable or taboo unions like that of Pedro and Juana. Clearly, for Margarita, a limit existed as to what was bearable, even as the pressures of economic necessity, family unity, and public standing collided.

Community Knowledge

Men's amasiato relationships—present or past and often well known in the community—could provide justification for the parents of young women to oppose a suitor's overtures. For parents hoping to provide better futures for their children, the prospect of a young daughter marrying a man who already had a family or, perhaps, who had abandoned one, was dubious at best. Furthermore, how men behaved as domestic partners shaped their public image. One mother opposed the courtship of her daughter with a man who "already had three children with [a woman] with whom he has lived in amasiato for five years."[33] Another wanted José Estrada "punished" for running away with her daughter because he was "in amasiato with another woman . . . who gets the *mala vida* from him."[34] One father, likewise, ended a rapto proceeding and simply wanted his daughter returned home when he learned that her intended already "had an amasia, a son, and another about to be born."[35] The urban poor accepted the possibility of multiple domestic and sexual partners, a sociocultural practice of everyday life eased by the fluidity characteristic of amasiato. But once a nonconjugal domestic relationship had been established, family and community expected monogamy from both partners because amasiato required a moral *and* an economic commitment.

In turn-of-the-century Mexico City amasiato represented the most common form of lower-class union, and it did so because it better matched the realities of popular life. In a society where divorce was an incredibly rare, expensive option available only to the middle and upper classes,[36] amasiato offered couples greater fluidity in forming and dissolving unions based on financial, emotional, or sexual needs. By allowing men and women to form new romantic and domestic relationships after an abandonment, a separation, or the death of a spouse, amasiato better met the needs of workers' lives where mutual household, financial, and emotional support could alleviate the hardships of an uneven Porfirian economy characterized by underemployment and the rising costs of basic goods.[37]

The Ideal of Marriage

Only state-officiated marriages performed by the civil registry were regarded as legitimate. The liberal state saw civil marriage as a remedy to the perceived immorality of the poor, characterized by the rise of prostitution, the disintegration of migrant families, and the increased number of begging and abandoned children on the streets. Primary and night schools, for example, taught a small number of working-class pupils that civil marriage equated with moral union. But the limited scope of the Porfirian school system and its inability to reach the majority of the working class meant that any overt and comprehensive effort to reconstruct the domestic lives of the poor would have little success.[38]

Many Mexicans continued to be married by the Church, although that practice appears to have waned among the poor during the Porfiriato. During those years, a struggle emerged between the Church and government over how people should marry. State officials maintained that men married by the Church gained tacit license to abandon their wives as ecclesiastical marriage had no legal standing. This perspective reflected the state's goal to use the law to promote male-headed households with family men as breadwinners. The Catholic press argued that civil union should be viewed as an impediment to Church marriage. As a result of this "marriage crisis," pundits claimed, immorality flourished among the popular classes who chose amasiato. Indeed, marriage had become a distinctly middle- and upperclass event with families seeking *both* Church and civil sanction. The marriage ceremony was a costly affair that required paying a priest and (outside of Mexico City) an officiating judge. Marriage celebrations were likewise expensive, with the purchase of wedding gowns, food, drink, and music.[39]

When they found themselves before a judge in a criminal proceeding, men rarely mentioned their having made a marriage proposal before sex, while women most often testified that they had received one.[40] Most men, when forced to make a marriage promise in front of authorities, pledged to take their lovers to the civil registry. Yet, as noted earlier, most men simply made an ambiguous "promise to marry," which most likely meant amasiato. In some cases, the promise to marry appears to have been a perfunctory statement men used to assuage concerned parents and lessen legal entanglements. For example, when arrested for rapto while at a hotel with his novia, Alejandro Alvarado swore he was about to take her to the civil registry, an unlikely claim as she was fifteen and required parental consent to marry.[41]

The liberal press—both state-sponsored and independent—universally promoted marriage through the civil registry. In 1909, an *El Diario* writer blamed the Mexican tradition of overly lavish weddings for causing "humble people" to undertake "marriage by rapto" or to eschew marriage altogether. He suggested that more modest marriage ceremonies and celebrations—events that honored the solemnity of the institution—would provide a better example to the poor.[42] As a means to promote marriage, the legal newspaper *El Faro* called on the president to abolish civil marriage fees across the country.[43] In an earlier article, *El Faro* had noted that while birth and marriage registrations were free in the Federal District, the same was "not true in the provinces where fees promote concubinage."[44] One man, when arrested for rapto because he had failed to marry in a timely manner, indignantly proclaimed that he had never meant "to make a mockery" of his intended. "As soon as I am out of jail," he vowed, "I will marry her through the civil registry and, finances permitting, I will also marry her in the Church."[45] The expense of undertaking both civil and religious marriage made it for some, in its rarity, a point of pride and social status. One reader-submitted poem to *La Guacamaya* reflected such self-satisfaction. The poetaster boasted that his wife was "well married" (*bien casada*)—the title of the poem and a play on words simultaneously meaning "well married" and "thoroughly married"—because he had taken her to the civil registry and the Church:

> Hermoso nombre, se llamaba Esther,
>   Solo por eso la hice mi mujer
>   Y con ella me uní por las dos vías . . .
>   La Iglesia y el Estado son mis guías,
>   Así cumpliendo como ciudadano
> Y cumpliendo también como Cristiano,
>   Decía mi suegra muy entusiasmada
>   Mi hija por las dos partes es casada.
>
> [Beautiful name, she was called Esther,
>   For that alone I made her my wife
> And with her I joined along the two tracks . . .
>   The Church and the State are my guides,
>   So fulfilling my duties as a citizen
>   And also as a Christian,
>   My mother-in-law says very enthused
>   My daughter is married on both sides.][46]

The penny presses presented civil and religious marriage in much less sanguine terms than the author of the poem "Bien Casada" above. In a bawdy exchange, also published, in *La Guacamaya*, two fictional characters, Pitacio and doña Timoteita, engage in a sexually charged exchange, full of innuendo, about food. Finding her cooking beans, Pitacio flatters: "I really appreciate a hardworking girl who knows how to take care of her old man." He then proposes that they run away together. Already in a relationship, he hopes to stress for Timoteita the seriousness of his offer by promising to take her to the civil registry. Offended, doña Timoteita interprets his offer as an accusation that she is a prostitute (prostitutes were inspected and "registered" by the Department of Sanitation). Pitacio begins the exchange:

—Lo que quero es que nos saquen en los periolicos cuando váyamos al Registro.
    —Oigasté, que yo no me he rupantiao nada pá que me registren.
    —No seasté tan madrota.
    —¡Ay no mas don Pitacio! No sea tan meco.
    —Pos qué l'hecho?
    —Me estasté insultando.
    —¡Ah qué usté! Si le adigo del Registro Cevil.
    —Güeno, y que es eso?
    —Pos es una oficina onde van los que se queren amancornar á que el juez les eche la bendición y los amarre del juerte.
    —Pero por qué ubres le llaman Registro?
    —Eso si no lo sabino, pero me afiguro qués porque lo registran á uno á ver si ya . . .
    —No reo tan groserote.
    —Esa es la neta.

[—What I want is that they put us in the newspapers when we get registered.
    —You listen up, I haven't broken the law for them to register (inspect) me.
    —Don't be such a dunce.
    —Hey, no more of that don Pitacio! Don't be such a wretch.
    —What have I done?
    —You're insulting me.
    —What do you mean? I'm just telling you about the civil registry.
    —Fine, and what is that?

—Well, it's an office where people go who want to tie the knot so that the judge will give them his blessing and tie them tight.

—But why do you think they call it the Registry?

—That I don't know, but I figure it's because they inspect you to see if you've already . . .

—Don't be so crass.

—That's the truth.][47]

In this humorous exchange, Pitacio proclaims the seriousness of his proposal not only by offering to get married through the civil registry but by noting that he wants the marriage advertised in the newspapers. Such advertisement was common practice among the middle- and upper-classes who announced wedding ceremonies in the city's dailies. Timoteita's suspicion of state authority is indicated by her umbrage when she misinterprets *Registro* as the department that inspects and registers prostitutes rather than as the office that performs state-sanctioned marriages. Her indignance and suspicion illustrates a sense among the lower classes that government involvement in the lives of the poor was inherently disciplinary, a result of their perceived criminality from the perspective of the state. Pitacio's choice of words to mock Timoteita's ignorance of government institutions when he calls her a *madrota* (a female pimp or madam) reinforces her assumptions. When Pitacio finally explains the role of the civil registry, he does so in a manner that mocks its pertinence to working-class life. When asked by Timoteita why it is called a "registry" (again confusing the meaning of the word in Spanish that can mean either "to register" *or* "to inspect"), Pitacio suggests that it is an office that verifies virginity ("they inspect you to see if you've already . . ."). Considering the narrative context, where Pitacio and Timoteita each already live in amasiato and where Pitacio seeks to steal Timoteita away for himself, the exchange ridicules the state's role in trying to protect men from marrying deflowered women, generally a concern of the propertied classes worried about illegitimacy and inheritance.[48] The passage implies that while the state has supplanted the Church in its authority to determine what counts as legitimate union, the state has failed to recognize and adapt its powers to the practices and environment of working-class life. Although completely different in tone, the two examples from *La Guacamaya* foreground the ideal of legitimate marriage. Both the amateur poet's braggadocio and the fictional couple's satiric dialogue that poke fun at the civil registry locate state-sanctioned marriage as an aspirational goal, yet one clearly beyond the means of most members of the working class.

Intergenerational Divides

The simultaneous legitimacy and unattainability of civil marriage explored in the penny press was reflected in the conflicts between parents and children found in the judicial record. Parental demands that young men civilly marry their daughters exposed an intergenerational fault line over the efficacy of state-sanctioned marriage. Yet the possible motivations driving parents' insistence on formal marriage through arrest were plenty: a naïve trust in a suitor's will or finances; a sincere claim to honor; a public demonstration of parental outrage; or, an effort to enforce parental authority.[49] After just five days of the couple's living in amasiato, the parents of Marina Romero had her lover arrested, compelling him to specifically avow to have a "legitimate union . . . before a civil judge."[50] One husband-to-be landed in jail after a miscommunication with his novia's father. The couple had already run away and been gone for over a week when they appeared before the girl's mother asking permission to go to the civil registry. On their way to get married in the municipality of Ixtalco, the couple ran into the girl's father on the street. Unaware of their plans, he had the suitor arrested.[51] Examples such as these show that some parents accepted initiation of sexual relations and cohabitation before official marriage, but only to a degree. Indeed, family and community acceptance of premarital sex among young couples, as long as a marriage was eventually celebrated, is well documented in the colonial period.[52]

In cases where parents completely opposed a marriage, arrest was preferable to marriage. María Dolores Rodríguez and Vicente Guadarrama arrived at the civil registry, having eloped two days earlier. They called on María's mother to witness the marriage. Instead, she had the couple dragged to the nearest police precinct in Colonia Guerrero where she accused Vicente of rapto.[53] One vindictive father used the legal system and marriage law to torment his daughter's suitor. The father, it appears from his daughter María Cordova's testimony, began to mistreat her due to her affection for Carlos Tovar, beating her when he learned of their relationship. The girl's grandfather was so concerned for her safety that he took the youngsters to the civil registry before María's father could "beat her to death" (*matarla a palos*). The grandfather calmed the situation, convincing María's father to attend the civil ceremony as a witness. His agreement to do so was apparently a ruse, as he failed to attend and foiled the marriage. He then called on authorities to arrest Carlos for rapto.[54]

Ambivalent Views of Marriage

Some men's actions demonstrated that marriage through the Church, to them, meant little. This seems especially true for the recently arrived migrant males who had left wives behind in the provinces.[55] Men's readiness to jettison established family ties and forge new conjugal lives in the city provided evidence for liberal pundits concerned about the legal insignificance of ecclesiastical marriage. Felipe Mora, a butcher from Colonia Indianilla, made clear how little he thought of his Church marriage when he told officials, "Although I am [ecclesiastically] married, I will marry Petra Torres through the civil registry (*por lo civil*). I have always behaved in good faith."[56] Similarly, Francisco Tovar, a shoemaker living in Tacubaya, dismissed his marriage stating that it had been performed six years earlier, that it was "only canonical" (*solo canónicamente*), and that his wife continued to live in his native city of Celaya, Guanajuato. Francisco, as well as his new lover, Crescensia Gutiérrez, both insisted that his original marriage was "only" through the Church. Her father, though, claimed he knew for a fact—it is unclear how, although Crescensia's family was also originally from Guanajuato—that Francisco was married both civilly and canonically. He refused to allow his daughter to make a life with Francisco and, as she was only fourteen years old, succeeded in bringing her back within parental authority. As he told officials in a letter, "Francisco should be put in liberty as long as he promises to not get involved with my daughter again."[57] In another case, although José Aguilar at first denied having had sexual relations with Beatriz Gutiérrez because he was already "married by the Church" to another woman, he later confessed to the "carnal act." The Church marriage meant little to Beatriz or her mother. They ended the investigation citing José's marriage offer.[58]

Originating in the municipality of Tacuba, northeast of Mexico City, one case offers an extreme example of the ambivalent views some individuals held about marriage as a solemn, life-long commitment. On the evening of February 24, 1901, fifteen-year-old Susana Mejía waited for her novio, Fidencio Ávila, behind her uncle's house. Because she had already been having relations with him for about a year, Susana had agreed to meet Fidencio one evening and suspected no ill intentions. He asked Susana to run away with him, but she declined. Suddenly, according to her testimony, in a fit of rage, Fidencio ripped off her rebozo and threw her to the ground. He pulled out a knife, threatening to kill her if she cried for help. He then dragged her to a friend's house where they spent the night, Fidencio "making use" of Susana "despite opposition." Afterward, he promised to take her back to his pueblo in the State of Mexico and marry her. They set off early the next morning on horseback.

Along the way, they stopped at an inn where Fidencio happened upon an acquaintance, Antonio Fonseca. What Antonio heard next must have shocked him. Fidencio explained that he had in his possession a girl he could not take to his pueblo because he was already married. He offered Antonio money to marry the girl instead. Antonio flatly rejected the bizarre proposal and Fidencio departed. Hours later, as Fidencio and Susana made their way over the difficult terrain, Antonio Fonseca caught up with them on the trail. Again, Fidencio proposed that Antonio marry Susana, this time in front of her, openly admitting that he was already married. Both Antonio and Susana rejected the idea "because they did not know each other." Irate at their refusal, Fidencio threatened to leave Susana alone in the mountains if she did not go with Antonio. Susana claimed that Fidencio had used a gun to make this threat. Antonio's testimony makes no mention of a weapon. Things apparently calmed down enough for the trio to stop and eat in a village where Fidencio bought bread and pulque. During their meal, Fidencio "without saying anything" mounted his horse and rode away, "not saying goodbye." Antonio later told officials that "alone with Susana, I decided to marry her . . . and she agreed." The two then spent the night at the home of Antonio's brother-in-law before going to the civil registry the next morning. Susana's testimony, though, made clear that although Antonio "did not touch" her that night, he used threats to get her to the civil registry and to falsely state she was twenty-two years old. (Individuals under the age of twenty-one required parental consent to marry.)[59] It took a bribe, according to Susana, for the officiant to look past Antonio's obvious lie.

The marriage, unsurprisingly, was an unhappy one. After just two weeks, Susana went to the house of her uncles who lived in the nearby town of Magdalena. Susana claimed that Antonio had driven her from the house. Antonio maintained instead that one night he had found Susana out on the street with a "bundle of clothes beneath her rebozo," planning to run away. Although he had convinced her to stay, Susana's aunt arrived the next day to take her home. At the family's behest, authorities eventually arrested Antonio for rapto (to which they added the charge of falsifying a civil registry document). But there, the file ends. The investigating judge forwarded the case to the municipality where the marriage had occurred.[60] The puzzling individual motivations that drove this strange drama shroud it in mystery.

Yet the case provides a strong example of individuals not treating civil marriage as a solemn, life-long commitment, even in a country where divorce was generally not permitted.[61]

While Fidencio's previous marriage made it impossible for him to legally wed Susana, Antonio's and Susana's decision to marry appears impulsive yet significant enough for Antonio to bribe a judge. Susana might have been motivated by the opportunity to form a legal union after having been deflowered by another man, a matter that did not dissuade Antonio from marriage. The couple's decision to readily and quickly separate, though, suggests that neither concerned themselves with how their actions could limit their future relationship prospects and social standing. On one hand, neither may have seen their legal marriage as an obstacle to forming future relationships as long as they did not seek to marry again. On the other, the fact that the family had Antonio and Fidencio both arrested for rapto suggests the parents may have sought one or more remedies: to enforce the marriage, to seek financial restitution from one of the men, or to have them punished. Because this portion of case file is missing, the family's exact demands cannot be known. Here, as in the cases already discussed, we find that for Mexico's poor—those who did not have concerns related to property or inheritance—civil and Church marriages could be treated quite casually and in a manner suggesting that some couples did not base their sense of self-worth on being legitimately married.[62] The absence of the kinds of financial commitments that concerned the well-to-do eroded for the working class the idea of legal marriage as the foundation of a traditional household. As a result, the lower classes primarily chose less formal domestic and romantic relationships and brought little solemnity to their views of marriage.

Casual Sex

The formulaic language of legal cases often obfuscates the romance and desire that courtship and sex kindled. Yet, at times, a close reading of judicial files sheds light on how the laboring classes enjoyed moments of bodily pleasure and emotional gratification in an otherwise grueling life. Case files offer glimpses of fleeting trysts, moments where concerns about neighborhood gossip, public reputation, or pregnancy were jettisoned for the thrill of romance and erotic satisfaction. Among the cases that particularly stand out are the criminal investigations of rapto and estupro where neither party makes reference to a marriage promise despite their sexual relations. While amasiato and formal marriage were the most common ways that couples came together, examples of casual sex emerge from the judicial record, albeit concealed by the legal strategies men and women mustered when they found themselves before an investigating judge. For example, Heriberto López and Cesárea Fragoso, after three months of courtship, made a date (*cita*) and ended up at a hotel where they had sex. The next morning, Heriberto went to work at 10 a.m. and Cesárea stayed at the hotel. No promise of marriage was given. It was only after his arrest, prompted by Cesárea's failure to return home the night before, that Heriberto "made arrangements" with her father.[63] For the Mexican lower classes, especially young girls, the delights and dangers of pursuing sexual adventure and the autonomy afforded by urban life reflected sociocultural changes that spurred the development of modern sexuality.[64]

Sixteen-year-old Concepción Cerón told officials that she had gone out one night with her novio of six months, Everardo Garduño. "I went to his house where he made use of me one time and I was a virgin," she explained, "This was done with my full will and consent without Everardo making any promise of marriage." After their nighttime tryst, the couple went their separate ways and did not see each other for over two weeks until Concepción's mother began a rapto proceeding. Concepción, who was now working at a brothel, was dragged to the police precinct against her will, not wanting to make any accusation against Everardo.[65] While similar to the Heriberto López and Cesárea Fragoso case above, Concepción's candid admission that she had had sex without a promise of marriage was surely eased by her employment as a prostitute. And, because the law only protected chaste women, her statement also completely undercut her parents' attempt to seek restitution from Everardo.[66]

Once in custody men might claim they had made a promise of marriage before sex. But cases where young couples parted ways after one-night trysts—not seeing each other again until both appeared at a police precinct days or weeks later—suggest that some couples did not equate sex with an obligation to cohabitate. Returning home late one night with her sister from the inn where they worked, Petra Gómez sneaked away and met Alberto Abogado on the street corner. Alberto, a regular patron at the inn, took Petra to an inexpensive hotel nearby to have sex. Although he planned to marry her, as he told officials, she left the hotel the day after their nighttime rendezvous and he had not seen her since.[67] Vicenta García left home after a fight with her parents, hoping to find work as a domestic servant. That night, she met her novio Alejo Ramos and they went on a stroll to Tacuba. The teenagers found a "secluded place" and had sex. The couple then separated and did not see each other again for two weeks. Vicenta, it appears, had succeeded in finding work and a place to live. Vicenta's mother "by chance" saw Alejo on the street in the Colonia Indianilla neighborhood. Recognizing him as Vicenta's novio, she confronted him as to Vicenta's whereabouts and about whether or not he planned to marry her. The mother's questioning caught Alejo by surprise. Having previously seen Vicenta only occasionally "on the street," he did not know where she lived. He denied that they had planned to run away or marry. Incredulous, the mother had him arrested for rapto. Alejo sat in the municipal jail for eight days until Vicenta finally arrived to provide testimony. She confirmed Alejo's claim that the couple had not seen each other since the night she was "deflowered." She had only learned of Alejo's imprisonment when, while visiting his apartment, vecindad neighbors informed her that he had been taken by police. After languishing for six weeks in prison, Alejo agreed to marry Vicenta, and her mother withdrew the accusation.[68]

Two cases, both involving police officers, show a similar pattern: couples having sex, parting ways, and not seeing each other again until coming face-to-face at a police precinct. Policeman Juan Gómez, after drinking pulque with his sweetheart and then taking her to a hotel to have sex, expected that the couple would now live together. But when he offered Eugenia Jiménez five pesos to find a room for them to rent, she declined and instead went to the home of her aunt near La Merced market. Juan had not seen Eugenia for four days when he was arrested at the behest of her mother.[69] Similarly, after a nasty fight with her mother, Juana Montes de Oca left home to find her novio, a policeman named Benito Galván. He took her to a hotel where they consummated their relationship. Afterward, each took separate *rumbos* (routes). Later, when he walked into the police precinct to start his shift, Benito found Juana's mother lodging a complaint against him, which forced him to go search for her daughter. In their depositions, Juana and Benito both showed a lukewarm commitment to marriage. Neither mentioned a proposal to wed in their testimonies. Juana declared that "she was willing to marry Benito, if he wanted." Benito provided an equally unenthusiastic statement, claiming that though he had never made a marriage promise, "if she got pregnant, he would give her a diario for her expenses."[70]

Even in cases where a marriage proposal was eventually made, the events and actions leading up to the agreement cast doubt as to whether or not the men and women involved sought anything more than a romantic rendez-vous. In 1907, Damiana Nápoles initiated a rapto investigation against David Morales. Damiana took care of her orphaned niece, seventeen-year-old María Guadalupe Castañeda. One Monday night, Damiana returned home to find her niece missing. She investigated the matter for a week, receiving tidbits of information from around the neighborhood about María Guadalupe's possible whereabouts and the young man with whom she might have absconded. Following her leads, Damiana discovered María Guadalupe working at a factory on Calle Guerrero. She hauled her niece to the nearest police station to make a deposition. María Guadalupe testified that she had had amorous relations with a young man named David but could not recall his surname. David Morales—as the authorities later identified him—had asked María Guadalupe to come live with him and she agreed. She further stated that when she initially left with David she was a doncella but had lost her virginity, allowing her novio to "make use of her body" one time after a promise of marriage. When asked by the investigating judge where they could find David for questioning, she replied that she did not know his address as they were not living together. The next day, María Guadalupe came back to authorities and changed her statement. She claimed that she had not gone with David willingly but only because he had enticed her using trickery (*engaños*) with a false promise of marriage. She now accused him of estupro.

The next day, fifteen-year-old David Morales appeared in court custody to provide a deposition. He defended himself against the accusations of rapto and estupro, telling authorities that, on the day in question, he had encountered his "friend" María Guadalupe on the street and had asked her to go for a *paseo* (stroll). She had agreed. The couple lost track of time and, as it was late and vecindad doors were locked for the night, the two decided to stay at a hotel. There, according to David, he had the "carnal act" with María Guadalupe. The next morning, the two said goodbye and parted ways taking different *rumbos*. He had not seen her since. Because of his young age, the judge sent David to the Escuela Correccional (correctional school) rather than to the municipal jail while the investigation took place. The following day, both Damiana and her niece withdrew their accusation against David who had made marriage arrangements in the meantime.[71]

Until the moment that María Guadalupe's aunt lodged a legal complaint against David, the couple, it appears, had engaged in an act of casual sex. Neither one knew much about the other—neither surnames nor addresses—and, after their night at the hotel, the pair had not seen each other again. María Guadalupe took the opportunity to live and work on her own, perhaps using the loss of her virginity to sever family ties. While her statements to legal authorities might have placated her aunt and secured a marriage proposal,[72] neither of the youngsters' actions suggested the goal of long-term union. Cases like this one disclose rare examples of how urban life—especially the availability of cheap hotels and rooms, but also opportunities for female wage work—promoted a freer sexual culture among the young working class. Nevertheless, this perhaps increasingly liberal attitude toward sex could collide with more traditional family expectations that linked the initiation of sexual life with marriage. Youthful indiscretion could bring about serious consequences and force unplanned commitments, as the youngsters in this case learned.

In other instances, not even the dry, formulaic language used by court scribes could obscure clear cases of casual sex completely free of familial or social expectations. Returning to her vecindad after drinking, sixteen-year-old Bárbara Torres encountered Ignacio Bejarano in the building's patio. They had known each other for about two years, both living in the same neighborhood. Ignacio was familiar enough with Bárbara, for example, to tell court officials that she had been in an amorous relationship with a mason who had previously lived in the building but that it "had not even lasted fifteen days." Whatever their relationship and whatever their conversation that night on the patio, it must have been of a romantic and arousing nature as it ended with Ignacio propositioning Bárbara to have sex. She had accepted. They agreed to meet later that night in Bárbara's vecindad apartment. Seemingly unconcerned that her sister slept in the same room, the couple "copulated" as planned. Bárbara's sister later testified that she had witnessed them fornicating but had said nothing in order not to "cause a scandal in the vecindad." She assumed that "Bárbara lent herself willingly since she did not put up any resistance."[73]

The urban environment offered some individuals bohemian lifestyles that included freer sexual expression than that typically exercised by convention. Details about sexual nonconformity rarely appear in judicial files because individuals were reluctant to admit taboo behaviors before officials. Fourteen-year-old Margarita Tesorero made at least two confessions that must have shocked investigators. Explaining to officials her relationship with her vecindad friends, Sara Dumant and Genoveva Méndez, Margarita admitted that the three occasionally drank together and that, while drunk, "Sara would put us to bed and have coitus with us, if that's what it's called when a woman gets between your legs like a man." She claimed that she had participated in these "lewd acts" (actos impúdicos) on five separate occasions. More recently, and the basis for her being brought before officials,

Figure 3. "Feminism Imposes Itself." Gendered anxieties depicted in the penny press after the Famous 41 incident. *La Guacamaya,* July 25, 1907.

Margarita and Sara had gone out drinking with a man named Alfredo Fonseca. At her friend's insistence, she claimed, she had sex with Alfredo while Sara had sex with another man in the same room. Arriving home late that night to a suspicious mother, Margarita drunkenly confessed *everything*. And although her admission prompted the arrests of Sara and Alfredo, the mother quickly withdrew the accusation.[74]

Accusations of rapto and estupro hinged upon perceived calamity in heterosexual relationships: such cases typically involved either a jilted woman or an aggrieved parent and are predominant in the judicial record. By contrast, same-sex relationships rarely emerge in the judicial files. Homosexual acts were easily hidden from normative heterosexual society because of the prevalence of same-sex sociability in tenements, workplaces, and on the street.[75] Yet the same-sex erotic pleasure glimpsed in this case was more common than judicial record reflects. Homosexuality emerged as a topic of discussion in the press and as an area of scientific and criminological analysis, especially after the shocking "Famous 41" incident when police raided

Figure 4. *"Juana la tortillera."* Middle-class press depiction of female same-sex affection. *El Colmillo Publico,* June 24, 1906.

an upscale, private, male-only party where half the men were dressed as women.[76] Both middle-class periodicals and the penny press openly discussed, mocked, or vilified homosexuality after the event, demonstrating both a bourgeois and working-class homophobia, albeit articulated in notably different ways.[77]

Similarly, for criminologists, homosexuality became a potent indicator of mental and moral degeneration, a cause of the antisocial and deviant behavior that they linked to the perceived wantonness of the working class and poor.[78] Lesbianism, likewise, was characterized as a lower-class phenomenon, not only by criminologists but also by the press. The middle-class periodical, *El Colmillo Público*, for example, offered readers a full-page illustration of poor women making tortillas, kissing, and embracing one another.[79] The drawing's caption referred to one woman as a *tortillera*, a vernacular term for "lesbian" that entered popular usage at the start of the century. (At that time, lesbianism was formally known as *safismo* or sapphism).

Likewise, the penny press's presentation of comic dialogues between women on the street, at times, featured homosexual innuendo in an effort

Figure 5. Penny press depicting "tortilleras" dancing together. *El Chango,* June 16, 1904.

to make readers laugh.[80] In the case of Margarita, her admission to authorities of sexual relations with Sara surely undermined any presumption of Margarita's chastity and virtue on the judge's part while it also reinforced classist assumptions about prevailing sexual vice among the poor. Whether an honest confession or an attempt to portray Sara as an immoral broker who led her astray, Margarita's admission is startling: it diminished any chance she had of seeking punishment for Alfredo or, at least, of obtaining financial recompense. Yet her admission also reveals a liberal sexual culture that existed, or, at the very least, could be imagined within the confines of the vecindad.

Conclusion

The cases explored here show that the working class shared a wide range of sexual values, practices, and behaviors. What stands out is the diverse array of relationship types, neither exceptionally wanton nor prudish, that couples formed and the different levels of intergenerational and community conflict such relationships could engender. This chapter has examined four ways that working-class couples formed unions, four ways of being together: amasiato, civil marriage, Church marriage, and casual sex. In each type of relationship, individuals showed themselves to be self-serving, pleasure-seeking, roguish, tender, caring, or committed. Yet, among all the diversity, the economic insecurity faced by the poor was the shared context that defined practice. While amasiato was the most common form of cohabitation because it allowed couples room to maneuver in a challenging environment of economic hardship, unsteady employment, and migratory life, marriage, whether state- or Church-sanctioned, did not always prove permanent either, often for the same reasons.

Examples of casual sex, and the risks it involved for women, likewise suggest that poverty shaped practice. As hypothesized of the working class in turn-of-the-century London, despite the risks of pregnancy that women bore alone, casual sex offered opportunities to interrupt the monotony and privation of daily life with moments of pleasure and immediate gratification.[81] The growing number of diversions and mixed-sex amusements that city life offered presented new prospects of personal freedom and unsupervised recreation. And while youthful actions pushed the boundaries of prudence in a liberalizing society, sexual self-determination spurred moments of intergenerational conflict where elders demanded the traditional resolution of marriage. In the following chapter, we will see how the diversity that characterized working-class romantic and domestic partnerships was also reflected in how men and women used sex strategically to achieve an equally diverse set of goals.

5

Using Sex

Beyond providing a window on how lower-class couples formed relationships, rapto and estupro cases also present examples of how sex could be used strategically to achieve a variety of goals such as adult independence, economic advancement, or romantic fulfillment. They demonstrate that sex was often a means to an end and not an end in itself. This chapter examines how the city's poor, especially young women, used sex to improve their plights as the city offered a range of new possibilities and opportunities to avoid parental vigilance and control. It argues that because poverty, hunger, underemployment, and cramped, unhygienic living conditions brutalized the lives of workers, they developed a range of strategies to mitigate the worst aspects of economic insecurity and to cultivate opportunities for self-fulfillment. The elite classes explained the plight of the poor—and by extension their perceived licentiousness—as a moral and physiological failing rather than as a result of economic and infrastructural policy that either ignored extreme socioeconomic inequality or assumed it as natural.[1] The same economic strains and social conditions that governed the types of relationships couples formed (the focus of the previous chapter) also shaped how they used sex as a form of self-management or for survival. Taken together, the heterogenous responses of common people to the social realities fostered by economic development and modernization shed light on how everyday interactions among romantic partners, family, neighbors, and state agents reshaped expectations about parental authority and gendered sexual norms.

Escaping Parental Authority

Within the taxing lives of poor women, running away and beginning sexual relations with a lover could mean better economic prospects or, at least, a reprieve from the grinding household work families often demanded. While previous chapters foreground examples of young women and girls running away, this section offers a closer look at that phenomenon. Working-class parents and surrogates such as uncles and aunts expected young women to contribute to household work or finances, to defer to parental discipline, and to respect family opinion about a potential suitor's acceptability. But when elders subjected female youths to excessive demands for labor or to physical abuse, running away with a lover offered an increasingly appealing option. Examination of criminal investigations where elopement led young couples to face judicial authorities may create an overrepresentation of intergenerational conflict, but it nonetheless sheds light on the dynamics of such strife. A young woman's leaving home and her initiation of sexual relations forced parents either to accept her coming of age or to fight for continued parental control. Within the context of female choice, families were positioned along a spectrum between liberty and tyranny. This can be considered a foundational spectrum as it comprised a range of actions in the exercise of parental authority. In households where elders demonstrated self-restraint, relying less on physical violence than, perhaps, persuasion, young women were less likely to flee. By contrast, families that exercised varying degrees of tyrannical control or that pressed daughters into labor to buoy family finances could easily erode paternal legitimacy.[2] It is little surprise, then, that domestic servants—often pressed into service by their families—represented the most common female occupation in rapto and estupro cases (21.4 percent). Mexico City domestics earned extremely low wages (and in some cases no wages at all) and often suffered verbal, physical, and sexual abuse from the families they served.[3] When parents and guardians ignored young women's complaints about their abuse at the hands of employers (*amos/amas*), it undermined the familial moral economy where daughters deferred to parental authority and contributed to household finances in exchange for parents' commitment to the welfare of their children.

In short, positioned along the foundational spectrum of parental authority we find families who allowed young people freedom in selecting romantic partners on one hand and families who limited or curtailed their children's freedom of spousal choice on the other. When the convictions of elders proved immovable, daughters simply eloped with the men of whom their families disapproved. As noted in chapter 2, while community and family may have censured such actions, the law maintained the right of young women over age sixteen to run away with lovers and claim their comings of age and independence. Where women exercised personal will in relationship choices, male deceit or seduction could not be assumed. As a result, parents had little recourse to the law in punishing abductors when daughters willingly initiated sexual relations with them. Such circumstances compelled parents to choose between accepting a daughter's decision or returning her home deflowered, which could mean family shame and humiliation by neighbors. For example, Luciana Villalobos told officials that she left her parental home with her novio, had sex with him, and "made marital life" because her father had "prohibited her from marrying him." Both noted in their testimony that Luciana had recently turned sixteen. Luciana's strategy worked, and her parents dropped their charge against her beau.[4]

When a daughter ran away with a lover it often forced her parents to accept him, if only reluctantly. Young women over age sixteen used the law as leverage to emancipate themselves from family authority and what some parents viewed as their right to choose—or at least sanction—a daughter's suitor. Agripina Arroyo, in 1905, told officials that, because her mother treated her badly and disapproved of her novio Gregorio Moreno, she had agreed to run away and leave the capital with him. When the couple returned to the city over two months later, Agripina's mother charged Gregorio with rapto but immediately rescinded the accusation, reluctantly accepting Gregorio as a son-in-law.[5] Parents came to accept unacceptable suitors, seeing marriage—and more than likely the financial commitment of amasiato—as an alternative preferable to having a sexually active, unwed daughter who could bring community scorn and a loss of social standing upon herself and her family.[6]

Because judicial cases more often present conflict than consensus, it is easy to overlook the possibility that true affection—rather than parental opposition, abuse, or economic exploitation—could drive a young couples' decision to elope. For example, Pilar Rodríguez, who lived just outside the middle-class neighborhood of Santa María la Ribera, walked into her local police precinct to report her daughter missing. She told them that her daughter "had no reason to run away from home" and it must have been the *amoreos* (love talk, courting) of Alfredo Villar, a train mechanic who worked at the nearby Buenavista Station, that enticed her to leave. The mother had learned that Alfredo probably had taken her daughter, Armanda Loaeza, to the State of Guanajuato. While the mother's information proved erroneous (the couple had in fact gone to Oaxaca), she managed to find them when they returned to the capital. Armanda and Alfredo had found an apartment just six blocks away from Pilar's home in the less prosperous Guerrero neighborhood.[7] Armanda's decision to elope with the working-class mechanic suggests her likely conflict with her mother over Alfredo's social standing. Both mother and daughter were literate, lived in a small house (as opposed to a tenement apartment), and did not need to work to sustain themselves. In her choice of Alfredo as partner, Armanda sacrificed relative economic comfort by leaving her middle-class home to live in a working-class vecindad.[8] The youngster's decision exemplifies how a deeply felt and personal romantic love could trump fulfillment of kinship obligations or family expectations. Whether real or perceived, Armanda's youthful intemperance must surely have caused her mother concern about her daughter's economic prospects and well-being.

As the cases examined so far demonstrate, one major goal pursued by young couples was emancipation from parental authority with its contingent opportunity to assert adult independence. For women, leaving the family home and challenging patriarchal or matriarchal authority often meant replacing one form of subjugation (to parents/guardians) with another (to amasio/husband).[9] The cases, nevertheless, make clear that young women sought to assert their own decision-making in matters of love and courtship. In this way, working-class women, especially those over the age of sixteen, had far greater autonomy in choosing life partners than their middle- and upper-class counterparts.[10]

The opportunity to break family ties deemed unduly oppressive led young women to make risky, perhaps impulsive, decisions that jeopardized their economic security in a society where mutual networks of support were crucial to survival. Investigations where runaway couples were not located, at least for the duration of the case, highlight young people's resolute aspiration to assert their adulthood. In 1885, Juana García returned to her vecindad in the rough-and-tumble Tepito neighborhood wearing two decorative shells her novio, Eulalio Flores, had presented her during Carnival. When her mother learned they were a romantic *obsequio* (gift) from Eulalio, she ripped them off and threw them to the ground. This gift would enrage her father, she admonished, as Eulalio had the "bad habit of frequenting pulquerías and drunkenness." That night, Juana and Eulalio disappeared not to be seen again.[11] In 1893, twenty-year-old Agustín González approached the Martínez family, offering to tutor their young son in carpentry. The parents later learned that this offer had been a ploy masterminded by their daughter Virginia and Agustín to run away together. The couple was not found.[12]

Middle-class families were not exempt from the intergenerational conflicts over partner choice that caused children to run away. Although rarely found in the judicial files because these families usually sought to keep such episodes private, some cases show that middle-class children also used sex to get their way. Carlos Delahanty, a merchant living near the Alameda, rebuffed Luis Vásquez's pretensions to his daughter Concepción as he was "too young," advising him instead to "wait three or four years . . . as he did not have any work prospects." Concepción's brother also counseled Luis, telling him that "they should not marry because he had no career or profession." Concepción, twenty years old, felt that she had waited long enough to start a new life. One night she slipped out of her house while Luis waited in a coach. They spent one night at Luis's house and, then, seeking to avoid capture, went to Ecatepec in the State of Mexico to stay with Luis's grandmother. Six days later, the young couple was discovered. Because of her age, as well as her admission that she wanted to marry Luis, the judge ended the case because no crime had been committed.[13]

Another middle-class family—propelled only by the *belief* that their runaway granddaughter had been deflowered—was likewise forced to accept her decision-making. When Dolores Ahedo spent two nights away from home, her brief absence was enough to prompt her grandmother's concession to Dolores's choice of partner. Manuel Gorostiza testified that although he had taken Dolores Ahedo to a hotel one night and, then, to the house of a family member the next, he had slept at his own home both nights and "did not make use of her." The grandmother, after having Manuel apprehended, dropped the charge against Manuel "since he is willing to marry Dolores and has offered as much."[14] While Manuel had made such offers to Dolores in the past, absconding with his sweetheart appears to have forced her grandmother into a reluctant acceptance of the relationship, given her belief that Dolores had initiated sexual life despite Manuel's claims otherwise.

For young women, though, escaping parental authority through the initiation of sexual relations was fraught with peril and could backfire, leading to domestic relationships disturbed by a man's neglect of economic support, his flimsy commitment to an unmarried partner, or his practice of physical abuse. One woman, after leaving her family, found herself forced to return to them for help. Delfina Pérez appears to have regretted her decision to run away. Her amasio had provided only one real (1/8 peso) a day for her needs (*alimento*), failed to fulfill his marriage promise, and kept another woman on the side. Disillusioned, Delfina returned to her mother one month later and, together, they went to the local police precinct to make a complaint against Albino Hernández. Delfina's legal challenge to her amasio worked. The investigation ended when Albino and Delfina's father agreed that the couple would marry in four months.[15] Delfina and her mother viewed a commitment to marriage as the best possible outcome, one that offered

Delfina the most promising prospect for financial security and, perhaps, although unlikely, marital fidelity.

Melesio Ramírez interpreted his novia's repeated complaints about her drunken father as an invitation to sex. His novia, Pomposa Saucedo, considered them a demand that he take her away and make married life. Melesio told the judge, "I encountered Pomposa Saucedo on the street and asked about her family and she said they were good, although her father was very drunk, which is why I asked her to go have the carnal act and she accepted. We went to a hotel and, after, I brought her back home. It was after the carnal act that she told me she did not want to return home. But I only asked for sex so I refused and took her home." Pomposa told officials that she had expected Melesio to provide a "house for them to live" but he instead took her to a casa de cita. Having failed to emancipate herself from her family through sex with Melesio, Pomposa told her father that her novio had deceived her. The father immediately searched for Melesio, found him at a neighborhood pulquería, and took him to the local police precinct "without resistance." After several depositions and, for Melesio, several days in the municipal jail, Pomposa's father dropped the charge against Melesio when he offered marriage.[16] This case, like the Delfina Pérez–Albino Hernández case above, exemplifies the situation where young women and their parents came to see marriage as the best possible outcome, even when suitors had demonstrated behavior that made future prospects for fidelity and economic security doubtful.

A couple's decision to run away was a consequential one that exposed intergenerational conflicts between parents and daughters over family expectations related to kinship obligations, economic responsibility, and how much control parents and guardians actually possessed in determining their children's marital futures. Such conflicts tended to trigger parents' resolve to assert dominion over daughters. Parental responses were guided by a range of motives and concerns. Some parents hoped to provide their children with better life prospects than lower-class families customarily enjoyed. Other parents thought it both their right and responsibility to claim patriarchal and authoritarian control over female autonomy. Still other parents, for their own survival in a precarious economy, wanted to continue relying on their children's financial contributions to the family. Pushing against parental tenacity, young women's principal motivations for exercising personal will usually took one or more of two forms. On one hand, they wanted the right to choose domestic and sexual partners on the basis of physical attraction, emotional intimacy, and authentic, personal feelings of romantic attachment. On the other, they saw the possibility that their initiation of sexual activity, their forging of consensual unions, or their getting married offered passage into adulthood.

Female Emancipation and Parental Opposition

Anxiety over their children's choice of partners or the prospect of losing a working daughter's income compelled some parents to go to great lengths to reassert paternal authority. While family opposition could run headlong into a young couple's unwavering romantic commitment and leave parents scant legal recourse, in some cases family financial needs unleashed in parents a dogged determination that thwarted juveniles' attempts to use sex as an emancipatory strategem. One such case took place in the summer of 1900 in the municipality of Tlapam, south of the city. Martina Verdiguel sat sewing with her mother in their vecindad apartment. The two women, it seems, were part of the large population of seamstresses who worked from home subcontracted by local textile factories.[17] Seventeen-year-old Martina anxiously awaited the arrival of her friend Mariana López. When the latter arrived, she did so on the pretense of borrowing sewing molds from Martina's mother. Martina and Mariana then walked outside, chatting. An hour later Martina had yet to return. Concerned, her mother stepped outside to ask neighbors of Martina's whereabouts. One informed her that Martina and Mariana had been seen running down the street away from the building. The mother then went to Mariana's apartment to investigate. Though she interrogated Mariana for hours, late into the night, Martina's mother received little information. The next day, feeling stonewalled, the mother made a report to the prefecture, and authorities apprehended Mariana for questioning. Under the investigation of local officials, Mariana was more forthright. She admitted that while she did not know with whom Martina had run away, she could provide the first name and a physical description of "a muchacho who had been making signs with Martina." With that information, the intrepid mother succeeded in finding the vecindad where Juan Martínez lived, the man she believed had possession of her daughter. On a rainy afternoon, Martina's mother approached the doorman and concocted a story that some of her chickens had made their way into the patio of the vecindad. "Once penetrating the building," she told officials later, "I found Juan and Martina who it seems had just arrived as their clothes were wet." The couple had moved in with Juan's family.

The case ended quickly, the judge determining that because of Martina's age and her willingness to leave with Juan, no crime had been committed.[18] The mother's actions may have been driven by parental concern or by the perceived economic necessity of Martina's hands to sew for outwork contracts or both. Whatever the reason, the case illuminates how a deeply felt mutual attraction could guide young women to choose conjugal partners and personal satisfaction over kinship obligations that helped maintain economic security in a family's household. Runaway youths could make worse the already-perilous economic conditions working-class families faced, either by bringing into the fold an individual of dubious financial prospects or by removing the money-earning labor that offspring provided. In some cases, a child's foolish romantic decision—in the eyes of the parents—could do both. As a result, the determination that some parents demonstrated in tracking down runaway lovers indicates that the stakes were high.

Family concerns over the lost honor caused by a daughter's deflowering meant little in the face of dire economic circumstances that required financial contributions contingent on a child's labor. Camila Palma had run away with her sweetheart and been gone two months when her father, inadvertently, found her washing the sidewalk outside the vecindad where she now lived. Her father was forced to recruit the help of a policeman to bring her to the local precinct. There, in front of the judge, she criticized her father because he had forced her to work as a domestic servant and, when she told him the family was abusing her, "he ignored it." Even though she was just fourteen, her admission that she had willingly run away and had sex mattered little to her father who did not seek legal retribution against the "abductor." Instead, he quickly withdrew the accusation, seeking only to bring Camila, and her labor, back under parental control.[19] Seventeen-year-old Paula de Jesús was similarly resolute about not returning to her family. She had managed to run away with her novio and avoid discovery for seven months. Her father, by chance, crossed paths with Paula on the street and was forced to rely on the assistance of a gendarme to apprehend her. Paula's flight had been spurred by her father's insistence that she work at a *fonda* (inn) that served local railway workers. Despite Paula's living in amasiato for six months with Gregorio Hernández, and despite Gregorio's declaration before the judge that he would marry Paula, the father told the court, "I make no accusation against Gregorio Hernández, but only want my daughter returned." The judge agreed, putting Gregorio at liberty and turning Paula over to her father.[20] Here, although Paula's age and willingness to have sex meant that seduction could not be assumed and that Gregorio, thus, could not be criminally prosecuted, the father was nevertheless able to secure his daughter's return to family authority. But the question, "for how long," surely weighed heavily on the father's mind. In the preceding two cases, the families were determined to bring underage daughters back home despite their loss of virginity, and the law supported the parents in doing so. Such examples expose the limits of young people's strategic efforts to use the law's age requirements to their advantage.

Juana Méndez sold tortillas at a colonia Guerrero market with her thirteen-year-old daughter, Agustina López, "both having to work to sustain themselves." When Juana could not go to the market herself, she would send her daughter alone to sell tortillas. One night, Agustina did not come home. Two weeks later, finding her daughter in the same colonia, Juana demanded that she return. But the girl refused, forcing her mother to call on a nearby police officer to apprehend her. Agustina had moved in with the family of her novio, Vidal Pérez. The angry mother demanded the return of her daughter and had a police officer arrest Vidal "so that he be punished."[21] While the outcome of the case has been lost from the file's tattered and missing pages, the mother's emphasis on the family's precarious economic circumstances highlights how one child's flight could jeopardize the financial prospects of a female-only household. Agustina and Juana formed one of Mexico City's many tenement households comprising varied combinations of young, single, separated, and widowed women, all in an everyday struggle for survival.[22] The potential loss of the thirteen-year-old's contribution to the family labor force, her availability to sell tortillas while her mother managed other responsibilities, surely would have been for her mother a considerable blow. But Agustina's young age gave her mother a good chance to secure her return and to shore up family finances.

In a similar case, one father explained that, as his daughter Simona Jiménez was younger than sixteen years, she was "not a free woman" and, therefore, "under the patria potestad of her parents." "A lack of money to sustain ourselves," he continued, "forced me to place her as a domestic servant, not suspecting that some individual was courting her, because I would have not allowed her to be away from the family." After Simona disappeared for several days, her novio Manuel Galván approached the father to make marriage arrangements. The father, livid, instead had Manuel arrested. Manuel swore that he and Simona had not had sex and, so, had committed no crime. Likewise, in her original deposition, Simona insisted the same. She also made clear her desire to accept Manuel's marriage proposal. It appears, though, that after talking with her father, Simona drastically changed her testimony. She claimed in her later depositions that, two nights in a row, Manuel had used pulque to get her drunk and have sex. It was out of "shame" she had lied to authorities, she said, not wanting her parents to know that Manuel "had abused her person." She recanted her desire to marry him. Instead, using language similar to her father's, she declared herself "a minor and not a free woman under the patria potestad," adding that "I did not agree to any arrangement with my novio and support the accusation put forward by my father." The father insisted that medical experts examine his daughter. They concluded that she had been recently deflowered. Facing four and a half years in prison, Manuel was relieved when a jury found him not guilty of seducing Simona because she had "consented" to her own rapto.[23] The radical reversal in Simona's testimony suggests the power that parents could exert over daughters, especially underage daughters, once they were returned to family authority. It also reveals the economic calculus of desperate circumstances that forced parents to accept a daughter's loss of virginity in exchange for her return to the family labor force. This case is exceptional because Simona's father pursued Manuel's punishment all the way to trial. Rapto and estupro cases rarely got this far: parents usually ended their complaints once a daughter returned to the family.

Mala Vida

Young women frequently cited their mala vida—at the hands of parents, siblings, guardians, or employers—as the reason why they chose to elope.[24] Corporal punishment, at least as administered by parents and guardians, was seen as a legitimate form of discipline and was rarely denounced by children to legal authorities.[25] But it was not only physical abuse that drove young women's attempts to escape parental authority. Youngsters also complained of parents who forced them to work or refused to allow them to see their love interests. Male suitors commonly reported their lovers' complaints of mala vida to officials when explaining why they had decided to elope or steal them away.[26] Men often portrayed themselves as the protectors of their novias, rescuing them from abusive or exploitative family members.[27] While men portrayed themselves in heroic terms, the events detailed in criminal cases suggest that women regularly leveraged their accounts of mala vida against their suitor's sense of masculine pride and responsibility to stir them to protective action and to start sexual relations, a strategy that served to emancipate young women.

The judicial record is replete with descriptions of family violence that young women did not see as legitimate. In 1889, María Dolores Rodríguez told officials that her brother's constant beatings were weighing heavily on her mind when she spontaneously ran away with her novio, Vicente Guadarrama. Accompanying a friend on an errand, she encountered Vicente in the market. Hearing of the violence was enough for Vicente to pledge to take her away. They went to the house of a friend to have "carnal relations." "Since that day," she stated, "we have lived matrimonially."[28] Hilaria Martínez, originally from the State of Hidalgo, was sent by her parents to live in Tacuba with her aunt, who proved to be a cruel guardian. She regularly abused Hilaria, for instance, by whipping her with a *reata* (thick rope or lasso), a common form of physical violence used by parents.[29] After three weeks of abuse, Hilaria ran away with her beloved to make "marital life."[30] Elvira López confided to her little sister that she planned to run away with her novio due to the poor treatment she suffered from their mother. The abuse must also have been a terrifying prospect to the younger sister who accompanied the runaway couple in their flight, knowing that she would be blamed and beaten for allowing her sister to leave.[31]

Some daughters detailed the brutality inflicted by stepfathers that necessitated the need to escape. Stepparents were common among Mexico City's poor families, the result of conditions where separation, abandonment, and widowhood compelled individuals to form new domestic arrangements for economic survival. Yet the introduction of stepparents could cause friction and divide blood relations.[32] Twenty-year-old Miceala Vásquez stated that her stepfather's physical abuse caused her to "abandon her family home." Out one night with her novio, neighborhood policeman Rafael Barriga, she agreed to spend the night with him at a cheap hotel where "he made use of her." Caught the next day by Miceala's stepfather, Rafael agreed to marry Miceala to regain his liberty.[33] Fifteen-year-old Josefina Cárdenas lived a difficult life. Her mother and stepfather drank too much. Josefina worked at a match factory to help supplement the family's income. Her mother, when inebriated, beat Josefina. Her stepfather often made sexual overtures. The final straw came when her stepfather arrived home drunk and tried to rape her. She left that night. Her boyfriend rented a room where they had sex. The next day, her mother had him arrested, but quickly accepted his marriage proposal.[34]

The words and deeds of some young women suggest that they viewed the start of sexual activity as a proclamation of adulthood and, as such, a powerful measure in escaping abusive family relationships. As the following two cases show, the desire to flee overly controlling parents demonstrated young women's tenacious resolve. Daniel Fuentes, a police officer stationed near the Tepito market, began courting Matilde López during his stints patrolling her neighborhood. She rebuffed his overtures. Undeterred, Daniel approached her mother to arrange a marriage. The mother went into a rage, replying that "she would rather poison herself than give her daughter to him."

Despite Matilde's assurances to her mother that the offer was made "without her knowledge or consent and despite not having amorous relations," the mother beat her as punishment. The beatings continued for several days, finally driving Matilde to run away. Her mother immediately suspected that the police officer had taken Matilde and called on authorities to arrest him. When dragged before a judge, Daniel denied any knowledge of Matilde's whereabouts. The judge, it appears, also suspected Daniel. He threatened to sentence him to one month in jail for each day he kept her in his possession. Daniel vehemently denied the accusation. After six days, Matilde appeared before the judge, confirming Daniel's innocence. She explained that, fed up with her mother's violence, she had run away to the house of a priest who was a family friend. She then stayed at various friends' homes until she learned that Daniel was in prison for her rapto. While away, she began "amorous relations" with a man named Policarpo García and "asked the authorities to allow her to marry García" as she "did not want to return to her mother."[35] Because parents and children viewed running away with a lover as a common tactic to escape parental authority, the mother immediately suspected Matilde of having done just that. Matilde, after just six days, was so resolved not to return home that she began a new relationship in order to sever her family bonds once and for all.

Like Matilde, María Santos Yepes was steadfast in her desire to escape home. But María's actions more pointedly demonstrate how some young women viewed sex—not marriage or amasiato—as an emancipatory act in itself. Older than María by ten years, her older sister Teresa served as her guardian. The sisters, who lived a seemingly middle-class life in the upscale Condesa neighborhood, appeared to have a contentious and, at times, violent relationship. A particularly fierce fight took place when Teresa learned of María's relationship with a local butcher named José González. Teresa threatened her younger sister with a knife, causing María to flee their home with help from their maid. María went to the butcher, imploring and baiting him: "if he was a man," he would not allow her to return home. At her wits end, María made the especially drastic threat that she would "live in a bordello" before returning to her sister. José, compelled, took her to Hotel Vienna, near the Zócalo. Neither José nor María mention that a promise of marriage preceded sex, yet María provided the court with her blood-stained underskirt as proof that she had been deflowered. The judge closed the case immediately.[36] Because of her age, her admission that she had willingly had sex, and her determination to show the court tangible proof of her deflowering (even in the absence of a marriage proposal), María's actions suggest that she equated the beginning of her sexual life with adult independence. As a middle-class woman, María's drastic actions probably jeopardized not only her own reputation but that of her sister/guardian. Whatever her sister's reaction—not detailed in the case file—María may also have acted, in part, out of a sense of righteous retaliation, seeking to bring community scorn upon her abusive older sibling.

Starting sexual relations with a lover, though, was not always enough to help young women forge new lives. The limited financial prospects of lower-class men made the decision to run away risky. Young women balanced their hope to leave their mala vida against the economic realities that required both men and women to work outside the home. Damiana Fortes, resolved to escape the mala vida inflicted by her mother, left home to live with her novio who then "promised to marry her and enjoyed her several times." By living in a one-room vivienda with her novio, Martín Alarcón, Damiana showed her commitment to emancipate herself. Because Martín lacked money, "in agreement with him," Damiana found work as a domestic servant to help the couple make ends meet. By the time Damiana's mother located them and brought them before authorities, Damiana was six months pregnant. The judge determined that as "she was older than sixteen and left voluntarily, there was no crime to pursue."[37]

As noted in chapter 1, one common justification runaway daughters gave to explain their actions was their fear that parents would reprimand and beat them if they arrived home too late, or the next day, because vecindad doors had locked them out for the night. Daughters' fear of parental violence was often weighed against the entertaining late-night diversions the city offered. Margarita Montenegro made an abrupt decision to leave home after staying out too late with her novio. Having lost track of time watching *tandas* (one-act plays) at the Teatro de Invierno, a venue popular among the middle and working classes, she "feared her parents would beat her." So instead of going home, she went to the Hotel Colón with her novio and had sex. This seemingly spontaneous decision by the couple ended with a marriage promise in front of authorities that led Margarita's father to drop charges against her novio.[38] Considering how consequential was the decision to form a domestic union, fleeing family on the pretext of punishments that might accompany staying out too late, perhaps, also offered a ready excuse for young women already determined to leave home.

The examples of young women beginning sexual relations as a means to escape the mala vida uncover the intergenerational fault lines that existed within families. There were varying degrees of how much abuse—verbal, physical, sexual—young women tolerated before running away. When their male lovers presented the opportunity to elope, it allowed couples to affirm their adulthood and reject family hierarchies that condoned the violent disciplining of children. Many young women surely endured abuse and never ran away while others absconded with lovers and did not end up before judicial officials. But, when they did, we see how young women used the state's legal apparatus and interventions to successfully emancipate themselves. At the same time, and in rarer instances, families were able to reassert paternal authority.

Male Benefactors

On March 13, 1889, a fight broke out in a vecindad patio on Calle de la Industria, a middle-class suburb near the San Rafael neighborhood west of Reforma Boulevard. The altercation between two older men brought police to the building. When they arrived, Gerónima Miramontes charged that one of the brawling men, Lisandro Lameda Díaz, a well-to-do fifty-five-year-old immigrant from Venezuela, had raped her twenty-year-old daughter. The investigation that followed is revealing. It shows how one working-class family sought to oblige a man of higher social station into marriage or, at least, to commandeer his financial support. The case also demonstrates how a well-to-do man could obtain sexual favors from a young woman in exchange for gifts and rent. Lisandro had known Gerónima and her daughter for fifteen years. The mother and daughter lived a life of economic precarity, working as *porteras* (housekeepers) at various tenement buildings throughout the city. Lisandro, it seems, had been their on-again, off-again benefactor over the years, helping the women financially. Over the past two years, Lisandro had rented Gerónima and her extended family a vivienda in an affluent neighborhood. In that two-bedroom apartment Gerónima lived with her amasio, José Cisneros, her son, Ángel Soria, and her daughter, Elvira Soria, the victim of the rape. Lisandro's financial support of the family, though, had strings attached. According to Gerónima, Lisandro had begun making offers to marry Elvira—whom he had known since she was five years old—demanding the sexual access that often accompanied a marriage promise. The previous month, according to both Gerónima and her daughter, Lisandro had taken advantage of Elvira while they were alone. He covered her mouth with a handkerchief, threw her on a bed, and raped her. Gerónima further claimed that Lisandro had offered her 3,000 pesos as well as the deed to a house in Mixcoac. He had failed to live up to any of his promises and had not married Elvira. Wanting to "save the honor of her daughter," Gerónima pleaded with Lisandro to hurry his marriage preparations.

Elvira provided an account similar to her mother's, adding that when Lisandro began making marriage proposals, "I denied them, believing I would not be happy." Elvira noted that Lisandro would spend two or three nights a week at their house, but that she would sleep "sitting up the entire night . . . because she did not want to give him carnal access." But after the rape, Elvira stated, they began living together and had consensual sex "many times . . . [as I was] animated by the promise of marriage." Elvira appears to have relented to Lisandro's demands in light of the financial security he offered. When she finally agreed to marry him, he provided the family with a new apartment in a nice neighborhood, bought 200 pesos worth of furniture for the family, including an 80-peso bed for his intended, and provided four reales a day for her expenses. As proof of the marriage proposal, Elvira showed the investigating judge a white dress that Lisandro had purchased her for the wedding.

When brought before authorities, Lisandro provided a different account of his relationship with Elvira and her mother. While he admitted to having helped them financially through the years, as well as to having recently provided an apartment and furniture, he denied that he had raped Elvira or made a marriage promise. He asserted that Gerónima, and her entire family, understood that his benefaction came with expectations: "they knew the use I would make of the daughter, having made an agreement [with the mother] beforehand." He denied that the white dress was for a wedding, explaining that he bought Elvira many clothes as a "friendly gesture." Finally, he brushed aside the rape allegation, claiming that Elvira was "not a doncella as her mother claimed" and that "anyone who lives in the vecindad, had I raped her, would know if she had screamed." Lisandro characterized the family as a group of schemers who had abused his good deeds and were always demanding more money while not abiding by his conditions. For example, he noted various instances where Gerónima had requested a deed to a house or 500 pesos to start a business, both "absurd" in their audacity. Moreover, Gerónima had ignored his demand that her amasio not live with them in the apartment which Lisandro paid for. Indeed, it was his finding Gerónima's partner living at the vivienda that triggered the physical altercation between Lisandro and José Cisneros, the amasio. After hearing Lisandro's testimony, the judge determined that the rape allegation "lacked merit."[39]

For poor women, finding a financial benefactor offered one economic solution to limited economic prospects. Elvira's sexual relationship with Lisandro appears to have been a financial bulwark for her family. And Lisandro's matter-of-fact account to the judge that financial support of the family included entitlement to sex suggests that such relationships were legitimate and, perhaps, common.[40] Elvira's mother had succeeded in gaining significant benefits from Lisandro, yet, in the end, his economic resources and social capital gave him legal leverage over the family once their demands became too burdensome or they ignored his rules. Middle- and upper-class men were well prepared to resist when expectations for support went too far. By contrast, poor women found themselves in weak legal positions when such relationships ended, having all the while faced the daunting risk of a pregnancy that they would undoubtably confront alone.

Attention, promises, and gifts from well-to-do men could obfuscate their cruel intentions. Power and wealth allowed men to successfully resist attempts by humble families to get justice. On February 19, 1910, a letter arrived on the desk of the Procurador de Justicia (Federal Prosecutor) of the Federal District. In it, a distraught father, Amado Solís, a sixty-six-year-old widower from Tlalmanalco, a small town in the State of Mexico, recounted the events that had led to the rapto of his fifteen-year-old daughter, Francisca Solís. Amado, who owned an inn that catered to travelers headed to and from Mexico City, had met two men on business in Tlalmanalco several months earlier. Ismael Reyes Retana and his assistant Enrique Romero gained the "confidence and esteem" of the innkeeper who invited them to lodge at his establishment, where he and his family also lived. Opening the doors of "my honorable and decent home," he wrote, the two men "committed a crime that would bring dishonor to my family." Amado claimed that Ismael began secretly courting his daughter, taking advantage of her "youth . . . and inexperience." Feeling increasingly suspicious about their intentions, Amado was relieved when the two men prepared to return to Mexico City. Days after they departed, his daughter Francisca also disappeared. The angry father's misgivings were confirmed when he learned that Ismael and Enrique, along with a woman named Ignacia Súarez who worked as a domestic servant for Ismael, had taken the fifteen-year-old to the capital.

The letter continued. In his investigations, Amado had searched his daughter's belongings and found two letters from Ismael and a ring with his initials (I.R.R.): proof of his seduction. Amado submitted the ring to the judge with his letter. About a month later, Amado found Ignacia Súarez, Ismael's domestic servant, in Tlalmanalco and had her arrested. The woman confessed that on January 19, 1910, she had accompanied Francisca to the train station and had brought her to the capital on orders from her employer. Weeks later, Ismael abandoned Francisca who returned to Tlalmanalco and confessed everything to her father. In her confession, which her father reproduced in his letter to the judge, Francisca recounted that a week before running away, she and her "novio" Ismael met in the corral behind her house. Ismael, knowing the "quiet solitude of the town," used his "power of suggestion" over Francisca to "consummate the assault upon her virginity despite the resistance that her weak sex allowed her to exert in such circumstances." Using all the wiles at his disposal—"promises of marriage, fears of [her father's] anger, and threats of abandonment"— Ismael convinced her to run away to Mexico City. The father implored the judge to apprehend all three individuals for rapto, especially noting the "villainy" of Ismael who had used "his wealth, education, and influence . . . with impunity against a humble, yet honorable, home." What Amado's letter did not mention was the extent of Ismael's power and wealth. The son of a senator, he was a successful engineer who often graced newspaper society sections.[41]

Francisca and her father arrived in Mexico City for the deposition, taking up residence at the Hotel Washington, a respectable establishment in the heart of the city. In her deposition, Francisca recounted how, that night in the corral, Ismael had used "promises, caresses, and threats" to convince her to have sex. The next day, he left for Mexico City. Over the following days, his assistant Enrique Romero visited Francisca twice, each time with a letter from Ismael. Enrique told her that if she did not come to Mexico City, Ismael would not marry her and would never see her again. Compelled by the threat of abandonment, Francisca allowed Enrique to arrange her trip to the capital, using Ignacia (Ismael's domestic servant) as the girl's chaperone. Once Francisca was in the city, Ismael rented her a house for twenty-five pesos, and there she lived for one month. As proof of the relationship's legitimacy and her hope to marry, Francisca made a point of highlighting her domestic role, telling the judge that, while staying at the city, "I made food, although Ismael sometimes brought it from the street." Ignacia returned to the capital and told Ismael of her arrest in Tlalmanalco, which led him to lament that "everything was now known." Francisca, he instructed, should return to her father. When Francisca bemoaned Ismael's refusal to accept her, he insisted she return to Tlalmanalco, promising that Enrique and Ignacia would accompany her. After reminding Ismael of his marriage proposal, Francisca must have been dealt a severe emotional blow when he told her his father would not allow them to marry (presumably because of their class difference). Francisca's abandonment became more obvious when Enrique and Ignacia simply left her at the station, "putting two pesos in her hand." "I returned home and told my father everything, asking his forgiveness," she said sadly, and "like all fathers, he forgave me." When the judge showed her the ring that had accompanied her father's letter, she confirmed it had been given to her by Ismael with a promise to marry.

In the following weeks, as the investigation proceeded, Ismael never once appeared before a judge. He neither sent a letter defending himself nor used a lawyer as a representative. What is striking is how little pressure the court put on Ismael to appear before authorities, a common requirement under such circumstances. Clearly, his wealth and social standing, as well as his political and legal connections (indeed, his father had served as a judge before entering politics),[42] allowed Ismael to avoid the public shame of testifying before a court. Officials only questioned his assistant, Enrique Romero. In his depositions, Enrique denied that either he or his boss had ever committed a crime. He characterized Ismael as an honest and decent man. He made a point of telling the judge that Ismael had saved him from drowning years earlier and that he owed him his life. Furthermore, Enrique divulged that Ismael paid him a considerable salary of 120 pesos a month, an indication of his benefactor's deep pockets. Enrique defended his own actions by stating he had only followed his employer's directions. Furthermore, Enrique described Francisca as eager to come to the city. As a sign of her complicity, he noted that when she arrived in Mexico City, she had asked the train's engineer to let her off at a garden just before the station in order to avoid suspicion or to evade people who might be looking for her. Then, on the orders of Ismael, he took her to the house where she would spend the next month. He did not see her again until Ismael instructed him to take her back to her father in Tlalmanalco. Enrique contended that while she was living at the house Ismael had rented, Francisca behaved in such a manner that she reportedly earned a "bad reputation" (*mala fama*) among the neighbors. One neighbor supposedly told Ismael to give her twenty pesos and send her back to her father, advice Ismael heeded.

Francisca's father demanded Enrique's arrest as an accomplice, telling the judge that failing to do so would "mock justice." The police obliged the father, placing Enrique in jail that same day. The investigation dragged on for another two weeks (although there is no indication the court made any attempt to apprehend Ismael) and, at length, Francisca's father appeared before the judge to show a complete change of heart. "Following the dictates of my heart that tell me to forgive," he explained, "I desist in this complaint in all forms."[43] As in the previous case of the Miramontes family and Lisandro Lameda Díaz, we find here the class inequalities that existed within the legal system and the impunity with which wealthy, powerful individuals could behave. It is also possible, considering Ismael's wealth, that he offered Francisca's father money to drop the case. The receipt of love letters and pricey gifts, the allure of city life, and the excitement of being desired by a wealthy and powerful gentleman must have surely enticed Francisca, blinding her to the possibility of roguish trickery. The events surrounding the deception of Francisca are strikingly similar to those in the era's most popular novel, *Santa*. Like Santa, the book's namesake, Francisca found no legal means to hold her social higher-up accountable for his deceit. In the novel, Santa's family cannot forgive her fall from grace. This rejection propels her into a life of prostitution in Mexico City that becomes her ultimate downfall.[44] Francisca, it appears, did not have such a dramatic and grim future in store. Her father showed empathy for his daughter, seeing her victimization as a result of youthful naivety.

The allure of adult independence (especially in a city that offered so much cheap amusement), the amorous pursuit of a male suitor, and the excitement of sexual experimentation and pleasure could make the enticement to run away too powerful to resist. As a result, some girls demonstrated a tenacious determination to permanently flee their parental homes. In some cases, poor girls accepted the overtures of well-to-do men who offered money, decent housing, and increased independence in exchange for sexual intercourse. One rather mysterious case hints at the seductive power of such worldly desires, although the young woman in question, Guadalupe Vilchis, was never found by authorities. Living with his daughter in the State of Mexico, Guadalupe's father had sent her to live and work in the municipality of Tacuba—but "not as a maid" as he stressed in his deposition. One month later, he was informed that she had gone missing. Rumors spread that a well-to-do merchant named Don Luis Morales was the author of the rapto. The father went looking for the merchant who also lived in the State of Mexico. He arrived at Don Luis's estate armed with a dagger. But, tipped off by his workers, Don Luis escaped on horseback. The enraged father, foiled, then went to Tacuba and denounced Don Luis to authorities. When finally brought before a judge one year after the incident, Don Luis stated that he often traveled to Tacuba and Mexico City on business. One day, he recounted, he had disembarked from a streetcar in the center of Tacuba when a young woman running errands in the market caught his eye. Believing her to be "one of the many free women who roam the streets," he invited her to accompany him to Mexico City. She accepted. Don Luis told officials that, before the two of them left Tacuba, he had told her he was married. He then asked her whether or not she was "running a danger [to her reputation]" by accompanying him. She had already been "dishonored" by a man named Luis Becerril, she supposedly confided to the merchant. With that assurance, Don Luis spent the day with and Guadalupe, strolling, eating, and drinking around Mexico City.

Infatuated by the young woman, Don Luis rented Guadalupe a "trusted house" in Naucalpan (State of Mexico) where he periodically visited her to "satisfy his carnal appetites." But, after two weeks, Guadalupe received news that the wife of Don Luis, having heard rumors about her husband's illicit relationship, was "indignant" and searching for the young woman. The news was enough to scare Guadalupe, who ran off suddenly. When Don Luis arrived at the house shortly thereafter looking for his lover, the housekeeper informed him why she had fled. Weeks went by. Then one day, while Don Luis was walking the streets of Tacuba, he again encountered Guadalupe. They chatted briefly and he learned that she now worked as a domestic servant in a house in Tacuba. Hoping to renew their sexual liaisons, Don Luis asked for her address, which she provided. But, he reported, he had not seen her since that day. When authorities followed up on the information, they found that Guadalupe had indeed been serving at that house but, again, had disappeared, which led officials to close the investigation.[45] Guadalupe's actions, although never recounted firsthand, suggest a young woman unwilling to return to her family and prepared to serve as a domestic or live in an adulterous casa chica to claim independence. While Don Luis's proposition provided her the initial impetus to break family ties and run away, the city offered enough opportunities to exercise initiative and make a living for Guadalupe to strike out on her own. In a city where women outnumbered men, especially men of marriageable age, and where economic opportunities for poor women were scarce, an amorous adventure with a married man could supplement income and lessen the possibility of destitution.[46]

Making Ends Meet

In an urban environment where indigence and unemployment always loomed, accepting money from lovers offered one way for girls and women to supplement their incomes.[47] Yet, by accepting money before or after sex, women undermined their legal standing in rapto and estupro cases. Judges, as well as parents, viewed women's acceptance of money from male sexual partners as a form of "clandestine prostitution." And, unsurprisingly, even implied prostitution discredited women before the law, where chastity was an expected condition of redress in a sex-based crime. Fifteen-year-old María Luisa Hernández swore that she and her novio Francisco Borja had been in an amorous relationship for nine months when he asked her to run away with him and promised to soon marry her. Both agreed on this plan, and the couple went to a hotel where María lost her virginity. By the next morning, Francisco was gone. María, abandoned, went to the house of her friend Otilia Sánchez and told her of Francisco's desertion. Moved and probably angered by her friend's plight, Otilia informed María's mother, who quickly went to a local police precinct to lodge a complaint. When brought before authorities, Francisco—a thirty-year-old middle-class merchant from Spain—denied any meaningful relationship with María. He denied that she was a doncella, calling her a *liebre corrida* (loose woman; literally, "runaway hare") and adding that "in the barrio, there is a lot of talk about her behavior." She had solicited from him twelve pesos, he claimed, which he had given her on the agreement that they go for a stroll and then to a hotel to have sex. "He only spoke to her with the intention of making use of her," he concluded in his deposition, "and paid her for the service." María vigorously denied his account, claiming that he had written her two letters promising marriage but that she had torn them to pieces to keep them secret.

When the medical exam corroborated María's claim and determined that she had been recently deflowered, the public prosecutor (*ministerio público*) was convinced of Francisco's wrongdoing. He concluded that, considering the results of the medical exam, the "spurious claims" made by Francisco, and María's age, the defendant was guilty and should serve the four-year prison sentence. Francisco's defense attorney argued for his acquittal. He attacked the class and reputation of María's family, noting María's status as an illegitimate child, as her mother had admitted in her deposition. He derided as "inconceivable" the notion that a young woman of María's "age, class, and morality was so innocent as to not know what the twelve pesos were for as she walked into a hotel without resisting." The judge agreed and acquitted Francisco.[48]

Based on the testimony provided in this case, it is difficult to determine whether the relationship between Francisco and María exemplifies male trickery or clandestine prostitution. In a society where social critics recognized that economic deprivation often pushed women into sex work, convincing a judge of a man's deception was a tough task.[49] Men, and in this case a middle-class man, exploited the social truism that lower-class women were licentious and sexually accessible to escape their own legal and financial responsibilities.[50] While it is difficult to assess exactly what role money played in this case, it is clear that the economic challenges and limited opportunities of the urban economy pushed women toward overt or clandestine prostitution. In other cases, young women accepted monetary gifts from men after sex as part of a broader survival strategy to makes ends meet.[51] For women, gift-taking was both a socioeconomic strategy of self-management and a means of bargaining with men in an environment where earning enough money to survive was arduous.[52] Because such strategies among the poor were well known to officials, María's case was all but doomed early on, despite the medical exam's corroboration of her recent deflowering that belied Francisco's testimony.

Yet, a strikingly similar case shows that some judges were *not* so willing to let men off the hook, even if money had changed hands. Notably, though, it seems that judges were more willing to believe that male deceit had taken place when defendants were from the lower classes. The case brought against twenty-two-year-old butcher Anselmo Orajudi likewise revolved around money, sex, and public reputation. Fifteen-year-old Sofía San Vicente told officials about her three-year "platonic relationship" with Anselmo and that he had offered her marriage verbally on various occasions. One afternoon, she encountered him on Calle del Factor in the heart of the city. The couple went for a stroll. Anselmo took her to a tenement apartment several blocks north of the Zócalo on the pretense that he was meeting a friend. While there, Anselmo offered Sofía several glasses of alcohol and after much canoodling (*caricias*), "he proposed the carnal act to which she agreed with her full will, losing her virginity."

Anselmo told a much different story. He stated that Sofía had been a regular customer at his shop for the past two years. He flirted with her—referring to it as *chanzas y bromas* (teasing and jokes)—but never promised marriage. One day, after shopping at his store, Sofía returned hours later "but without her basket." She begged him to take her for a stroll and, after finding someone to cover his shift, he obliged. Not wanting to incite gossip, he told Sofía to walk on the opposite side of the street until they reached Calle de la Amargura, several blocks north. He then took her to a "clandestine house used for prostitution" to which he had taken other "women on other occasions." After sex, he paid Sofía three pesos and they left the hotel.

When Sofía failed to arrive home, her mother suspected Anselmo. She denounced him at the local police precinct, telling the judge about the years-long amorous relationship between Anselmo and her daughter. Days later he was arrested for rapto. Anselmo testified that not only did he pay Sofía for sex, but he had also given her mother five pesos and, then again, eight pesos in the days before his arrest, "presuming it was because she understood what had taken place between him and her daughter." While Anselmo sat in prison, Sofía's mother visited him to ask for another seven pesos to pay for an abortion.[53] (The case file is unclear about the details surrounding this request.) Anselmo further claimed that he knew two other neighborhood men who had had sex with Sofía and demanded that they be questioned. One of the men was located but denied the allegation. The medical exam, though, appeared to corroborate Anselmo's claim, showing that Sofía's deflowering was not recent. Nevertheless, the judge, despite the results of the medical exam and the defense attorney's pleas, prepared Anselmo to stand in a jury trial. The defense attorney called for the decision to be overturned. Because of the "vice of her origins, her race, and her lack of education," he wrote, "[Sofía] easily trespassed the limits of prudency and . . . did it for her own convenience." Her parents had failed to provide the proper moral guidance, his argument ended, "necessary to sterilize bad behavior rather than breed it . . . and with the goal of pleasing and gratifying her lover, she gave herself without reservation." The case file ends there, without recording the jury's decision.[54]

While the outcome of the trial remains unknown, Anselmo's testimony depicts a poor, female-centered household using sex to secure money from a man of somewhat elevated social standing. Even if his is a fabricated or partially fabricated account, it brings to light the kinds of financial negotiations that took place behind the scenes between parents and the men unwilling to marry their daughters. Comparing the court's treatment of the butcher Anselmo to its treatment of the middle-class merchant Francisco Borja from the previous case underscores the disparities and, as a result, the inconsistencies that existed within the Porfirian legal system. The medical exam used to determine the state of the victim's hymen achieved different legal outcomes in each case. For the middle-class merchant, the medical report incriminatingly refuted his claim of María's "looseness" and sexual experience, yet the judge ignored its findings by acquitting the man anyway. The butcher's testimony, by contrast, supported his claim that Sofía was not a virgin when they had sex. The judge, nevertheless, sent his case to trial. These evident disparities reveal themselves along class and gender lines. A man's employment record, education, and social standing determined his credibility before the law, a fact that demonstrates how, on the basis of class, men could experience unequal access to justice or impunity.[55] Yet, because civil society—with its established gender norms—expected females to protect their chastity, men from any class background generally found themselves in advantageous positions vis-à-vis their accusers, whose very appearance before a court undermined their respectability in the eyes of the law. Revelations that women had received money from their lovers only served to further entrench the law's bias against them.

Fourteen-year-old Josefa Herrera's admission to twice receiving money after having sex with a neighborhood store owner doomed her chance to gain a marriage proposal, both from the perspective of the law and of her family. The case is worth elaborating as it reveals the interconnections among money, nonmarital sex, and patriarchal authority. Josefa had begun a sexual relationship with Luis Rubín, the owner of a store located in the main plaza of Azcapotzalco, a municipality north of Mexico City. Neighborhood rumors circulated that a relationship existed between Josefa and Luis. This gossip was even known to Josefa's father who immediately suspected the storeowner when his daughter disappeared one night. While the testimonies of Josefa and Luis contradicted each other on several points, the pair agreed that a sexual relationship had started between them two months earlier. Accompanied by her five-year-old brother, Josefa had visited Luis's store to buy *manteca* (lard). Luis had gestured to Josefa to meet him outside, behind the store. While her brother waited, Luis took her to a deserted alley where they had sex. Josefa claimed to have been a virgin at the time. Luis denied it. They both agreed, though, that after sex, Luis had given her one peso. The couple continued to have sex until the day Josefa left home. What caused Josefa to leave was disputed. Luis claimed that after a fight with her family, she decided to stay with her cousin Petra and, after six days, came to his shop where she spent the night and again had sex with him. The next day, Luis gave her six pesos and told her to go back to her family. At this point, their accounts diverged. Josefa claimed that Luis had sent messages to her, through Petra, instigating her to leave home. But then, after sex, he told her to "scram" (*que se largara*). At no point, though, was marriage discussed between them. Josefa's admission that she had taken money from Luis twice after sex, along with her making no mention of a marriage proposal, doomed her case, both in the eyes of the law and of her family. Her father notified the court that, "believing that the dishonor of his daughter cannot be vindicated," he was withdrawing the accusation.[56]

The need for varied financial streams to support economic survival blurred the lines between committed relationships and sex for hire. Gumecinda Tapia, a thirteen-year-old working as a domestic in Santa María la Ribera, near the Buenavista Railroad Station, testified that she had met her novio of four months, Róman Reyes, near the station. He had asked her to run away with him, she claimed, after a promise of marriage. When Gumecinda agreed, Róman rented a room nearby where they had sex. Two days later, Gumecinda's aunt, who served as her legal guardian, found the youngster hanging around the train station workshops. After questioning her, the aunt went to the police precinct and made a complaint, demanding that Róman marry the girl "so that she could regain her honor." Róman, when brought to the precinct by police, provided a radically different story from Gumecinda's. He claimed that he had never met her before the day in question, when she had introduced herself to him under the false name, Luz. Describing their interaction as transactional, Róman maintained that he had paid her two pesos for sex "as they agreed . . . and reimbursed her as he would anyone else because she was not a doncella." He had not seen her since and was surprised when police arrested him. Indignant, Róman demanded a "thorough medical exam" and "justice for the damages against him." The medical exam, though, contradicted his claim, showing that Gumecinda had been recently deflowered. The aunt, two days later, nevertheless withdrew the accusation against Róman as it was "convenient to her interests."[57] Although Gumecinda made no mention of receiving payment for sex and insisted that she was driven by Róman's promise to marry her, it appears the aunt did not believe her niece's account. Or perhaps the aunt felt there was little legal recourse to be gained by pursuing the matter further, presumably because she was aware that most judges—as members of the respectable classes—would see Gumecinda's domestic service as one step away from prostitution.[58]

The precarious economic situations of domestic servants indeed pushed some of them into sexual transactions. In 1888, fourteen-year-old Sabrina Esparza worked as a domestic servant at a house in the affluent Bucareli neighborhood. Her surroundings were a far cry from the ramshackle home (*jacal*) where she lived with her mother in the Tacuba municipality. Sabrina claimed that while she was out on an errand buying bread and candles Antonio Salcedo raped her. He had pulled her into a carpentry workshop and "violated her, making her lose her state of girlhood" (*perder su estado de niña*). Antonio declared that, over the past three days, he had been chatting with Sabrina on the street while she ran errands. At one point he offered her four reals (half a peso) to have sex with him and she agreed. When confronted by authorities with Antonio's testimony, Sabrina recanted her original story. Her mother dropped the charges "after talking with her daughter and learning she had not been raped."[59] Seemingly ashamed that she had accepted money, Sabrina lied. Beyond the poor pay domestic servants received—and sometimes, no pay at all—it is conceivable that Sabrina's affluent surroundings at the center of a new consumer culture deepened the allure of subsidizing her paltry income by selling sex. Indeed, working girls received mixed messages about the value of virginity.[60] While parents, community elders, and religious figures might stress the virtue of chastity, girls also experienced sexual attention and harassment in the workplace and understood that sexual favors could be exchanged for money.[61]

On a September evening in 1900, fourteen-year-old Concepción Aroas stumbled drunk into her vecindad apartment on the south side of the city. She and her mother lived in the working-class Indianilla neighborhood near factories and a tram depot. Enraged at her child's behavior, Concepción's mother beat her with a stick. The girl immediately ran away and, one month later, she had still not been found despite her mother's frequent searches. Then, one day, a neighbor informed the mother that Concepción was living on the other side of town in the Guerrero neighborhood near Plazuela Martínez de la Torre. Concepción had found work as a domestic servant in the home of a middle-class family. The resolute mother walked to the north side of the city and hid among the market stalls until she caught a glimpse of her daughter. Grabbing her, the mother demanded to know why Concepción had left home. Concepción confessed that she had lost her virginity the night she came home drunk. Seeing the initiation of sexual life as her coming of age and a marker of independent adulthood, she had severed her family bonds. The mother dragged Concepción to the nearest police station to find out more about the assailant.

In front of a judge, Concepción admitted that she had lost her virginity to an American streetcar mechanic named Benjamin Tanner. (He was actually British.) That night, while out on an errand, Concepción encountered the Brit who invited her to drink liquor at the tram station. She agreed. Once Concepción was drunk, the man "abused her, making her lose her status as a doncella." Concepción recounted that, since leaving home and working as a domestic, she had visited the mechanic on three more occasions, each time drinking and having sex with him at the depot. She added that he had provided her three pesos on each occasion. Young women's admissions of receiving money after sex often led judges to end investigations immediately because they regarded such acts as prostitution, not crimes of rapto. Remarkably, in this case, the judge ordered the foreigner's arrest.

In his short deposition, Benjamin Tanner—twenty-eight years old and married—rejected vociferously the allegation that he had had sex with the girl. He even denied knowing her name. He only recognized her, he claimed, because she had often hung around the depot. The judge, nevertheless, placed him in prison while the investigation proceeded. For a week the judge waited on Concepción to get a medical exam, which she eventually refused. Then, in a short letter addressed to the judge, Concepción's mother explained that she had reached an agreement (more than likely financial) with the British mechanic and, as a result, was dropping the accusation against him.[62] Although only fourteen years old, Concepción demonstrated a desire to strike out on her own as an independent adult, a goal that required earning money. She did start earning, when she took work as a domestic servant far from where her mother lived. At the same time, if we believe her testimony, Concepción supplemented her income by returning to the British mechanic to trade sex for money. Such cases would have surely cemented the belief among Porfirian social critics, such as Luis Lara y Pardo, that domestic servants were "consummate parasites" who produced nothing and lived off the benefaction of the well-to-do.[63] Yet even Lara y Pardo acknowledged that the dearth of economic opportunities for women, especially the recent migrants from the countryside, pushed them into sex work.[64] Rather than demonstrating moral failing, the cases explored here reveal the economic strategies poor women and girls used to integrate themselves into the urban economy through self-employment. Short on economic opportunities, poor women demonstrated resilience in their ability to eke out livelihoods from their extremely marginalized social positions in a city that offered limited and low-paying employment options.

Pleasure

Beyond their strategic uses of sex, women, it should be no surprise, expected passion and pleasure from romantic relationships. And while such desires were most often obfuscated in the judicial record, the penny press's sex-laden comedic dialogues and articles openly addressed what was, for most other publications, a taboo topic. Humor allowed penny press writers and editors to engage topics avoided by more respectable publications. And, in so doing, the penny press characterized women as individuals in search of sexual fulfillment and pleasure. While its comedic and satiric bent allowed the penny press to make political and economic critiques—within limits—of the government,[65] its tales of relationships between the sexes, at times, offered implicit critiques of the gendered double standards related to domestic relationships, romantic trysts, and sexual gratification. In contrast, the era's most popular self-help book on love and courtship, Condesa de Tramar's *El Amor Obligatorio*—a publication that exclusively targeted the middle and upper classes—condemned any form of female sexual expression outside of marriage. And, even within the confines of nuptial union, de Tramar's book suggested that a woman's sensual pleasure was only acceptable when it met the "physical and moral needs of her husband."[66] Alternatively, the working-class penny press presented women who discussed erotic pleasure and had sex either without being married or extramaritally. In 1906, for example, *Don Cucufate* published a short dialogue between a mother and her about-to-be-betrothed daughter. The mother, with great seriousness, tells her, "On your wedding night there will be grave consequences. Your husband will . . ." The daughter cuts her off and says exasperatedly, "I know mother, enough! I know this perfectly well. I know the theory well! It's the practice I need!"[67]

The following week, the same publication offered readers a poetic dialogue between a "neighborhood Tenorio" (the comedic Don Juan of the vecindad)[68] and Chloe, the object of his desire. He tries to regale her with compliments about her beauty and proclaims his love. In response, she calls him a *lepero* (leper), a *majadero* (idiot), and complains that his breath stinks. He then breaks her bodice, trying to undo it with "his hands of iron," which prompts her to further protest his unwanted attention. Promising to stop smoking and to only "suck candies" (*chuparé caramelos*, a double entendre hinting at cunnilingus), he piques her interest. Aroused, Chloe changes her mind and declares, "Oh God, what delights I feel . . . listen up! Take me to your room now!"[69]

Penny press portrayals of pleasure-seeking women stood at odds with the gendered legal scripts women and men used in criminal investigations. As noted in earlier chapters, these scripts emphasized males' "natural" libidinal drive and females' passivity. *El Chile Piquín*, for example, published a poem about a wife whose husband has grown tired of sex. The despairing woman looks for advice. Her friend suggests that, while in bed, she should toss and turn, pretending to be cold. After waking her husband, she should ask him to cuddle and keep her warm. This advice works for several weeks and reignites the couple's love life. That is, until the husband "realizes her ruse" and returns to rebuffing her attempts at lovemaking.[70] This poem stands out for two reasons. First, it acknowledges women as pleasure-seeking, sexual beings. Second, it suggests that men are not necessarily driven by their sexual appetites and thereby challenges the gendered assumptions that undergirded government policy on prostitution and laws related to sex crimes. By marshaling humor, the poet—who surely sought comic effect in reversing the gendered expectations surrounding male and female sex drives—highlights that conjugal responsibilities related to sexual gratification are a two-way street and not simply defined by male needs.

Penny press content satirized traditional notions of manhood, especially male domination over women, and suggested the possibility of modern, companionate relationships.[71] *La Guacamaya*, for example, portrays a gender role reversal similar to that featured in the *El Chile Piquín* poem. *La Guacamaya*'s poem likewise tells the story of a man who has lost his passion and no longer makes love to his "beautiful and attractive" wife. The poet tells the reader that the man works too hard, which leaves him completely "lame" in the bedroom. As a result, the disappointed wife begins an affair with a man from another vecindad. When the husband finds out, he barges into the building, gun in hand, "to avenge his defamed honor." But even though the door is open, the cuckolded husband finds himself impotent to "penetrate" the room and fails to avenge his wounded honor.[72] By ending with the impenetrable door as a symbolic representation of the husband's impotence, the poem tacitly legitimizes the wife's need to find physical pleasure elsewhere. Like the poem in *El Chile Piquín*, the poem here defies the gender stereotypes articulated in elite publications and, in so doing, presents a class critique of social "higher-ups." On one level, by focusing too much on work and the accumulation of wealth, the cuckolded husband loses sight of the emotional and physical bonds of marriage and, perhaps, represents the emasculated dandies (*rotos*) so often the targets of scorn in popular publications. At the same time, by stressing female sexual desire and the husband's failure to meet his wife's needs, the poem implies the value of marriages based on *mutual* love and pleasure.

While the penny presses portrayed women as individuals who experienced sexual desire and sought sexual pleasure, women rarely presented themselves or characterized their rapto dramas in ways suggestive that any of their actions were driven by desire for physical gratification. Indeed, such an indication to judges or juries would inevitably undermine women's positions before the court and dash their already-slender chances of getting monetary or legal indemnification. Nonetheless, as described in their testimonies, some women's actions hint at moments where they sought premarital or nonmarital sexual gratification. The claim that women enjoy sex or seek sexual gratification is by no means a radical one. Like the examples of casual sex in the previous chapter, the cases discussed here underscore how desire drove some women to engage in sexual activity despite the serious consequences it could have. The severe consequences women risked by nonmarital sex have led scholars of colonial-era society to suggest that the very act of sexual intercourse represented, for women, a form of female rebellion.[73] By the turn of the nineteenth century, lower-class women were less concerned about social stigma, although pregnancy and venereal disease remained very real hazards.

One evening in 1905, Dolores N., a domestic servant who worked for a middle-class family living in a respectable vecindad two blocks south of the Alameda, accompanied sixteen-year-old Ángela Salazar to the store to buy a light bulb (*lámpara*), or so Ángela told her mother. Once on the street, Ángela informed her criada that they were going to the Alameda instead. Arriving at the park, Ángela instructed Dolores to find a bench and wait. Ángela then approached a stagecoach where she was greeted by "a white youth with blond hair, about twenty-four, elegantly dressed." They spoke briefly, and the young man helped Ángela into the coach and they rode away. Dolores waited. At length surmising that they were not coming back, Dolores returned to her employer who demanded to know what had happened to her daughter. The mother, after making some investigations, walked into the local police precinct and made a complaint. Although she did not know the name of the mystery man, she did learn (it is unclear how) that the couple might be lodged at the Hotel Madrid. Days later, she returned to the police station and informed officers that her daughter had returned home and confessed to having had "illicit relations" with Mario

Bulnes for over a month. She stated confidently that Ángela was a doncella before her "dishonoring" by Mario, a man she had never met and who "had never visited their home."

Ángela portrayed herself as the naïve dupe of a dashing rogue. She recounted that Mario had been her novio five years earlier (when she would have been eleven) but that she had not seen him for years. Then, by chance, she had recently encountered him on the street. He regaled her with "love talk," and she swooned. He invited her for a stroll the next day and she accepted. That day, after a coach ride, he took her to a "house" (more than likely a casa de cita) where, "after much caressing, she agreed to give him carnal access, losing her virginity, and committed by the impulse of affection." Over the next several weeks, they continued to have sex in the same house. Mario finally asked Ángela to run away with him and they went to the Hotel Madrid—the incident that had occasioned the investigation in the first place. After spending several days at the hotel, Ángela was dismayed when Mario told her that he planned to leave for Veracruz for work and would return in one month to marry her. (The case file does not make clear when or whether he returned as promised.) Weeks later, she accused him of rapto and estupro, believing he had deceived her. She added that Mario had offered marriage in a letter but she had lost it. When the judge asked for the address of the house where they met for their trysts, Ángela could not verify it "as it was always night" and she "did not pay attention to the number or the street."

When Mario Bulnes testified, he not only rejected Ángela's account but enlisted the help of several men who claimed to have had sex with Ángela. She seemed, he said, to be an "accessible woman" (*mujer accesible*), adding that they had met several times the week of the Hotel Madrid incident. The night she went missing, the couple had dined at the fancy Chapultepec Restaurant where Ángela lamented that, having fought with her mother, she did not want to return home. Mario rented a room at the Hotel Madrid where he lodged Ángela for several days and visited her on various occasions late at night to have "casual copulation." He insisted that he had not made a promise of marriage and had used neither "seduction nor trickery." He was sure, so he claimed, that Ángela was not a doncella, a supposition, in Mario's view, "confirmed by the ease at which she allowed herself to me." He denied "courting" her or having had prior amorous relations with her. He further claimed knowing two men to whom she had allowed "carnal access" without their "seduction or trickery." "Ángela," he gravely asserted, "played the game of loose morals, flirting, and the like . . . trafficking in the commerce of men."

One of the men Mario identified, twenty-six-year-old Emilio Sola, an architectural engineer, testified days later. He claimed that he had known Ángela for over a year as they lived in the same neighborhood and that she "was a woman of doubtful conduct." He had met her months ago at the Teatro Principal and, after the show, had invited her on a stroll. She agreed and "was in his company for one night and two days." (Here, of course, Emilio implies that the two of them had had sex.) He knew several men, he claimed, who had "cohabitated" with Ángela. As a result, Emilio doubted that Mario could have committed the crime of rapto, though Emilio admitted that he and Mario were not well acquainted. Instead, Emilio recommended that the judge interview Carlos Navarro who had also had relations with Ángela.

Twenty-two-year-old Carlos Navarro appeared before the judge, offering an account of how he and Mario had first met Ángela. Months back, he recalled, they were walking around the Centro Mercantil when they first saw her. Ángela "smiled and then began to flirt" (*darles cara*). The two young men had invited her to eat with them and to stroll the Alameda, and Mario eventually spent several days with Ángela at the Hotel Madrid. He had then approached Carlos saying he "no longer wanted to sleep with her" (*ya no quería ligarse más*), which had prompted Carlos to go to the hotel and "proposition her." When she agreed, Carlos and Ángela began a sexual relationship that lasted fifteen days. Ángela's behavior convinced Carlos that "she was of bad conduct and trafficked with her body." On the same day that Carlos testified, one last man provided an account. José de Haro told the judge that Ángela was known in the neighborhood for her "bad conduct." He noted that although he had not had sex with her, "she was a woman perfectly accessible and had been seen at various times and hours of the night with different men . . . and never accompanied by her family." José was convinced that Mario had not had "amorous relations" with Ángela. Instead, he told the judge, "those were momentary relations that one has with a woman of bad conduct." Immediately following this litany of male condemnations aimed at her sexual behavior, Ángela appeared before the judge to drop the complaint because she had reached an agreement with Mario, more than likely a financial one.[74] The testimonies of the men in this case provide a glaring example of the well-documented sexual double standard that existed in Mexico.[75] Neither they nor the judge questioned or condemned male pleasure-seeking sexual behavior while they demonized Ángela for the same conduct. In the face of that double standard, it is worthwhile to consider the possibility that Ángela rejected the middle-class strictures that governed her social group and simply enjoyed sexual adventure and being treated by a variety of men to restaurants, hotels, and good times.[76]

Fourteen-year-old Natalia Cosio lived with her father and stepmother in a vecindad on the south side of the city. Natalia regularly quarreled with her stepmother and, sometime in December 1901, a violent fight broke out between them that caused her to leave home. Natalia moved in with her friend Ángela Alemán, an unwed mother who lived with her parents, siblings, and baby in the working-class Guerrero neighborhood on the other side of town. Natalia's boyfriend of six months also lived in the Guerrero neighborhood, just two blocks away from Ángela's family. One Saturday afternoon after leaving work, Marcelo Paredes, a mechanic at the Buenavista Railway Station, met his novia Natalia, who was accompanied by Ángela and her baby. They had waited for him outside the station. Natalia asked Marcelo to take them to the theater. Marcelo agreed, but told them to meet him later at Jardín San Fernando, a few blocks west of the Alameda, so that he could go home and wash up.

Hours later, the group met and headed to a cantina. In his later testimony before a judge, Marcelo claimed that while he was drinking he had asked Natalia whether or not she had conserved her virginity and, after some prodding, she admitted she had not. Both Natalia and Ángela, later recalling the same conversation, insisted that Natalia had assured Marcelo that she was indeed a doncella. The trio then went to watch a *zarzuela* at the Teatro Principal, located between the Alameda and Zócalo in the heart of the city. At around 10 p.m., the group boarded a coach to return home, but, according to the testimonies of both Marcelo and Angela, Natalia had said it would be best to stay at a hotel because the doors of the vecindad would be locked. Marcelo agreed, found a nearby establishment, and rented two rooms. Again, both Marcelo's and Ángela's testimonies agreed on the point that they had expected Natalia to sleep in one room while Ángela and the baby slept in the other. Marcelo had planned to return home. Natalia, according to Ángela's testimony, insisted that Marcelo stay with her. Ángela tried to intervene, telling Natalia that if she was "supposedly a doncella," she should let Marcelo leave. Natalia replied: "nothing matters to me and I do what I want." As Ángela later told officials, because of her friend's remark, she was not sure whether Natalia was, indeed, a "girl" as she had claimed at the cantina. Early the next morning, Ángela came to Natalia, advising that they should leave because, if anyone saw them, they would assume them to be *clandestinas* (prostitutes).

In their statements, both Marcelo and Natalia gave similar, short accounts of what had transpired that night. Both agreed that they had twice had sex with each other. Neither noted that a marriage proposal had been offered before sex, although Natalia ended her deposition with the statement that Marcelo had promised her marriage the next day and that she was willing to marry him. The couple disagreed vehemently on whether or not Natalia was, in fact, a virgin before they engaged in sexual relations. In what appeared to be a heated careo, the judge noted that Marcelo and Natalia had both kept to their statements after "much debating" (a detail rarely mentioned in case files) but that Natalia had insisted that Marcelo had seen the blood on her underpants. After that night, Marcelo avoided Natalia for two weeks, which led her to return home and tell her father about her seduction.

Natalia's father had a police officer arrest Marcelo and bring him to the 4th Precinct on the south side of the city where father and daughter lived, far from Marcelo's home. He accused the mechanic of deceiving and seducing his daughter. The father, well prepared, brought Natalia's birth certificate, proved parentage, and agreed that she be medically examined. The exam, performed now two months after the sex act, determined that Natalia's deflowering was not recent, although the exam's conclusion was meaningless given medical experts' agreement that a recent deflowering could only be accurately identified within ten days of sexual intercourse. The case proceeded slowly. Marcelo languished in Belén prison for two months. Then abruptly, Natalia's father appeared before officials to end the complaint, stating that he did not seek to harm Marcelo any further.[77] While it appears that Natalia threw caution to the wind, seeking sexual adventure and pleasure, her attempt to get a marriage proposal from her lover suggests she was also aware of the consequences of nonmarital sex. Indeed, her friend Ángela, a single mother herself, was surely a strong reminder of that. The explanation as to why young women engaged in nonmarital sexual relations despite the repercussions involves a combination of factors: the low social value of virginity, the drudgery of working-class life, and the possibility of immediate sexual gratification. All of these coalesced in a freer expression of sexuality among the poor than among the middle and upper classes.[78] At the same time, for those seeking sexual adventure, the harsh realities of life endured by unwed mothers who lived in the same neighborhoods and tenements counterbalanced young women's romantic yearnings with fears of pregnancy and grinding economic hardship.

Conclusion

Poor and working-class women of Porfirian Mexico City could use sex strategically in the hope of improving their financial or social lots or of simply escaping (momentarily) the bleakness of economic deprivation. Whether the initiation of sexual relations created opportunities for young women to flee abusive or exploitative parental relations, to earn extra income, or to enjoy moments of amusement and pleasure, sex was a risky proposition where women could be deceived and abandoned by men to face alone such serious repercussions as unwanted pregnancy. Nevertheless, unsteady employment, low wages (which in some cases went directly to family), and the monotonous labor women and girls faced as domestics, seamstresses, or factory workers could make the strategic use of sex worth its risks. Running away and forming a domestic partnership provided young women the chance of freedom from family control of their bodies—especially through corporal punishment—and of their wages. Likewise, the occasional exchange of sex for money or gifts offered women a broader strategy for economic survival. It also allowed them moments of physical and emotional gratification, a reality the penny press openly acknowledged without moral indignation. Yet because sex offered poor women one among very few avenues to—perhaps—improve their prospects, we must acknowledge here the exploitative nature of Porfirian patriarchy and capitalist development that limited female opportunities so severely.

6

Shameless Love

The nature of courtship, romance, and sex differed greatly between Mexico City's working class and the well-to-do. Honor, too, varied greatly in its meaning, articulation, and public performance among different social groups. For the middle and upper classes, the protection of a daughter's chastity before marriage was crucial to maintaining family respectability and ensuring good marriage prospects.[1] The courtship rituals of the respectable classes reflected these concerns and were demonstrated by the practices of chaperoning, sequestering, and surveilling that safeguarded their daughters against acts that could cause family shame or even ruin.[2] Popular novels and etiquette manuals, targeting both the sons and daughters of the well-to-do, detailed a comprehensive set of rules and dictates for proper behavior leading up to marriage.[3] Foreign travelers often noted, with surprise, the conservative and meticulous character of Mexican courtship among the respectable classes. Such refinement and conservatism sharply contrasted with the courtship practices of the poor, for whom "free love" was the norm.[4] Elite families, outside observers agreed, kept young women locked inside their homes and, when their daughters ventured out in public, the families insured that they were chaperoned.[5] Courtship, one traveler observed, was conducted through windows protected by "gratings of iron."[6] The patient practice of a romantically interested man was to wait beneath his love interest's balcony, "walking to and fro, like the caged or tied animal." This ritual was known as "playing the bear."[7] Balcony courtship reflected the strict rules elite families enforced that forbade young men from visiting or "interviewing" ladies without family permission.[8] Foreign travelers were occasionally given extreme examples of Mexican courtship: one man visited a young woman's balcony for four years before the parents allowed "him to call"; another wooed a woman for seven years "without ever speaking to the lady."[9] Although these are probably exaggerated accounts, tuned for dramatic effect, there is no doubt that reigning courtship ritual among the elite was stricter than that among the common classes.[10]

Bourgeois protection of female chastity and virtue reflected elite-class concerns about honor that dated back to the colonial era and the maintenance of public and private distinctions related to race, social hierarchy, and female virtue. Patriarchal honor was tied to control of female sexuality because the protection of racial lineage, legitimacy, and inheritance were all crucial to family interests and the politics of marriage.[11] Colonial era signifiers of honor continued to exist among the elite into the late-nineteenth century and fostered a "cult of virginity." For the poor and working classes, ideas of sexual honor necessarily took a back seat to concerns about basic survival despite recent scholarly claims that sexual honor and virginity were values shared "by all social classes."[12] While a shared, trans-class language related to honor may very well have existed among victims, defendants, families, lawyers, and judges,[13] the actions of lower-class women, men, and families do not suggest that female sexual purity was a governing feature of public reputation among the poor.[14]

The lower classes, as this chapter illustrates, articulated conventional values related to female sexuality and respectability. Surely, in many cases, the poor and working classes used conventional, gendered values strategically to make judges and other court officers relatively receptive to their legal claims and self-representations. Nevertheless, among the city's urban poor many individuals and families *did hold* traditional values related to courtship, marriage, and sex. Outstanding, though, is the fact that the lower classes did not necessarily possess a distinct value system. What they possessed instead was a clear-eyed understanding of their vulnerabilities and of the impossibility of adhering to "respectable" courtship practices under strained economic and social circumstances. The lower classes recognized the traditional values related to sexual behavior; they may even have believed in and aspired to them; but they knew the limitations economic hardship placed upon their performance of what must have seemed, at times, like "luxury ideas." The respectable classes could strive to maintain a greater degree of self-mastery and privacy than their less fortunate fellow citizens. The poor suffered no such illusions. Instead, the working classes adopted a contingent and reflexive approach to honor and shame, sex and courtship, love and marriage, and, in so doing, demonstrated complex, contradictory, and always shifting responses to the circumstances they faced. This reflexive and flexible approach to intimate matters set the lower classes apart from their social higher-ups in ways that characterize a "modern" subjectivity.[15] This chapter's examination of the often-overlapping themes found in the penny press and judicial record highlights a fundamental ambivalence at the heart of popular attitudes about honor, shame, virginity, marriage, and sex.

When the idea of honor was invoked in criminal investigations, it was most often fathers and mothers who summoned it on behalf of a disgraced daughter. When a young couple's premarital sex pushed parents to accept a marriage proposal, judicial scribes recorded the standard refrain for ending investigations: the marriage would "cover the honor" of the victim. Similarly, when male suitors failed to marry in a timely manner, parents often initiated court proceedings to "cover the honor" lost. Male suitors, indignant at their arrest for rapto, commonly claimed that they had no intention "to make a mockery" (burlar, dejar burlada) of the beloved. Using similar language, parents, too, complained to authorities about men whom they felt had "made a mockery" of their daughters. Young women sometimes characterized their loss of virginity through male deception, inebriation, or violence as "being dishonored." Even so, the formulaic, and suspiciously consistent, language of judicial cases calls into question the degree of confidence historians can assume when ascribing those words and values to their lower-class deponents.[16] Instead, close examination of the actions taken by families—both in the rapto dramas themselves and in their legal decision-making—suggests that the call to legal authorities to initiate investigations was driven less by family concerns over a daughter's sexual purity—the negative impact it might have on family honor or future social prospects—and more by the need to do something in an environment where lack of privacy fueled circulation of the neighborhood gossip that could affect an entire family's social standing.[17] But even in a culture where family honor hinged upon a man's capacity to protect the chastity and virtue of female family members, the predominance of female-headed households recorded in rapto investigations suggests that, while community reputation surely mattered, working women neither aped nor shared elite mores about sexual purity.[18] Middle- and upper-class expectations about proper sexual behavior did not align with the social environments and material conditions that made adherence to such strict norms unachievable among the lower classes.[19]

The testimonies of certain parents make clear that they genuinely valued honor and worried about the stigma and repercussions a deflowered, unwed daughter might face. For example, one father lodged a criminal complaint against a young man "to have him apprehended so he will marry [my daughter] so she can regain her honor."[20] Bringing a criminal case forward, one widow noted: "my only objective is to protect the virginity and honor (*honra*) that I gave to my daughter."[21] A dejected father ended an investigation lamenting, "the honor of my daughter cannot be vindicated."[22] One young woman returned home to her father before she was married. She abandoned her amasio because of his violent behavior when, one night, brandishing a knife, he threatened to kill her. The despondent father told the judge that he had no choice but to "take her back" and "accept the disgrace."[23] Even in cases where honor is never mentioned, the actions of aggrieved parents make clear the interconnection between loss of paternal power and public humiliation. In the rural *chinampas* (agricultural plots on lake beds) of the Xochimilco municipality, Joaquín Medina was approached by the man he believed had stolen his daughter and was "greeted by him in a mocking manner." Joaquín told the perpetrator to leave immediately because he had "offended him by robbing his daughter." Then, pointing his rifle at the man, Joaquín threatened to "offend him in a different manner."[24]

References to the loss of family honor are extremely rare in the judicial record and, generally, are made only by members of the middle class. That said, it is also possible that, in the documentation of cases, the language and tropes of family honor were reserved for families whose social standing, from the perspective of judicial officials, merited them. One middle-class father told an investigating judge in Tacubaya that the man who had absconded with his daughter "mocked her honor, mine, and that of my family." He referred to the culprit as the "thief of *our* honor," which he had "conserved with great sacrifice."[25] Another middle-class father lamented that a lodger staying at his home had taken advantage of his hospitality and convinced his daughter to run away, thereby "bringing dishonor to the family."[26] Angered that a judge had freed the young man who had deflowered his daughter, one father bemoaned in an appeal that the court had left "his family mocked."[27]

While lower-class youths cited honor less frequently than middle-class youths, some suitors made known their honorable intentions when they promised marriage. For example, after engaging in premarital sex with his novia, one man stated, "so that [my novia] will not be damaged, I told her mother that I had the best intentions of marrying her."[28] An illiterate potter from the municipality of Guadalupe Hidalgo denied having had sex with his intended, insisting, "I absolutely have not touched her because I want her as my wife. I want to receive her with honor."[29] But just as often, men invoked honor as leverage vis-à-vis parents, exploiting parental fears about having a deflowered, unwed daughter. José Galván took revenge on his girlfriend's middle-class family when they publicly shamed him with an arrest. He exploited their concerns over honor and reputation by retracting his marriage proposal—despite his having lived with her for three weeks—as retaliation.[30] Another suitor, upset that the father of his novia had besmirched his reputation with complaints that he had not yet married her, threatened to renege on his marriage promise altogether, despite his having already consummated the relationship.[31]

These tactics expose an intergenerational divide over the significance and social value of honor. A candid conversation between one couple showed that while youths might not put much stock in female sexual honor, they recognized that parents did. Celestina Paredes's boyfriend, after having sex with her one night at a mesón (restaurant/hotel), promised that if, when she got home, her parents "reprimanded her for not being careful," he would "save" her by offering marriage.[32] Celestina's beau clearly did not seek to "save" her honor or reputation—or his, by association. Rather, he recognized that the yoked ideas of honor and virginity mattered to elders. His promise of marriage was merely a strategem proposed to mitigate the physical or verbal abuse that Celestina might suffer from parents whose family reputation hinged on their ability to protect their daughter's sexual purity.

Young women and girls rarely elaborated on how initiating sexual activity affected their public reputations and honor. Usually, women simply referred to the sex act as "being dishonored," formulaic language that might have reflected the semantic preferences of investigating officials. When women *did* specifically discuss their honor as related to their public reputations, they did so by emphasizing their work ethic and honesty, not their sexual honor. One runaway daughter noted that she had not left home with a man but had gone with a friend to Amecameca in the State of Mexico to find factory work. "There were no men," she explained: "the goal was to live honorably by our work."[33] Men likewise tied their sense of honor to their work ethic. Insulted that his sweetheart's mother opposed their relationship because she thought him a *ratero* (thief), José González, a carpenter, insisted he was an "honorable man and worker, making seven *reales* a day."[34] Alejandro Alvarado told officials that as a "man of honor and hard worker," he planned to marry his novia who had been "deposited" at the home of his aunt.[35] Although members of the middle class targeted the lower classes for moral reform and inculcation of a sound work ethic in order to make them honorable and productive citizens,[36] Mexico City's poor likewise defined their honor through labor. Whether workers portrayed an honorable work ethic strategically to make points with middle-class judges or whether such values were truly engrained in them, the discourse tying honor to work ethic stretched across all social groups.

Honor and the *Diario*

The high percentage of rapto and estupro cases stemming from working-class households (91.5 percent) reflects the discomfort that most middle- and upper-class families had with publicly airing private sexual matters or having their daughters undergo intrusive medical exams.[37] According to *Diario del Hogar*, when elite families *did* seek legal recourse for sexual crimes, their cases could be kept secret by having the trial testimony restricted from government officials and workers.[38] Newspapers, likewise, kept names private when reporting on matters involving the city's prominent families,[39] a courtesy not extended to the lower classes. An *El Nacional* writer made the seemingly contradictory claim that middle- and upper-class families no longer filed rapto or adultery cases because they did not want the public ridicule and because there was among them a more relaxed attitude toward sexuality.[40] Indeed, the increasing connection between honor and public opinion during the Porfiriato made newspaper publicity of family scandal a potentially serious blow to reputation.[41]

While the well-to-do continued strenuously to identify male honor in terms of the sexual virtue of female family members, the working classes identified male honor in quite different terms. Here, in the context of amorous relationships, a man's financial support of his partner in the form of the diario was his primary obligation. And, often, the fulfillment or non-fulfillment of this duty formed the context in which working-class male honor was defined and discussed. Penny press writings regularly satirized men's financial responsibilities and, by acknowledging their centrality to domestic bonds, mirrored the working-class sensibilities revealed in legal cases. Humorous dialogues between women often satirized men's lack of financial accountability and the measures women needed to take, and endure, to make ends meet. One such dialogue featured two women discussing how "men were all terrible," only willing to provide a "public woman" with a "great house and lots of furniture."[42] In another, two women are forced to buy horse meat to feed their families because their men fail to provide.[43] *La Guacamaya* offered a dark take on the theme with one woman asking another why her husband had publicly beaten her at the market.

The woman explains that he had spent all his money getting drunk and that because her children were crying from hunger she was forced to go "to the street to make some money," a less-than-subtle reference to clandestine sex work.[44] In *El Hijo del Fandango's* recurring section "Quejas Populares" (Common Complaints), women lament that their husbands never provide them enough money to meet even basic needs.[45]

That disputes over men's financial support emerged routinely in judicial cases indicates that penny press editors were keenly aware of the everyday struggles that defined popular domestic relations. Working men tied their sense of honor to their ability to provide for partners and children. Whether they were formally married to their partners or not, in front of judges men emphasized their commitment to the economic support of women. Cristóbal Buendía openly admitted that he wanted to marry a woman who was not a virgin when they had sex (although he was already married himself). Yet he took great offense when his novia Guadalupe Villegas claimed that while they "lived as married" he did not provide money, starving her for three days. He insisted that he had given "her money for the *gasto* for the food to make him meals and treated her very well."[46] Benito Galván insisted that he had not made a promise of marriage to convince Juana Montes de Oca to sleep with him. But he did assure her that, if she got pregnant, he would provide her a diario for her expenses.[47] Félix López told officials that his novia was not a virgin when they began to live in amasiato. But he insisted that he had provided her two reales every day that they "made marital life."[48] Ignacio Mejía insisted that because Cesárea Calderón was not a virgin when they had sex, and because she came to live with him willingly, he had committed no crime. Despite this, he told the investigating judge, "I admit having given a promise of marriage various times and I am willing to comply because I make enough money to support her."[49] Ignacio's capacity to financially support Cesárea—not her sexual past or how it reflected on his manhood—defined his sense of honor.

The families of women whose partners failed to provide financially could use rapto and estupro accusations to force the men to maintain their economic commitments. Such legal pressure did not necessarily include the enforcement of marriage. When Celso Cano failed to meet his promises to provide Luz Saavedra "one peso daily for her needs," her parents immediately charged him with estupro to force him to realize his obligations.[50] Similarly, the mother of Leonarda Venegas was not specifically interested in having her married. Instead, when she had Ignacio Tenorio arrested, accusing him of impregnating his daughter after a false promise of marriage, she asked only that he "cover her costs after she leaves his care and that he compensates her for the loss of her virginity." In a letter to the judge, Leonarda's mother calculated that he owed 504 pesos for "damages and harms," a hefty sum for Ignacio who worked as a mechanic. In his testimony, Ignacio pledged to "cover all the costs associated with the birth" and to "provide a diario, as long as circumstances permit it." In the end, the judge ordered him to pay an undeclared amount to cover the "costs of the pregnancy."[51] Unable to provide a home for his intended, although they had already consummated their relationship, Gregorio Moreno gave her twenty-five centavos daily as her diario. Because she continued to live with her mother, Gregorio hoped to demonstrate his conjugal commitment. But when he failed to provide money for three days straight, he was "chased and insulted" by his mother-in-law-to-be who then had him arrested.[52]

Virginity

Among the middle and upper classes, social convention dictated that virginity determined women's marriageability. The lower classes did not share this view. Although the claim that a woman was not a virgin could serve as a legal strategem by which men might avoid marriage or compensatory payments, most cases demonstrate that they did not see a woman's nonvirginity as an obstacle to marriage or amasiato. Some unscrupulous men claimed that the absence of bodily proof—especially blood—after sex justified their decision to retract a marriage proposal, but in Mexico City this was exceedingly rare.[53] In the seventy-three cases where men claimed that the female plaintiff was not a virgin, marriage offers were nonetheless made in forty of them (54.8 percent).[54] In contrast, only eleven men (15.1 percent) retracted or denied making a marriage proposal and only five (6.8 percent) explicitly stated that the woman's failure to show physical proof of virginity had prompted them to retract or deny a nuptial commitment. And, in two of those five cases, the men continued to live in amasiato with their partners. Similarly, in the rare instances—eleven cases—where *women* acknowledged having lost their virginity to another man, marriage offers were, nevertheless, forthcoming in six cases (54.5 percent). These numbers suggest that meaningful relationships—presumably characterized by feelings of affection, "longing for association," or a desire to mutually fulfill gendered domestic responsibilities—mattered more to men than bodily proof of virginity. Moreover, a man's public declaration—at least before the judge and scribe—that he planned to marry a woman whose first sexual experience was with another indicates that female sexual history did not affect his masculine pride.

Men repeatedly made clear testaments that their novias' sexual pasts did not deter forging long-term partnerships with them. Andrés Franco testified: "I made use of [my novia] and judge that she was not a doncella, nevertheless I offer to marry her."[55] Speaking about his novia who sold tortillas in the Guerrero neighborhood market, one man said, "after fifteen days I made use of her, not finding her to be a doncella, but this wasn't problematic in keeping our relationship so we moved into a home together and I gave her the title of wife" (*le dio el título de esposa*).[56] Antonio Arévalo took his sweetheart to a hotel to have sex and "didn't find her to be a doncella." He still "found himself wanting to marry her."[57] Another man, when testifying about the woman with whom he was having an affair, had the boldness to state, "when we had sex she was not a virgin, but I don't care, if I wasn't married I would give her my name."[58] While we might suspect that these men publicly committed to marriage or amasiato because they only *presumed* that their lovers had a sexual past, the judicial record suggests otherwise.

Verbal admissions and medical "proof" of women's previous sexual experience likewise did not deter men from forming long-term unions with them. Calixto Martínez testified that his novia had admitted to him that she "did not protect her state," yet he offered to marry her.[59] Antonio Guerrero did not mind that his sweetheart had already been deflowered by a railway brakeman named Hilario Sánchez, something his novia acknowledged in her testimony. He offered to marry her nevertheless.[60] Fifteen-year-old Carmen Flores, after a medical exam disclosed her "old" deflowering, was pressed by the judge to admit that she had lied about being a virgin in her initial testimony. She conceded that she had had sex two years earlier with another youth who lived in her vecindad. This admission did not change her novio's wish to marry her, however.[61] The environment in which the poor formed relationships made expectations of sexual purity unrealistic and untenable. Men and women understood that domestic and sexual relationships—whether long or short term—offered opportunities to alleviate economic hardship through shared gendered household responsibilities and united income streams.

Beyond strictly economic concerns, sincere and deep feelings of affection moderated or dissipated male concerns about how a partner's sexual past reflected on a man's public honor or reputation. This seems to be the case for José Aguilar and Beatriz Gutiérrez who lived in the same vecindad on the south side of the city. One afternoon, they made their way to a cantina after Beatriz ended her shift at a factory on San Antonio de Abad. After several hours of drinking, they spent the night in a vecindad accesoria, which José had rented for the night. José claimed that the couple did not have sex. Beatriz was not completely sure. She told officials, "I didn't feel deflowered, and I didn't have a hemorrhage," which led her to conclude that the "coitus was not verified." To be sure, she requested a medical exam because she wanted José punished after learning he was already ecclesiastically married. The exam, though, determined that Beatriz had been deflowered prior to her assignation with José and that it was not recent. The judge, in light of the medical exam, questioned Beatriz's mother about whether the girl had engaged in any previous "illicit" relationships. The mother did not know. The medical report, as well as the mother's uncertainty about her daughter's sexual past, did not inhibit José's desire. He ended the ordeal, making a promise to the mother that he would marry Beatriz through the civil registry.[62] Although the medical exam results could have absolved José legally by "proving" he had not deflowered a chaste woman, either José's attachment to Beatriz or his skepticism about the accuracy of the medical findings superseded everything else.

Because the law aimed to protect chaste women from male deceit and from deflowerings unaccompanied by marriage proposals, the language linking virginity to honor could get confused when women were, at least by traditional standards, nonvirgins. One man noted that he did not believe his novia was a virgin when they had sex, but he was "still willing to cover her honor and marry."[63] Andrés Resa promised to repair the honor of his novia although she was "already a woman of the world." He offered to marry the thirteen-year-old after her medical exam corroborated his claim and determined that her deflowering was "old."[64] Whether a man's promise to "cover the honor" of a nonvirgin was based upon his reconceptualization or misunderstanding of that traditional concept, the promise nonetheless suggested his quest to remedy the dishonor caused by another man. Such deeds were surely interpreted by parents and partners as chivalrous. More likely than not, they also positively reflect a male self-worth based on noble actions rather than on a woman's virginity or lack thereof.

Varying Views of Virginity

In the cases examined so far, working-class men did not hang female honor and respectability on the hook of proven virginity. Likewise, working-class women's sense of personal honor and respectability also did not hinge upon their own virginity. Even so, the gendered scripts women were often compelled to use in their legal self-defense could also obscure their actual values. Nevertheless, along with the cases of casual sex and sex for pleasure explored in chapters 4 and 5, the cases discussed here—demonstrative of women's actions in romantic relationships—also indicate the low value of virginity from a working-class, female perspective. For example, the behavior of sixteen-year-old Juana López suggests that her sexual past would not affect her future prospects: personal, social, or romantic. After six months of amasiato, she returned to her mother because her partner, Domingo Olmos, "had avoided his [financial] obligations," and she would not marry him civilly as a result. When brought before authorities at the behest of Juana's mother, Domingo claimed that although Juana had not been a virgin when they began their relationship, he nonetheless planned to marry her. Unwilling to return to Domingo, Juana apparently convinced her mother to drop the accusation against him because she did just that, without securing a promise of marriage or financial support for her daughter.[65] Many case files make clear that a woman's being deflowered seldom dissuaded a suitor from making a marriage proposal. Had the issue of nonvirginity been consequential for Juana, she would have been unwilling, or at least reluctant, to refuse to marry or to leave Domingo. The very fact that she refused him on the basis of his failure to support her reinforces the idea that financial stability carried greater weight for working-class women than the possible social consequences of alleged nonvirginity.

In February 1905, fourteen-year-old Magdalena Galicia told officials that after drinking at a cantina with her novio Alberto Sierra, they had gone back to his vecindad apartment and had sex. Although she insisted that he had promised her marriage, she did not see Alberto again for three months. Magdalena had not wanted to report the matter. But her father learned about Magdalena's lover when his daughter-in-law—to whom Magdalena had confided—exposed the secret. Once located and brought to a police precinct, Alberto agreed to marry Magdalena "in the hope of ending the ordeal against him."[66] As in the previous case, like Juana's, Magdalena's decision not to force the issue of marriage suggests that she was not seriously concerned about having lost her virginity. Instead, she appears to have engaged in premarital or nonmarital sex without any expectation of immediate marriage or amasiato.

While parents exhibited greater concern than their daughters over their virginity and its impact on marriageability, the actions of many fathers and mothers caution us against assigning too much importance to that connec-

Table 5. Legal Outcomes

Desist	77
Promise to marry	56
No crime committed	46
Case file incomplete	37
Guilty verdict	8
Not guilty verdict	6
Daughter not found	4
TOTAL	**234**

Source: Archivo General de la Nación, Archivo del Tribunal Superior de Justicia de la Ciudad de México and Archivo del Tribunal Superior de Justicia del Distrito Federal.

tion. Parents regularly dropped charges against perpetrators who had allegedly deflowered their daughters and instead sought financial compensation or, simply, their daughters' return home. Indeed, guardians' terminations of cases without their securing marriage promises was the most common outcome in rapto and estupro cases. The seventy-seven cases that conclude in this manner represent 33 percent of the 234 examined in this study. If we subtract the thirty-seven cases where a resolution cannot be determined (because the case files were in poor condition or missing pages or had been sent to another court), then that number increases to 36.8 percent.

Considering the precarious economic and social conditions that defined lower-class life, profound concern over a daughter's virginity ranked low among day-to-day priorities. As discussed in chapter 5, the penny press reflected such realities, usually characterizing working-class men and women as people with sexual pasts, as demonstrated by their open acknowledgment of amasios, lovers, or children. And despite their pasts, the penny press, shows these individuals forging new relationships without social stigma.

Vicenta Rangel, a thirteen-year-old seamstress living in the Tepito neighborhood, flouted the marriage proposal of Luis Velásquez as well as her father's acceptance of it. She admitted that she and Luis had had sex in a hotel and that "he made me lose my virginity." "Despite this," she continued, "I am not willing to marry him because I don't have affection for him and because we never had amorous relations." When pressed by the judge to explain her decision to have sex with Luis, she explained it was "a simple agreement because he lived in the same vecindad."[67] Indeed, parents could be hard pressed to force daughters into marriage when they refused, which compelled elders to accept—if they did not already—that nonmarital sex was a fact of life. Feliciana Jiménez and Paula Valencia, domestics in the house of the well-to-do Buenrostro family, briefly ran away with their boyfriends, both of whom worked at the same home. When their mothers had the men arrested for deflowering the girls without a promise of marriage, they quickly retracted their legal complaints "adhering to the wishes of their daughters" who were "not willing to marry."[68] Similarly, Feliciano Nava did not seem to care that his daughter had lost her virginity to a neighborhood coach driver; he wanted her back home and not to go through with the marriage.[69]

Some parents accepted their daughters' decisions neither to get married after sex nor to return home after living in amasiato. Lack of financial support, domestic abuse, alcoholism, and infidelity represented the most common factors that drove women to leave their partners. The period that couples spent in amasiato, at times, revealed the abusive nature of some men, which prompted women to abandon the relationships before undertaking legal marriage, if such had ever been the goal. After having lived with him for four months, María Gutiérrez decided that she would not be happy with her husband-to-be and returned to her family.[70] Although María Martínez was originally willing to marry her novio, eight days of his drunken violence convinced her to leave. Her family also rejected his proposal and instead made a financial arrangement with his family.[71] Concern for the safety and health of daughters shows that some families placed sexual honor second to well-being. It is also possible that parents who ignored the plight of a daughter suffering from a domestic partner's physical abuse or financial neglect faced scrutiny from the neighbors who viewed them as incapable of safeguarding their children. Tenement gossip surely concerned itself with more than a parent's capacity to control a daughter's sexual purity and public behavior.[72] A parent's display of forgiveness for or protection of a child probably also shaped the family's public standing, revealing the calculus some parents faced over how to respond to matters tied to honor, sex, and a daughter's emancipation.

The prospect of infidelity or the financial burden created by a second family when men established a casa chica, also led parents to prefer that a deflowered daughter return home. After insisting that his daughter's novio commit to marriage after deflowering her, one father quickly changed his mind when he learned that the man already had "an amasia, a son, and another about to be born." He dropped the rapto charge against the suitor and demanded that his daughter return home.[73] The parents of Romana

Montaño ended the investigation against their daughter's abductor when they discovered that he had recently committed another rapto of a neighborhood girl.[74]

In rarer cases, middle-class families were forced to calculate how the loss of a daughter's virginity weighed against other prospects such as marriage or getting an education. Agustín Monteverde, an employee of the courts, ended the rapto investigation against his daughter's lover once she was returned to paternal custody. At first, the father seemed determined to punish the young man and paid for six copies of his photograph to be distributed to police to ensure his apprehension. Yet once the father recovered his daughter, he was more interested that she return to school and dropped the charges immediately.[75] In a letter to a lover who refused to wed, one young woman of middle-class background lamented: "It makes me very sad that you are going to harm me without cause. I ask you dearly to do me the favor and make me yours." In a second letter, dated the very next day, she addressed her "beloved boy" and asked why he refused to marry her. The court saw her as a "libertine," she bemoaned, pleading "make good on your promise to marry . . . even if after eight days you leave me." This would "uplift" her honor, which is what her mother "wanted most."[76] In the cases that issued from middle-class families, a consistent concern for honor is demonstrated by both parents and daughters in counterpoint to the less restrictive courtship culture of the poor. Furthermore, as the young woman's letter makes clear, public reputation (the indignity of being seen as a "libertine") and parental opinion weighed heavier on the minds of middle-class youths than it did on those of working-class young people.[77]

As noted, working-class men seldomly claimed that a woman's past sexual history made marriage, or at least long-term union, impossible. A man's resolve not to marry an allegedly sexually active woman could prove easy to undo while also revealing a range of male responses. Manuel García, for example, denied ever having promised to marry Felisa Sánchez: "she had already been with a man," he protested. He admitted not knowing what kind of relations she had had with her former novio, but "he feared" she was not a virgin "because of how easy it was to make use of her." The discovery of a stash of signed love letters and, perhaps, two days in prison changed the sixteen-year-old's mind.[78] Another man noted that although he had originally offered to marry his intended, when he learned she was not a virgin, he "only offered to give her a home" (*ponerle casa*) and to live with her in amasiato.[79] Similarly, judging that his novia was not a virgin the first time they had sex, Miguel Espíndola decided that he would "nevertheless take care of her (*sostenerla*), but not marry."[80] Perhaps because of the flexibility that characterized amasiato, some men viewed concubinage as the preferred form of union for women with sexual history with the more solemn institution of marriage reserved for virgins. The popular practice of amasiato also appears to have diminished the importance of female virginity among the working classes. If so, the cases discussed here highlight the sexual double standard that favored men and could serve as their legal pretext to avoid a binding union. Further, these cases also reveal the much broader range of responses articulated by working-class men, responses that acknowledged and accepted female sexuality, as compared to those of their middle- and upper-class counterparts for whom nonvirginity was, more often than not, a nuptial death sentence.

Middle-Class Sexual Values

Indeed, most examples of men who reneged on marriage promises on "discovering" their lover's sexual past involved members of the middle class or professionals and entrepreneurs with middle-class aspirations. The testimony of Daniel Peres—a literate, private employee living in the respectable working-class Guerrero neighborhood—demonstrated the sexual double standard that shaped some men's thinking about female virginity. He refused to marry Josefina Márquez, his novia of two years, because when they had had sex "she did not scream" or "make any demonstration of pain." The day after their sexual relations, Daniel sent her a letter ending the relationship. After Daniel's arrest, a medical exam confirmed that Josefina had been "recently deflowered." This revelation prompted Daniel to tell officials, "I believed that Josefina wasn't a doncella because she didn't scream once. But seeing the result of the medical exam, I am disposed to make good on the promise of marriage."[81] José González—a literate butcher shop manager—articulated a similar double standard. After his arrest for deceiving a young woman into sex without a marriage proposal, he defended himself by proclaiming, "had she been a doncella I would have never dared violate her because of the responsibility that would incur." As evidence of his accuser's lack of chastity, José claimed that he had had "no trouble undertaking the material act of coitus."[82]

The case of middle-class pastry chef, Arturo Guevara, provides one of the rare examples of a man resolutely opposed to marriage when he came to believe his novia had known a previous lover. He and María Felipa had spent the night driving around the city in a coach. While inside, he had "the carnal act with her, not finding her to be a doncella." The next day, the coach dropped them off at Chapultepec Park where they spent the day strolling until two friends appeared, telling them that María's mother demanded her return. Two days later, Arturo received a message from María's mother "reproaching his conduct and demanding that he marry María." Arturo refused "because he did not find her to be a doncella." Despite her repeated threats to have him arrested for rapto and estupro, Arturo rejected her demands. His steadfast refusals led to his detention and a drawn-out legal battle that required him to post a 300-peso bail.[83]

All three of these cases present examples of men who either put great stock in the value of female virginity or who sought to marshal nonvirginity as a legal strategy to avoid marital commitment. Assuming that Daniel's and José's apprehensions about their lovers' nonvirginity are genuine, their anxiety arises in both cases from disappointed, and, probably misinformed, expectations about how a woman should react on her deflowerment. Both men misinterpreted the absence of physical pain or resistance as evidence of their novias' nonvirginity. As other cases have shown, the absence of female bleeding on deflowerment was also misinterpreted by other men the same way. In both cases, the suitors' disappointed expectations expose a fragile masculinity tied to notions of sexual conquest. Male expectations about and arousal over the anticipated physical proof of sexual conquest are laid bare in Francisco Flores's study *El hímen en México* where he proclaims: "the young man who marries dreams of his wedding night and the resistance he will encounter when he goes to satisfy his ardent passions."[84] If it was a legal strategy, "proving" that a woman had been deflowered prior to the sex act in question ended an estupro accusation by default because the law held that only "chaste and honest" women could be victimized.[85] While the legal wording for the crime of rapto did not specifically mention "chaste and honest" women, the law fell under the legal category of "crimes against morality and good manners," which, again, by definition, assumed the sexual purity of the victim.[86]

Bodily Truth

The sexual double standard also opened up opportunities for females to take advantage of male expectations, whether personal or legal, regarding the assumption that deflowered women were sexually available. One young woman exploited this expectation to coax her reluctant beau to have sex with her and to commit to a marriage proposal. As María Guadalupe Rodríguez explained herself to officials, she suggested she had lied to her lover only to calm his fears. Having already spent time in prison, he worried that deflowering María might lead to a rapto investigation or, worse yet, a conviction that could leave him to suffer years in prison. María admitted to investigating officials that she had lied to her beau, telling him that she had already been deflowered six months earlier by a blacksmith who got her drunk and took her to a field to have sex. The lie worked. The medical exam corroborated her claim that she had been only recently deflowered, and a readily forthcoming marriage proposal ended the investigation.[87]

Physical evidence of female virginity could belie the acts of sex under legal investigation. Testimonies reveal a fetishization of the intact hymen by women, men, and parents who all viewed hymenal integrity both as the ultimate proof of chastity and as a marker of morality inscribed on the female body. Manuel Gorostiza explained that his novia confessed that she had "lost her virginity by accident," not by sex but "by other means." Manuel was "willing to marry despite her confession."[88] Another man felt exempt from lawful punishment because the young woman with whom he had had sex was "not a virgin." She had told him that "One night while dreaming she introduced her finger and that is how she lost her virginity."[89] Vicente Guerrero—who was already married—noted that he had "no intention to mock" his lover. But she had "confessed" that her cousin had "introduced his fingers into her parts," and, as a result Vicente told the judge, "I knew that I would have no responsibility."[90] Margarita Flores's daughter was raped by a houseguest while she was working as a domestic servant for a well-to-do family. Margarita took her daughter's assailant to court but dropped the charge when the medical exam determined that the fourteen-year-old girl's hymen was intact. As a result, Margarita came to believe that the houseguest "did not deflower my daughter."[91] For Margarita, verifying the physical proof of her daughter's virginity mattered more than her rape.

The significant leeway the law offered men—placing the onus on young women to prove their virtue and sexual purity—created opportunities for unscrupulous men to use a woman's allegedly bad reputation to escape the legal repercussions of sexual misconduct. The tryst between Gala Perantes and José Fernández offers such an example. Gala worked and lived at an inn three blocks south of the Alameda with her grandmother. She caught the eye of José, a regular patron. Though he had sent her flowers and other *requiros* (gifts), José claimed that, during this courtship period, "he never had relations with her." One day, during their chance meeting on the street, he invited her to his house to drink beer. She declined. Two weeks later, outside the inn, José invited her again and, this time, she agreed. Worried that her grandmother might see her leave with a patron, Gala departed in a hurry "without her *rebozo*."[92] Gala went to her novio's tenement building where, with her consent, the couple had sex twice in José's one-room vivienda. Although she made no claim that José had deceived her by promising marriage, he nevertheless disputed her account. He claimed that he had left her waiting in the zaguán while he went to his vivienda. After waiting for a long time for José to return, Gala entered his apartment to look for him. This action, according to José, showed her eagerness for sex. José, believing she was not a doncella, now felt emboldened to have sex, without repercussion. As proof of Gala's nonvirginity, he asserted that it was well known that Gala "strolled with many men" and had spent time in a casa de asignación (brothel). Convinced that Gala had been willingly deflowered, the grandmother withdrew the accusation she had brought against José.[93]

The case of twenty-seven-year-old Demetrio Morales and thirteen-year-old María Contreras highlights the complex ways that individuals treated sex and virginity. A variety of issues explored thus far coalesces in their case. María, a domestic servant, left work to visit her sister as they had made plans to brush each other's hair. On the way, she passed Demetrio's carpentry workshop and stopped to chat. She testified that, there, he made a marriage promise and asked her to enter his shop, presumably to have sex. She initially declined, but Demetrio persisted, finally convincing her to spend the night. Only wearing her undershirt to bed—at his insistence—she "woke up screaming because Demetrio was on top of her . . . by which time he had already taken her virginity." Having already lost her status as a doncella, María agreed to have sex with Demetrio three more times over the next two days. María's mother, learning that her daughter had disappeared from work, eventually found the couple at Demetrio's workshop. Although María admitted to having willingly stayed with Demetrio, she emphatically rejected his marriage proposal and wanted him punished for rapto and estupro.

When authorities hauled Demetrio into the local police precinct, he put forward a different story. He asserted that María had come to his shop upset. She had been reprimanded by her employer who had heard unflattering "gossip" about María among the domestic staff. Not wanting to return to her job, she asked to spend the night at Demetrio's workshop. He agreed, later taking her to eat breakfast and, afterward, to the Villa de Guadalupe where they spent the day strolling. At some point, María divulged that she had lost her virginity in Texcoco, Mexico, before migrating to the city. A youngster named Ponciano had "taken her to a dance and then to his home where he enjoyed her, [although] he was put in jail for two months." It was with this "confidence," Demetrio claimed, that he had sex with María. "In fact, she was not a doncella," he continued, "for no blood came out [the scribe underlined these words] during the moments of the carnal act, but despite this, if she wants, I am willing to marry her." A medical exam appeared to confirm Demetrio's statement, determining that María had "signs of deflowerment not totally recent." The mother and daughter insisted that María would not marry Demetrio, and they exerted much effort to have him punished. The case ended when María's mother failed to procure María's birth certificate to prove her parentage. Despite her taking the trouble to call on two neighbors to testify that she was indeed María's mother, she was forced to drop the investigation, which set Demetrio free.[94]

Demetrio's claim that María was not a virgin at the time they had sex was supported on several points: by her alleged admission that she had already had sex before migrating to the city; by the absence of female bleeding during penetration; and by the medical exam's finding of her "not totally recent" deflowering. But like most lower-class men, Demetrio was undeterred from offering a young woman marriage, in spite of her sexual history, before a judge. Though the medical examination that corroborated Demetrio's assertions offered him an obvious opportunity to deny María a marriage promise, he did not. Rather, it was María who rejected Demetrio's offer. Under other circumstances, either the results of her medical exam or her admission of willingly having had sex with Demetrio (even after he'd raped her) surely would have doomed her case. On one hand, the fact that María continued to live with Demetrio might suggest that her testimony was a gendered script through which she sought to highlight her vulnerability and initial chastity. On the other, María's insistence that Demetrio be punished and her refusal to marry a willing suitor seem to undermine that hypothesis. While María's specific motivation proves difficult to discern, her case demonstrates, once again, that a woman's sexual past did not necessarily undermine her marriage prospects.[95] Furthermore and for whatever reason, for parents and daughters, the quest to punish a man for his sexual misconduct could outweigh the quest to "cover honor."

Working-Class Sexuality

The penny press tackled the topics of working-class romance, relationships, sex, and sexuality in ways that often mirrored the culture of courtship brought to light in the judicial record. It proves difficult to verify whether or not penny press editors were members of the working class as they often purported. Whether penny press portrayals of working-class people derived from editors' lived experience or observation, the parallels between penny press satires and stories and the attitudes and practices of the lower classes as documented in legal cases suggest the penny press's intimate familiarity with barrio and street culture.[96] Comedic dialogues and waggish poetry offered readers characterizations of working-class love, sex, and relationships that highlighted promiscuity but rarely with moralizing objections. Instead, the penny press depicted bohemian lifestyles involving tawdry entertainments at cantinas, neighborhood dances, and civic festivities—all of which offered the lower classes a few moments of reprieve from an otherwise harsh life of grinding poverty and social subordination. In its tragicomic or melodramatic presentations of popular sexual mores and practices, the penny press accentuated, both implicitly and explicitly, the plight of the poor and the drastic social inequalities to which they were subject.[97]

Don Cucufate, for example, offered readers "La mujer caída" (The Fallen Woman), a somber poem about "fallen women," either those who had lost their virginity outside of wedlock or, worse yet, had succumbed to prostitution. It beseeches readers not to "insult" them as men can never know the burdens and trials of a woman's life. Instead, the poem instructs that with "love and light . . . everything regains new life."[98] The poem reinforces the belief—one that was certainly not borne out in the judicial record—that deflowered, unmarried women were "fallen" in the eyes of most potential working-class suitors. At the same time, of course, by imploring men to look beyond a woman's sexual past, the poet foregrounds what appears to have been an already-established social practice. The anonymous poet's middle-class sentimentality and the subject of lower-class promiscuity perhaps suggest that working-class readers of the tendered advice would have found it less subversive than the author intended.

Among its melodramatic fare, the penny press regularly portrayed men and women whose sexual lives preceded their current partners. In one poem, "Romance Callejero" (Street Romance), the protagonist Prudencio encounters a past lover, Beatriz. He hopes to regale her with memories of their love, reminiscing about romantic interludes of kissing beneath a tree near a "crystalline brook." It was there, he recalls, that Beatriz first expressed her love for him. Yet now, he laments, she ignores him "because of his misery . . . and because he does not have work." Beatriz—dressed in fine clothes—reminds the heartbroken wooer that it was at his insistence that she became the amasia of a "drunk butcher" who could financially support her. Ignoring Prudencio's vows that he can offer her true love despite his poverty, Beatriz leaves him some money and walks away.[99] In its poetic, dialogic, or discursive presentations of romantic entanglements and domestic squabbles, penny press fare matter-of-factly posited that the poor, both men and women, had multiple domestic, amorous, and sexual relationships throughout their lives.

La Guacamaya's recurring feature "Desde la estaca" (From the Stake), a humorous dialogue between two men, Chema and Pitacio, usually at a bar or on the street, consistently and casually presents men and women moving in and out of romantic relationships. As an example, Chema might ask Pitacio, "who's your jaña [girl] these days?"[100] One of the "Desde la estaca" dialogues features one man telling the other that he is broke after spending the cash his jarana (woman) had been saving to give to her chamaco (kid). (The dialogue's language makes clear that the child is from the jarana's previous relationship.)[101] Similarly, in the humorous dialogue "Entre Cotoras" (Between Parrots), as two lower-class women chat, one notes in passing that she has been with her current man for one year.[102] In another example, two men talking on the street turn to the topic of their novias. One asks the other, "Who are you with nowadays?" His friend replies, "Catarina, she used to be with our pal Cotorrón."[103] These casual, non-moralizing portrayals of transitory domestic and romantic relationships reflect the flexibility and freedom that amasiato offered individuals to seek out new amorous partners according to the dictates, disappointments, and needs of daily life. While the question of whom, exactly, penny press editors targeted as their readership remains difficult to fully answer (wage laborers, artisans, or middle-class bohemians?)[104] the similarities between its comedic dialogues and the practices and values documented in the judicial record offer one potential reason for the penny press's popularity. It offered a counter-discourse to more respectable publications that made working-class sexuality a target for scorn and reform. The penny press instead presented working-class sexuality in all its ambiguity, contradiction, and freedom. It offered audiences vignettes and portraits that could simultaneously mock the lower classes' lust and promiscuity while reveling in their resourcefulness and capacity to survive.[105]

Another recurring dialogue in La Guacamaya features a man and woman who live in the same vecindad. Theirs are innuendo-laden conversations, heavy on sexual themes. In one such dialogue, don Cañuto talks to doña Rosita at the door of her vivienda. She complains that her husband often leaves her in a shaky financial position; he's always traveling for work but never leaves her money for expenses while he's away. Cañuto lavishes her with compliments about her beauty before proposing to whisk her away. He offers her the dream of a better life, fancying that they will open a market stand to sell mole and pozole and live like *rotos* (affected or haughty middle classers). Although at first worried that people will call her an "adulteress," Rosita quickly agrees. Cañuto then rushes off to find his boss to ask for an advance on his pay so that he and Rosita can find a new home.[106] The financial hardships faced by the poor—hunger, unemployment, illness, and death—were a common theme in the penny press. Doña Rosita's decision to leave her deadbeat husband foregrounds the kinds of choices that working-class women faced when a husband or amasio did not meet his diario obligation. Even if only satirically, the dialogue also exposes how economic strain promoted ephemeral domestic bonds. Don Cañuto's desperate rush to get a pay advance to finance the elopement gives scant hope that doña Rosita's financial troubles are truly over.

The Penny Press and Popular Attitudes Toward Sex

The working-class courtships and domestic relations that the penny press tackled satirically nevertheless reflected the lives we find documented in the judicial record, where the real-life stakes of crime and punishment, abandonment and destitution, self-determination and family conflict always loomed. Many parents, as noted, lived in amasiato themselves alongside their children from previous relationships. Men abandoned women and children to find work elsewhere or to forge ties with new lovers. Teenagers admitted openly to having had previous sexual partners before planning to marry. What appeared to elite observers and social reformers as the lasciviousness and promiscuity of the poor instead reflected the unsettled and migratory life of the lower classes where even temporary bonds provided opportunities for mutual financial, domestic, and emotional support. For example, when Dolores Sánchez revealed to her lover, Manuel Olivares, that she had already had a sexual relationship with a "man in the service," he did not care and offered her marriage nonetheless. Manuel also disclosed his own previous relationship, admitting that he was already married canonically to a woman in Puebla whom he had not seen in two years.[107] The legal or economic oaths that bound middle- and upper-class marriages were rarely exercised among the poor, which allowed them greater fluidity in spousal choice, especially in an environment where men and women interacted more regularly and intimately with each other on a daily basis than did members of the affluent classes. The case of twenty-nine-year-old Vicenta Alonso highlights such interaction and the sad consequences she faced as a result. She suspected her amasio, José Rendón, of running away with her daughter from a previous relationship, testifying that "one day I surprised him, finding him with his hand on my daughter's knee." The daughter, fifteen-year-old Juliana Muñoz, told investigating officials that she had agreed to run away with José because he promised marriage. She added that she had not been a virgin at the time, having already had a sexual relationship a year earlier. José openly admitted to the judge that he had been in amasiato with Vicenta for over three years but had fallen in love with her daughter—whom he knew was not a doncella—and planned to marry her. With no legal recourse, Vicenta dropped her complaint.[108]

Few women, though, openly admitted before a judge to having had previous sexual relationships.[109] Over the course of an investigation, some women eventually acknowledged prior lovers, especially after a medical exam concluded that their deflowering was "not recent." In other cases, novios, friends, and family claimed to know about a young woman's sexual history. Case examples suggest that many women had notably more sexual experience than their initial statements to judges indicate. For example, having suffered repeated beatings from her father, Rafaela Pacheco left her home and went to the Buenavista train station to find her novio, a railway brakeman. She told him to "take her wherever he wanted because her father mistreated her." Antonio Guerrero knew of Rafaela's previous relationship with another brakeman (presumably at the same train station). Rafaela, though she had originally claimed that Antonio had deflowered her, later admitted that she had had sex with another railway worker. She had little choice: her medical examination showed that her deflowering was "antigua" (old). Antonio agreed that Rafaela would live with him but was unequivocal—as was Rafaela—about the fact that he had never made a promise of marriage, verbally or in writing.[110] The wrongful arrest of Juan Flores provides another glimpse at the relative freedom of the lower classes' sexual lives. Arrested for the rapto of Manuela Rodríguez, Juan acknowledged that he had had an amorous relationship with her but insisted that he was not the culprit in the alleged rapto. As Juan explained it, he was on his way to visit Manuela when he saw her leave "with another man named Juan Vargas and she went with him quite happily." Manuela's mother confirmed Juan's account and admitted to having had the wrong man arrested.[111]

In its satires of popular sexuality, the penny press commonly covered the themes of adultery and infidelity, deeds that were rarely documented in judicial cases. *El Chile Piquín* offered a short, humorous story about vecindad living. Fretting to her friend in the vignette, a married woman recounts how she had entered the wrong vivienda apartment, gotten naked, and slipped into bed with another man. Delivering the punchline, the woman worries that she has deceived her husband, especially because this was the second night it happened.[112] In a short dialogue, also in *El Chile Piquín*, one man tells another that Hermenegildo, an "ugly and stupid" hotelier, is about to marry Francisca, a thirty-year-old fishwife, but who has "a great body." The other man asks, "how do you know, did Hermenegildo tell you?" Delivering the punchline, the other responds: "no . . . I've been told by several friends."[113] *La Guacamaya*'s "Desde le estaca" feature offered dialogues between men who mock each other over their partners' infidelity, described as *ponerlo cuernos* (literally, putting horns on him; that is, cuckolding). And rarely do the protagonists deny the accusation or get angry.[114]

Ever lampooning, *La Guacamaya* tackled the topic of female infidelity in the context of economic insecurity, sexual exploitation, and women's financial self-management. In "Entre Cotoras," the recurring comedic dialogue between two women, one woman boasts that she saves her *gasto* (the money provided by a husband or partner for food and other necessities) by dealing with the merchant don Bernardo, a *gachupín* (Spaniard). Using heavy sexual innuendo, she tells her friend that she "takes out his beans and garbanzos" (*le saco los frijoles y garbanzos*)—an idiomatic expression meaning to make a man ejaculate—and she allows him to put his "chile" in her "basket"—the quoted nouns being oft-used placeholders for "penis" and "vagina." Wishing that she could find such a merchant, her friend responds that "rather than sell biscuits all day, I want a man to put me in a house, even if I have to live there alone, making tortillas." (Idiomatically, "making tortillas" refers to masturbation or lesbian affection.) The first woman concludes the conversation with the well-known saying, "alone, the ox licks himself fine," an idiomatic phrase that simultaneously emphasizes the value of independence and the worth of self-pleasuring.[115] This particular "Entre Cotoras" dialogue highlights how the exigencies of poverty and a multifarious urban environment allowed the lower classes sexual freedom in ways that were simultaneously exploitative and liberating. On one hand, the friends' dialogue reveals, matter-of-factly and without shame, the economic hardship and exploitation Mexico City's poor women routinely faced.[116] On the other, the friends' conversation also reveals an ease in discussing female sexuality and masturbation, an ease that *La Guacamaya*'s writers expected readers to recognize and appreciate as a reality as commonplace as economic struggle.

Candid discussion of sexual life in the penny press also exposed the indignities and dangers faced by the working classes, especially women. In another dialogue, also published in *La Guacamaya*, two men—one a womanizer, the other faithful— while drinking at a bar discuss the former's sexual adventures. The womanizer tells of meeting a *gatota* (attractive woman) and using "love talk" to convince her to follow him to an empty field where "they went hard at affection." But then, a police officer shows up at the assignation spot and arrests the lothario for canoodling in public. When the keen listener asks the womanizer what happened with the girl, he responds that the "cop must have finished what I started."[117] The story's punchline somewhat obscures whether the incident emphasizes the sexual eagerness of the woman or a sexual assault by the policeman. The highly negative depictions of city police in penny press pages suggest the latter. If we take the latter meaning, the dialogue uses humor to expose the daily injustices faced by the poor: men's lack of power in the face of authority and women's susceptibility to sexual violence. For male readers, the story's symbolic force lies in its personification of assault on working-class masculinity: a state agent "robs" the womanizer of the fruits of his labor, a woman attracted and open to the lothario. In a social context where working-class men found limited arenas in which to exercise agency and power, the demonstration of sexual prowess and conquest—aspects central to the notion of *machismo*—offered men one such domain. Yet the story spotlights that the ubiquitous state always looms large, ready to emasculate men and violate working-class women. While the implied rape is minimized in the narrative's male-centered focus, its humor—the presentation of probable rape as punchline—arouses reader awareness, an awareness honed by the womanizer's glib acceptance of injustice and brutality as everyday realities.[118]

The penny press portrayed the vecindad as a milieu of loose morals and sexual promiscuity—a characterization strikingly similar to that presented by Porfirian moral reformers but, as already noted, without the moral remonstrances. One vignette in a recurring "Street Romance" feature titled "A Popular Baptism," tells the story of Guadalupe "Sargenta" and Felipe "Rebocero" who live in a Colonia de la Bolsa tenement. Guadalupe, described as light-skinned and *sazona* (sexy), is chased by many men in the barrio but has "great affection" only for Felipe. Another vecindad couple, Luisa "Mecates" and Serapio "Cargador," the latter described as a "worthless drunk," are soon to have a child and make Guadalupe and Felipe the godparents. Once the baby is born, Guadalupe and Felipe throw a lavish party in honor of the newborn. After all-night revelry with food, dance, and drink, the foursome, badly hungover, take a coach to the church to have the baby baptized. These are, after all, the raconteur tells the reader, "popular customs." The narrator ends the poem by exposing a secret: "Let me tell you / Although it might anger our godfather / That the baby of that mother / Was actually the child of Felipe . . . / For 'Mecates' made / A cuckold of the 'Cargador'/ And the traitor 'Rebocero' / Was the lover of 'Mecates.'"[119] Just as the narrator links drunken revelry and religious tradition as "popular customs," the poem's author also links infidelity and loose morals to vecindad culture. The verses play with the same stereotypes of lower-class life denounced by social reformers—drunkenness, wantonness, and improvidence—yet, unlike the reformers, without the moral revulsion. Depiction of the characters' lasciviousness does not promote social rot or erode the social fabric. Instead, the tale shows that despite people's human and ethical failings, the vecindad's networks of mutual support and comradery remain the foundation of the working-class neighborhood and community.

The legal case of Felipa Salas and Tiburcio Navarro similarly serves to portray the liberal sexual culture of the working class that the penny press so often represented. In it, we find a young man seemingly unconcerned with the sexual history of his partner. The case begins with Soledad Salas's learning, through neighborhood gossip, that her daughter Felipa has been having amorous relations with Tiburcio, her childhood friend. While Soledad had been unaware of any relationship between the two, several neighbors informed her that Tiburcio and Felipa's relationship was well known publicly. One neighbor passed along a rumor, which he'd heard from a local puppet-theater owner, that the young man planned to take Felipa to Pachuca where Tiburcio's brother operated his own puppet theater. Since her daughter had failed to return home after running an errand eight days earlier, the mother lodged a complaint with the Ministerio Público in Mexico City, on June 26, 1902, accusing twenty-three-year-old Tiburcio of the rapto of her fifteen-year-old daughter.

Just one day later, Soledad Salas, with the help of a police officer, brought the young couple to the neighborhood police station near Lagunilla Market for questioning and to officially charge Tiburcio. Both youngsters gave short statements in order to end the ordeal quickly. Felipa told authorities that because she had left home of her own free will, her boyfriend should not be held responsible for a crime. She further ended any chance of continuing a criminal complaint, stating that she had lost her virginity six months earlier, also willingly, to another neighborhood "muchacho." To verify her statement, she agreed to a medical exam. When questioned, Tiburcio, who identified himself as a shoemaker by trade, declared that he and Felipa had been amorously involved for two months and that he had taken her from home to live in amasiato because of the poor treatment (mala vida) inflicted by her mother. Moreover, he announced confidently that he had had sex with Felipa who was not a doncella, and that she would state the same. The case ended when the medical exam confirmed the couple's claim that Felipa's deflowering was indeed "antigua" (old).[120]

Even when her family deployed legal authorities to return Felipa to the family home, she succeeded in ending a drawn-out case by declaring her sexual history—to her family, her boyfriend, and the authorities—seemingly unconcerned with a public reputation based on sexual purity. As this and other cases suggest, too, the speed with which local gossip notified parents about the possible whereabouts and amorous relationships of their children may also have made even the notion of a private sexual past nearly unthinkable. Felipa's willingness to have a medical exam to demonstrate that she had already lost her virginity, as well as her boyfriend's knowledge of her sexual history, demonstrate how public and private declarations of a sexual past could become a useful legal strategy in ending court proceedings. Far from revealing a shameful aspect of female public reputation—either to neighborhood peers or the elite officials adjudicating the matter—Felipa's and Tiburcio's testimonies demonstrate that the poor did not rely on traditional assumptions about sexual honor's connection to identity or self-worth. As documented in judicial record, the real-life attitudes and actions of working-class couples embody a sexual culture quite similar to that articulated in the poems and dialogues of the penny press. Determining how great a part working-class courtship played in informing penny press content is less relevant than acknowledging that—on the streets and on the page—popular culture was for the working classes relatively unencumbered by the rigidity of the honor/shame complex and by family, community, and social expectations about how people should behave. Like the characters portrayed in the penny press, real-life couples took control over their own circumstances by continually adapting to shifting challenges. The stability of traditional societies is often sustained by human reliance on already-established norms and group identities. In contrast, one of the principal characteristics of modern societies according to social theorist Anthony Giddens is an individual capacity to develop personal identity and self-mastery in negotiations of the day-to-day world.[121] The adaptive and expanding sociosexual freedoms of Mexico City's working classes developed in relation to the Porfirian project of modernization, even as those freedoms were reviled by state officialdom and disrupted long-standing traditions fixed in middle- and upper-class culture.

Conclusion

In his seminal philosophical text, *Being and Time*, Martin Heidegger explores the meaning of human existence and the different modalities of how we exist. Each mode can be authentic or inauthentic or undifferentiated. For Heidegger, freedom and self-awareness are central to authenticity. He goes on to argue that the authentic/inauthentic divide is defined by how individuals avow (authentic), disavow (inauthentic), or fail to take a stance (undifferentiated) on what it means to exist in a particular manner and, by so doing, to determine how they engage the social possibilities available to them.[122] Heidegger found that, most often, humans exist inauthentically, rarely taking a stand on their existence, identity, or actions. The more that people view existence, identity, and action as their very own, the more freedom they experience and the more authentic that experience becomes.[123]

Central to Heidegger's authentic/inauthentic existence spectrum is the idea of "the they" or the "they-self" (*Das Man*). Heidegger argues that in their everyday existences, individuals typically do not act as themselves but as "the they." People are lost in the impersonal prattle of the crowd; their actions and ideas are not their own but rather subsumed within the everydayness of what people generally do. As Heidegger states, "Everyone is the other, and no one is himself."[124] In other words, while humans have the potential for resolute action of their own accord, most often, in the commotion of everyday life, they behave or exist in a manner that adheres to prescriptions and assumptions about what people do in general (to expected social practices, customs, behaviors, and so on). Heidegger emphasizes how human existence always teeters between accepting a life governed by external circumstances beyond our control (inauthentic) on one hand and the possibility of acting determinedly in the face of entrenched norms (authentic) on the other. When compared to the rigid social, class, and family rubrics that defined romance and marriage for the upper classes, lower-class courtship and romantic partnership is far less dominated and determined by strictures imposed by family and social expectations.

Penny press personifications of popular sexual norms quite remarkably reflect the actions and statements of the individuals whose cases are documented in court record. Subaltern sexuality and its culture of courtship stirred penny press editors and writers to satirize and celebrate the more authentic disposition of the working class in the face of tradition and social convention. And while there surely existed a wide range of behaviors that plebeian people deemed either acceptable or despicable, we find a popular culture defined by greater sexual freedom than that of their middle- and upper-class counterparts. The lower classes' rejection of the elites' concept of honor and its so-called cult of virginity allowed for more authentic action, action less constricted by social pressures about how one *should* behave. Lower class life was governed instead by its own material conditions and by more individually oriented decision-making in matters of love, romance, and sexual pleasure.

Conclusion

The close examination of lower-class courtship, love, and sex made possible by rapto and estupro cases reveals a world of contradictions and practical diversity. Amid the everyday struggles faced by Mexico City's poor, we discover that sexual life was defined by a series of contrasts: lasciviousness and morality, honor and shamelessness, strategy and whim, cruelty and tenderness, suffering and joy, and so on. The contrasts and ambiguities disclosed in the historical judicial record are far from surprising as they reflect remarkably the experiences of our own *real* lives.[1] As argued throughout this book, the ways that Mexico City's urban poor comported themselves in matters of courtship, love, and sex were shaped by the material conditions that defined lower-class life. The middle and upper classes, by contrast, were subject to the stricter conventions that governed their intimate lives. Of course, these conventions were by no means accepted or applied universally, as some cases in this study have shown. Nonetheless, the well-to-do served as the model to policymakers and social critics of how to promote the modern, bourgeois family as the bedrock of a civilized nation.

Porfirian Mexico's brand of rapid modernization and export-driven economic development fostered a highly unequal distribution of national wealth where grinding poverty, uneven employment, cramped housing, and unsanitary living conditions defined urban, lower-class life. Instead of acknowledging how economic inequality cultivated these social conditions, policymakers and reformers blamed lower-class immorality as the root cause. Targeted for social and moral elevation by an increasingly hegemonic state, the poor were subjected to new disciplinary and surveillance techniques that aimed to reshape their productive and reproductive practices. Paradoxically, it was those very living conditions and state interventions that helped create the kinship structures and social environments that nourished a sexuality deemed deviant. Mexico City's varied enticements to adventure and waywardness created space for sexual freedoms and possibilities where women and men, if only temporarily, deliberately transgressed the boundaries of what was expected.[2]

Yet amidst the multifaceted ways that common people experienced romance and behaved in their sexual lives, we find a remarkably modern and authentic sensibility. It was the very social and economic precarity of working-class urban life that provided the context for a distinctly modern, reflexive, and ambiguous courtship culture. In her groundbreaking study of popular love in turn-of-the-century Rio de Janeiro, Martha de Abreu Esteves notes that the sexual mores and values held by the city's working-class women were relatively unshackled by elite concerns over honor and bourgeois morality, which allowed for a freer sexual culture among the poor. She provocatively suggests that the girls and women in her study presaged the twentieth century's so-called sexual revolution insofar as they eroded or rejected traditional concerns about honor and its relation to female sexuality and the veneration of virginity.[3] This study, too, finds that Mexico City's lower classes expressed values, beliefs, and behaviors that were much more similar to modern-day expectations about sexual life than those espoused by their social higher-ups. While these values, beliefs, and behaviors at times could be ambiguous and demonstrate individuals' ambivalence about matters of honor and shame, the urban poor nevertheless often showed little concern about female chastity and sexual history while exhibiting more freedom in choosing paramours and partners based on their own needs and desires. As a result, we find among the lower classes a more authentic and individually oriented approach to matters of love and sex. Strong scholarly arguments about bourgeois sexual morality's filtering down to plebian society—especially the idea of virginity as a prerequisite for marriage—while true for some of the people examined in this study, do not reflect the values generally espoused by the poor.[4] Moreover, such claims ignore the material conditions that characterized life among the lower classes and made their adherence to bourgeois sexual values and behaviors impractical, if not impossible.

Anthony Giddens has emphasized how a weakening of family control over women's sexuality and an evolving female sexual liberation represent important social changes that help define modern life.[5] The individualistic ideology that characterizes modern sexual and family values appears to have been well entrenched among Mexico City's lower classes during the Porfiriato. In his seminal study on marriage, sex, and family life in early modern England, Lawrence Stone claims that modern individualism related to "internal and external family relations" developed first among the "professional and upper bourgeois classes, not among the propertyless industrial poor."[6] In a more recent study of sexuality in the United States that focuses on the sexual revolution of the 1960s, while the authors recognize how 1960s cultural icons help to shape modern sexual values, they neglect to foreground the role played by the sexual freedoms practiced by turn-of-the-century working classes—a group discussed in their study—in initiating and driving that values-shift and its contingent modernity.[7]

Recent anthropological and sociological research on gendered relations, sexuality, and family life in late twentieth-century Mexico City has called attention to the persistence of conservative sexual values, especially among the poor and least educated. A continued sexual double standard that defines masculinity by sexual aggression and femininity by sexual passivity has cemented traditional expectations of male promiscuity and female chastity before marriage.[8] These studies, at the same time, argue that because members of the middle and upper classes have enjoyed significant access to higher education they have come to hold more liberal and progressive values—values less defined by family control and conservative social norms—than they did prior to and at the turn of the twentieth century. As a result, among the middle and upper classes today, women are more likely to have premarital sex, to reject any conditional link between marriage and virginity, and to question values that associate sex with marriage and marriage with child-bearing. Their male counterparts, likewise, hold more progressive sexual views and acknowledge female sexual desire and pleasure.[9] Some of these studies, though, also highlight how younger working-class generations are beginning to evince more liberal sexual values—no longer expecting, for example, female virginity before marriage—while also holding cultural values that celebrate so-called virtuous women.[10]

Influenced by the theories of Néstor García Canclini, Ivonne Szasz has recently argued that a "sexual hybridity" defines Mexico today insofar as the modern values of an industrialized society have been superimposed on a culture with a long history of conservative Catholic mores and indigenous folkways. This hybridity manifests itself in ambiguities and tensions among different social groups where the educational opportunities provided by the modern state clash with inequitable gendered relations dictated in social and cultural norms. As an example, Szasz notes that while Mexican women are open to the use of contraceptives, they continue to ignore or dismiss the importance of personal pleasure. While she identifies a freer sexual culture among the middle and upper classes, she also finds a persistent expectation, for example, that male partners should initiate sex. Szasz likewise argues that socioeconomic and class divisions are central to differences in sexual values but often in contradictory ways. For example, the transmission of modern concepts through privileged access to higher education has not so much freed middle- and upper-class women from the constraining values of the past as to accomplish women's internalization of traditional social control mechanisms. This suggests that middle- and upper-class women have yet to fully experience the liberation accompanying an actual democratization of intimacy. In contrast, despite their limited educational access, lower-class women can dispense with social controls and experience an individualization—a freedom from sociocultural expectations and norms—similar to that of their middle- and upper-class counterparts.[11]

In matters of courtship and sex, many of the intergenerational tensions identified in late-twentieth-century Mexico between so-called traditional and modern values appear to have been well in place in Porfirian Mexico City among its lower classes. Similarly, the freedom of young women today in Mexico City to form personal lives unconstrained by patriarchal domination and parental authority and to control their own sexuality and intimate relationships[12] was demonstrated in the actions and decision-making of nineteenth-century working women. And while the double standard comprising expectations of male sexual experience and female chastity before marriage continued to exist among working-class men in the 1990s and 2000s,[13] one hundred years earlier, many poor men made known that their partners' sexual pasts neither encumbered nor tarnished their sense of personal honor or manhood.

Just as ambiguities and contradictions persist in modern-day sexual practice and values, the experiences of working-class Porfirians also disclose the tensions between conservative social and family norms on one hand and a greater range of freedoms offered by the modernizing urban metropolis on the other. Even so, the nineteenth century offers valuable counterpoints that challenge conclusions about the role played by the middle and upper classes in liberalizing sexual norms. It was the working class, for example, whose everyday practice under oppressive material conditions challenged the normative sexual values championed by the elite, a phenomenon not lost on policymakers who sought to curb, if not extinguish, the perceived lasciviousness and immorality of the poor. By studying cases that directly and indirectly exemplify such challenges, this study hopes to open new avenues of exploration and stir new insights with regard to lower-class culture as a possible model for modern romance and sexuality. Indeed, we may consider the possibility that, in some respects, nineteenth-century popular sexual values and behaviors were freer and less constrained by gendered social expectations than our early twenty-first century sexual values and behaviors.

We may also consider the likelihood that, within the domains of social life and custom, ebb and flow governs human receptivity to and exercise of traditional and modern perspectives rather than a teleological drive toward modern selfhood and social practice that emerged after the consolidation of the Revolutionary State.[14] It is also worth considering the ambiguities, contradictions, and reflexivities that shaped, and continue to shape, gendered expectations of sexual life among individuals of all social groups in different eras. Nineteenth-century sexuality among the poor and working classes presaged the expectations, values, and practices shared by middle- and upper-class Mexicans, as well as younger generations, today: an individually oriented romantic decision-making; an acknowledgment that partners, male *and* female, have sexual pasts; a willingness to form multiple long-term unions over a lifetime; and a disposition toward companionate relationships. While building a genealogy that traces Porfirian to modern-day sexual values is beyond the scope of the current study, this book has, at the very least, put a spotlight on how the poorest and most marginalized citizens of the Porfirian era participated in creating modernity through their everyday romances.

NOTES

Introduction

1 Federico Gamboa, *Santa: A Novel of Mexico City* [1903]. translated and edited by John Charles Chasteen (Chapel Hill: University of North Carolina Press, 2010), ix; Debra A. Castillo, "Meat Shop Memories: Federico Gamboa's *Santa*," *Inti* 40–41 (1995): 175.

2 Castillo, "Meat Shop Memories," 175; Carl J. Mora, *Mexican Cinema: Reflections of a Society, 1896–2004* (Jefferson: McFarland & Co. Inc, 2005), 35–36.

3 Gamboa, *Santa* [1903], reprint (Mexico City: Ediciones Botas México, 1938). For an excellent English translation, see Gamboa, *Santa: A Novel of Mexico City.*

4 For a discussion of the penny press's "Street Romance" feature, see Robert Buffington, *A Sentimental Education for the Working Man: The Mexico City Penny Press, 1900–1910* (Durham: Duke University Press, 2015), 178–193.

5 Paul Garner, *Porfirio Díaz* (London: Longman, 2001), 70.

6 Garner, *Porfirio Díaz*, 89.

7 William Schell Jr., *Integral Outsiders: The American Colony in Mexico City, 1876–1911* (Wilmington: Scholarly Resources, 2001); John M. Hart, *Revolutionary Mexico: The Coming and Process of the Mexican Revolution* (Berkeley: University of California Press, 1987) and *Empire and Revolution: The Americans in Mexico since the Civil War* (Berkeley: University of California Press, 2002).

8 Claudia Agostoni, *Monuments of Progress: Modernization and Public Health in Mexico, 1876–1910* (Calgary: University of Calgary Press, 2003), 52; Matthew Vitz, *A City on a Lake: Urban Political Ecology and the Growth of Mexico City* (Durham: Duke University Press, 2012), 40–41.

9 See for example: Allen Wells and Gilbert M. Joseph, "Modernizing Visions, 'Chilango' Blueprints, and Provincial Growing Pains: Mérida at the Turn of the Century," *Mexican Studies/Estudios Mexicanos* 8, no. 2 (1992): 167–215; Michael Johns, *The City of Mexico in the Age of Díaz* (Austin: University of Texas Press, 1997); Robert Buffington, *Criminal and Citizen in Modern Mexico* (Lincoln: University of Nebraska Press, 2000); Pablo Piccato, *City of Suspects: Crime in Mexico City, 1900–1931* (Durham: Duke University Press, 2001); Mark Overmyer-Velázquez, *Visions of the Emerald City: Modernity, Tradition, and the Formation of Porfirian Oaxaca, Mexico* (Durham: Duke University Press, 2006); Elisa Speckman Guerra, *Crimen y castigo: Legislación penal, interpretaciones de la criminalidad y administración de justicia, Ciudad de México, 1872–1910* (Ciudad de México: El Colegio de México, Centro de Estudios Históricos: Universidad Nacional Autónoma de México, Instituto de

Investigaciones Históricas, 2007); James Alex Garza, *Imagined Underworld: Sex, Crime, and Vice in Porfirian Mexico City* (Lincoln: University of Nebraska Press, 2009); Emily Wakild, "Naturalizing Modernity: Urban Parks, Public Gardens and Drainage Projects in Porfirian Mexico City," *Mexican Studies/Estudios Mexicanos* 23, no. 1 (2007): 101–123; Anna Rose Alexander, *City on Fire: Technology, Social Change, and the Hazards of Progress in Mexico City, 1860–1910* (Pittsburgh: University of Pittsburgh Press, 2016); Diana J. Montaño, *Electrifying Mexico: Technology and the Transformation of a Modern City* (Austin: University of Texas Press, 2021), chapters 1–4.

10 Michael Matthews, *The Civilizing Machine: A Cultural History of Mexican Railroads, 1876–1910* (Lincoln: University of Nebraska Press, 2013); William H. Beezley, *Judas at the Jockey Club and other Episodes in Porfirian Mexico* (Lincoln: University of Nebraska Press, 2018). Bárbara A. Tenenbaum, "Streetwise History: The Paseo de la Reforma and the Porfirian State, 1876–1910," in *Rituals of Rule, Rituals of Resistance: Public Celebrations and Popular Culture in Mexico,* edited by William H. Beezley, Cheryl English Martin, and William E. French (Wilmington: Scholarly Resources, 1994); Tony Morgan, "Proletarians, Politicos, and Patriarchs: The Use and Abuse of Cultural Customs in the Early Industrialization of Mexico City, 1880–1910" in *Rituals of Rule;* William H. Beezley, "The Porfirian Smart Set Anticipates Thorstein Veblen in Guadalajara" in *Rituals of Rule;* and William E. French, "*Progreso Forzado:* Workers and the Inculcation of the Capitalist Work Ethic in the Parral Mining District" in *Rituals of Rule.*

11 Mauricio Tenorio-Trillo, *Mexico at the World's Fairs: Crafting a Modern Nation* (Berkeley: University of California Press, 1996), 64–65, 82–83, 123–124.

12 Stephen B. Neufeld, *The Blood Contingent: The Military and the Making of Modern Mexico, 1876–1911* (Albuquerque: University of New Mexico Press, 2017); Mary Kay Vaughan, "Women, Class, and Education in Mexico, 1880–1928," *Latin American Perspectives* 4, no. 1/2 (Winter-Spring 1977): 135–152; William E. French, *A Peaceful and Working People: Manners, Morals, and Class Formation in Northern Mexico* (Albuquerque: University of New Mexico Press, 1996); Overmyer-Velázquez, *Visions of the Emerald City.*

13 Michel Foucault, *The History of Sexuality,* edited by Gros Frédéric and translated by Robert Hurley (New York: Vintage Books, 1990). For studies on Mexico and Latin America, see, for example, Claudia Agostoni, "Discurso médico, cultura higiénica y la mujer en la Ciudad de México al cambio de siglo (XIX-XX)," *Mexican Studies/ Estudios Mexicanos* 18, no. 1 (Winter 2002): 1–22; Donna J. Guy, *White Slavery and Mothers Alive and Dead: The Troubled Meeting of Sex, Gender, Public Health, and Progress in Latin America* (Lincoln: University of Nebraska Press, 2000).

14 Michel Foucault, *The Birth of Biopolitics: Lectures at the Collège de France,* edited by Michel Senellart and translated by Graham Burchell (New York: Picador, 2008).

15 Martha de Abreu Esteves finds similar dynamics at play in late-nineteenth-century Rio de Janeiro. See *Meninas perdidas: Os populares e o cotidiano do amor no Rio de Janeiro da belle époque* (Rio de Janeiro: Paz e Terra, 1989), 27–32.

16 Abreu Esteves, *Meninas perdidas;* Eileen J. Findlay, "Courtroom Tales of Sex and Honor: *Rapto* and Rape in Late Nineteenth-Century Puerto Rico," in *Honor, Status, and Law in Modern Latin America,* edited by Sueann Caulfield, Sarah C. Chambers, and Lara Putnam (Durham: Duke University Press, 2005); Catherine Komisaruk, "Rape Narratives, Rape Silences: Sexual Violence and Judicial Testimony in Colonial Guatemala," *Biography* 31, no. 3 (Summer 2008): 369–396.

17 Kathryn A. Sloan, *Runaway Daughters: Seduction, Elopement, and Honor in Nineteenth-Century Mexico* (Albuquerque: University of New Mexico Press, 2008).

18 William E. French, *The Heart in the Glass Jar: Love Letters, Bodies, and the Law in Mexico* (Lincoln: University of Nebraska Press, 2015).

19 Honor, as an analytical and historical category, has received a great deal of scholarly attention among Latin Americanists. See, for example, Patricia Seed, *To Love, Honor, and Obey in Colonia Mexico: Conflicts over Marriage Choice, 1574–1821* (Stanford: Stanford University Press, 1992); Ann Twinam, *Public Lives, Private Secrets: Gender, Honor, Sexuality, and Illegitimacy in Colonial Spanish America* (Stanford: Stanford University Press, 1999); Lyman L. Johnson and Sonya Lipsett-Rivera, (eds.), *The Faces of Honor: Sex, Shame, and Violence in Colonial Latin America* (Albuquerque: University of New Mexico Press, 1998); Nicole von Germeten, *Violent Delights, Violent Ends: Sex, Race, and Honor in Colonial Cartagena de Indias* (Albuquerque: University of New Mexico Press, 2013); Sueann Caulfield, *In Defense of Honor: Sexual Morality, Modernity, and Nation in Early-Twentieth-Century Brazil* (Durham: Duke University Press, 2000); Caulfield, Chambers, and Putnam, (eds.), *Honor, Status, and Law;* Pablo Piccato, *The Tyranny of Opinion: Honor in the Construction of the Mexican Public Sphere* (Durham: Duke University Press, 2010); Sonya Lipsett-Rivera, *Gender and the Negotiation of Daily Life in Mexico, 1750–1856* (Lincoln: University of Nebraska Press, 2012). As noted by Víctor M. Macías-González and Anne Rubenstein in their edited volume, most agree that the honor/shame complex represents an ideology and not a "reality." See *Masculinity and Sexuality in Modern Mexico* (Albuquerque: University of New Mexico Press, 2012), 7–8. Much of the discussion has been in response to Julian A. Pitt-Rivers pioneering work: "Honour and Social Status," in *Honour and Shame: The Values of Mediterranean Society,* edited by Jean Peristiany (London: Weidenfeld and Nicolson, 1965). In this classic work, Pitt-Rivers defines honor as a person's "estimation of their own worth, his *claim* to pride but it is also the acknowledgment of that claim, his excellence recognized by society, his *right* to pride" (21).

20 Buffington, *Sentimental Education,* 8.

21 John Lear, *Workers, Neighbors, and Citizens: The Revolution in Mexico City* (Lincoln: University of Nebraska Press, 2001), 60; Susie S. Porter, *Working Women in Mexico City: Public Discourses and Material Conditions, 1879–1931* (Tucson: University of Arizona Press, 2003), 15–48; Carlos Illadies and Marion Barbosa (eds.), *Los trabajadores de la Ciudad de México, 1860–1950* (Ciudad de México: El Colegio de México Universidad Autónoma Metropolitana-Cuajimalpa, 2013); Buffington, *Sentimental Education,* 8.

22 Lear, *Workers, Neighbors, and Citizens,* 62–63, 73, 77–78.

23 Ingrid Bleynat, *Vendors' Capitalism: A Political Economy of Public Markets in Mexico City* (Stanford: Stanford University Press, 2021), 4.

24 John Tutino, "Power, Marginality, and Participation in Mexico City, 1870–2000," in *New World Cities: Challenges to Urbanization and Globalization in the Americas,* edited by John Tutino and Martin V. Melosi (Chapel Hill: University of North Carolina Press, 2019), 78.

25 Lear, *Workers, Neighbors, and Citizens,* 54–82.

26 Alejandro Tortolero Villaseñor, *Notarios y agricultores: Crecimeniento y atraso en el campo mexicano, 1780–1920* (Iztapalapa: Universidad Autónoma Metropolitana, 2008), 94, 159.

27 Tutino, "Power, Marginality, and Participation," 80; Tortolero Villaseñor, *Notarios y agricultores,* 282–283.

28 On the development of Porfirian Mexico's internal economy through railroads, see Sandra Kuntz Ficker, *Empresa extranjera y mercado interno: El Ferrocarril Central Mexicano, 1880–1907* (Ciudad de México: El Colegio de México, 1995). On the role of the canal system, see Alejandro Tortolero Villaseñor, "Canales de riego y canales navegables en la Cuenca de México: Economía, patrimonio y paisaje en el México porfirista," *Historia Caribe* 10, no. 26 (Enero-Junio, 2015): 75–105.

29 Nora E. Jaffary, *Reproduction and Its Discontents in Mexico: Childbirth and Contraception from 1750 to 1905* (Chapel Hill: University of North Carolina Press, 2016); Ann Blum, *Domestic Economies: Family, Work, and Welfare in Mexico City, 1884–1943* (Lincoln: University of Nebraska Press, 2009); Katherine Elaine Bliss, *Compromised Positions: Prostitution, Public Health, and Gender Politics in Revolutionary Mexico City* (University Park: Pennsylvania State University Press, 2001); Robert Buffington, "Homophobia and the Mexican Working Class, 1900–1910" in *The Famous 41: Sexuality and Social Control in Mexico, 1901,* edited by Robert McKee Irwin, Edward J. McCaughan, and Michelle Rocío Nasser (New York: Palgrave Macmillan, 2003); James Garza, "Dominance and Submission in Don Porfirio's Belle Époque: The Case of Luis and Piedad," in *Masculinity and Sexuality in Modern Mexico,* edited by Víctor M. Macías-González and Anne Rubenstein; Robert Buffington and Pablo Piccato, "Tales of Two Women: The Narrative Construction of Porfirian Reality," in *True Stories of Crime in Modern Mexico,* edited by Robert Buffington and Pablo Piccato (Albuquerque: University of New Mexico Press, 2009); Michael Matthews, "Deadly Words, Deadly Deeds: Honor, Sexuality, and Uxoricide in Porfirian Mexico," *Journal of Social History* 51, no. 2 (Winter 2017): 341–363.

30 On gender as a category of historical analysis, see Joan W. Scott, "Gender: A Useful Category of Historical Analysis," *American Historical Review* 91, no. 5 (December 1986): 1053–75 and *Gender and the Politics of History* (New York: Columbia University Press, 1988). On the complex construction of gendered identities and gender performativity, see Judith Butler, *Gender Trouble: Feminism and the Subversion of Identity* (New York: Routledge, 1990).

31 Gabriela Cano, Pamela J. Fuentes, Anne Rubenstein, and Nicole Sanders, "On the History of Sexuality in Modern Mexico City," *Mexican Studies/Estudios Mexicanos* 36, no. 1–2 (Winter/Summer 2020), 160.

32 Kate Weston, *Long Slow Burn: Sexuality and Social Science* (New York: Routledge, 1990), 20; Robert Buffington, "Introduction," in *A Global History of Sexuality: The Modern Era*, edited Robert M. Buffington, Eithne Luibhéid, and Donna J. Guy (Chichester: Wiley Blackwell, 2014), 2; Jeffrey Weeks, *Sex, Politics and Society: The Regulation of Sexuality since 1800* (London: Longman, 1989).

33 Cano et al., "On the History of Sexuality in Modern Mexico City," 156.

34 *Las siete partidas del Sabio Rey D. Alfonso el IX: Cotejados con variants de mas interés y con glosa* (Barcelona: Imprenta de Antonio Bergnes y Compañía, 1843), Ley III, Título XX, Partida VII, 325; Lara Putnam, Sarah C. Chambers, and Sueann Caulfield, "Introduction: Transformations in Honor, Status, and Law over the Long Nineteenth Century," in *Honor, Status, and Law*, edited by Caulfield, Chambers, and Putnam, 4.

35 Putnam, Chambers, and Caulfield, "Introduction," 4. On the colonial era specifically, see Verena Martínez-Alier, *Marriage, Class and Colour in Nineteenth-Century Cuba: A Study of Racist Attitudes and Sexual Values in a Slave Society* (Cambridge: Cambridge University Press, 1974); Ramón A. Gutiérrez, *When Jesus Came, the Corn Mothers Went Away: Marriage, Sexuality, and Power in New Mexico, 1500–1846* (Stanford: Stanford University Press, 1991); Seed, *To Love, Honor, and Obey*. On the national era, see Sloan, *Runaway Daughters*; French, *Heart in the Glass Jar*.

36 Asunción Lavrin, "Introduction: The Scenario, the Actors, and the Issues," in *Sexuality and Marriage in Colonial Latin America,* edited by Asunción Lavrin (Lincoln: University of Nebraska Press, 1989), 10.

37 Cheryl English Martin, "Popular Speech and Social Order in Northern Mexico, 1650–1830," *Comparative Studies in History and Society* 32, no. 2 (1990): 305–324; Richard Boyer, "Honor among Plebians: *Mala Sangre* and Social Reputation," in *The Faces of Honor: Sex, Shame, and Violence in Colonial Latin America,* edited by Lyman Johnson and Sonya Lipsett-Rivera (Albuquerque: University of New Mexico Press, 1998), 152–178.

38 Sonya Lipsett-Rivera, "A Slap in the Face of Honor: Social Transgression and Women in Late-Colonial Mexico," in *Faces of Honor,* 179–200; Nancy E. Van Deusen, "Determining the Boundaries of Virtue: The Discourse of *Recogimiento* among Women in Seventeenth-Century Lima," *Journal of Family History* 22, no. 4 (1997): 373–389; Arlene J. Díaz, *Female Citizens, Patriarchs, and the Law in Venezuela, 1786–1904* (Lincoln: University of Nebraska Press, 2004).

39 Johnson and Lipsett-Rivera, "Introduction," 3–4.

40 Lavrin, "Introduction," 10.

41 Seed, *To Love, Honor, and Obey,* 63–64.

42 Putnam, Chambers, and Caulfield, "Introduction," 4.

43 Juan Pedro Viqueira Albán, *Propriety and Permissiveness in Bourbon Mexico* (Wilmington: Scholarly Resources, 1999).

44 For the most comprehensive exploration of how the colonial honor system was redefined in the national period, see *Honor, Status, and Law,* edited by Caulfield, Chambers, and Putnam.

45 Piccato, *Tyranny of Opinion;* Sarah C. Chambers, *From Subjects to Citizens: Honor, Gender, and Politics in Arequipa, Peru 1780–1854* (University Park: Pennsylvania State University Press, 1999); Matthews, "Deadly Words, Deadly Deeds," 341–363.

46 Piccato, *Tyranny of Opinion,* chapter 6.

47 Lavrin, "Introduction," 10; Seed, *To Love, Honor, and Obey,* 64; Catherine Komisaruk, *Labor and Love in Guatemala: The Eve of Independence* (Stanford: Stanford University Press, 2013), 206.

48 Lavrin, "Introduction," 10; Gutiérrez, *When Jesus Came,* 209–226; Seed, *To Love, Honor, and Obey,* 157; Twinam, *Public Lives, Private Secrets,* 60.

49 Ann Twinam, "Honor, Sexuality, and Illegitimacy in Colonial Spanish America," in *Sexuality and Marriage in Colonial Latin America,* edited by Lavrin, 129.

50 Twinam, *Public Lives, Private Secrets,* 39.

51 Kathy Waldon, "The Sinners and the Bishop in Colonial Venezuela: The *Visita* of Bishop Mariano Martí, 1771–1784," in *Sexuality and Marriage in Colonial Latin America,* edited by Lavrin. 172.

52 Findlay, "Courtroom Tales of Sex and Honor," 211; Abreu Esteves, *Meninas perdidas,* 120, 182.

53 Sueann Caulfield, "The Changing Politics of Freedom and Virginity in Rio de Janeiro, 1920–1940," in *Honor, Status, and Law,* edited by Caulfield, Chambers, and Putnam, 229–231.

54 Jaffary, *Reproduction and Its Discontents* 35–37, 41.

55 Blum, *Domestic Economies,* 27, 30.

56 French, *Heart in the Glass Jar,* 173.

57 French, *Heart in the Glass Jar,* 61.

58 Sloan, *Runaway Daughters,* 2–3, 38.

59 See, for example, *Gender, Sexuality, and Power in Latin America since Independence,* edited by William E. French and Katherine Elaine Bliss (Lanham: Rowman & Littlefield, 2007).

60 Sonya Lipsett-Rivera, *The Origins of Macho: Men and Masculinity in Colonial Mexico* (Albuquerque: University of New Mexico Press, 2019), 52–53; Steve J. Stern, *The Secret History of Gender: Women, Men, and Power in Late Colonial Mexico* (Chapel Hill: University of North Carolina Press, 1995), 270–272.

61 Silvia Marina Arrom, *The Women of Mexico City, 1790–1857* (Stanford: Stanford University Press, 1985), 129–153; Bliss, *Compromised Positions,* 41.

62 Abreu Esteves, *Meninas perdidas,* 119–120, 155.

63 Komisaruk, *Labor and Love,* 186, 199.

64 Bliss *Compromised Positions,* 46; Abreu Esteves, *Meninas perdidas,* 41.

65 Buffington, *Sentimental Education,* 184, 203–212.

66 Agostoni, "Discurso medico," 4; Guy, *White Slavery,* 124–125, 136.

67 On the process of state formation and its limits in Mexico, see Raymond Buve and Romana Falcón (eds.), *Don Porfirio president . . . nunca omnipotente: Hallazgos,*

reflexiones y debates, 1876–1911 (Ciudad de México: Universidad Iberoamericana, 1998); Gilbert M. Joseph and Daniel Nugent (eds.), *Everyday Forms of State Formation: Revolution and the Negotiation of Rule in Modern Mexico* (Durham: University of Durham Press, 1994).

68 See, for example, Blum, *Domestic Economies;* Bliss, *Compromised Positions;* Agostoni, "Discurso médico"; French, *A Peaceful and Working People;* Overmyer-Velázquez, *Visions of the Emerald City;* Piccato, *City of Suspects;* Buffington, *Criminal and Citizen.*

69 See, for example, Mary Kay Vaughan, "Modernizing Patriarchy: State Policies, Rural Households, and Women in Mexico, 1930–1940," in *Hidden Histories of Gender and the State in Latin America,* edited by Elizabeth Dore and Maxine Molyneux (Durham: Duke University Press, 2000), 199, 208–209; Nichole Sanders, *Gender and Welfare in Mexico: The Consolidation of a Postrevolutionary State* (University Park: Pennsylvania State University Press, 2011), 6–7, 51.

70 Vaughan, "Modernizing Patriarchy," 199; Sanders, *Gender and Welfare,* 51.

71 Vaughan, "Modernizing Patriarchy," 208–209.

72 Sanders, *Gender and Welfare,* 18, 87; Bleynat, *Vendors' Capitalism,* 92; Buffington, *Sentimental Education,* 16–17.

73 See, for example, Susan K. Besse, *Restructuring Patriarchy: The Modernization of Gender Inequality in Brazil, 1914–1940* (Chapel Hill: University of North Carolina Press, 1996); Barbara Weinstein, *For Social Peace in Brazil: Industrialists and the Remaking of the Working Class in São Paulo, 1920–1964* (Chapel Hill: University of North Carolina Press, 1996); Mary Kay Vaughan, *Cultural Politics in Revolution: Teachers, Peasants, and Schools in Mexico, 1930–1940* (Tucson: University of Arizona Press, 1997); Eileen J. Findlay, *Imposing Decency: The Politics of Sexuality and Race in Puerto Rico, 1870–1920* (Durham: Duke University Press, 1999); Karin Alejandra Rosemblatt, *Gendered Compromises: Political Cultures and the State in Chile, 1920–1950* (Chapel Hill: University of North Carolina Press, 2000); Elizabeth Quay Hutchison, *Labors Appropriate to Their Sex: Gender, Labor, and Politics in Urban Chile, 1900–1930* (Durham: Duke University Press, 2001); Heidi Tinsman, *Partners in Conflict: The Politics of Sexuality, Gender, and Labor in the Chilean Agrarian Reform, 1950–1973* (Durham: Duke University Press, 2002); Elizabeth Dore, *Myths of Modernity: Peonage and Patriarchy in Nicaragua* (Durham: Duke University Press, 2006).

74 Elizabeth Dore, "One Step Forward, Two Steps Back: Gender and the State in the Long Nineteenth Century," in *Hidden Histories of Gender,* edited by Dore and Molyneux, 26.

75 See, for example, Richard Boyer, *Lives of the Bigamists: Marriage, Family, and Community in Colonial Mexico* (Albuquerque: University of New Mexico Press, 1995); Stern, *Secret History;* Lipsett-Rivera, *Origins of Macho;* Twinam, *Public Lives, Private Secrets.*

76 Richard Greenleaf, a pioneering scholar of Inquisition records in Mexico, stresses the value of these sources. See, *The Mexican Inquisition of the Sixteenth Century* (Albuquerque: University of New Mexico Press, 1969), 1–2.

77 Arlette Farge, *The Allure of the Archives,* translated by Thomas Scott-Railton (New Haven: Yale University Press, 2013), 33.

78 Elizabeth Dore, "The Holy Family: The Imagined Households in Latin American History," in *Gender Politics in Latin America,* edited by Elizabeth Dore (New York: Monthly Review Press, 1997), 101–102.

79 Farge, *Allure of the Archives,* 29. Here, Farge refers to Michel Foucault's "La vie de hommes."

80 Piccato, *City of Suspects,* 123.

81 Farge, *Allure of the Archives,* 6.

82 Natalie Zemon Davis, *Fiction in the Archives: Pardon Tales and Their Tellers in Sixteenth-Century France* (Stanford: Stanford University Press, 1987).

83 Buffington, *Sentimental Education,* 15–26; Guy, *White Slavery,* 15; Vaughan, "Modernizing Patriarchy," 199.

84 Sloan, *Runaway Daughters,* 42–43.

85 Here, this book follows Richard Boyer's approach where he reconstructs the testimony of Inquisition bigamy trials in the first person. See *Lives of the Bigamists,* 10–11.

86 Buffington, *Sentimental Education.*

87 Archivo del Tribunal Superior de Justicia del Distrito Federal, Siglo XX, 1909, caja 0846, expediente 149797 (hereafter, TSJDF/sXX/year/caja/exp.).

88 For an examination of the erasure of the inappropriate by colonial scribes, see Zeb Tortorici, *Sins against Nature: Sex and Archives in Colonial New Spain* (Durham: Duke University Press, 2018).

Chapter 1. City of Sexual Danger, City of Sexual Delight

1 The Federal District was composed of the municipality of Mexico (the historic city center), Azcapotzalco, Guadalupe Hidalgo, Iztapalapa, Mixcoac, Tacubaya, and Tacuba. The city was also divided into seven administrative districts, each with its own legal jurisdiction: the municipality of Mexico and the prefectures of Guadalupe Hidalgo, Azcapotzalco, Tacubaya, Coyoacán, Tlalpan, and Xochimilco.

2 Lear, *Workers, Neighbors, and Citizens,* 25–32.

3 Alan Knight, *The Mexican Revolution* (Cambridge: Cambridge University Press, 1986), Vol 1, 511 (ft. 152); Moisés González Navarro, "La vida social," in *Historia moderna de México,* edited by Daniel Cosío Villegas (Ciudad de México: Editorial Hermes, 1955–1972), Vol 4: 198; Robert H. Holden, *Mexico and the Survey of Public Lands: The Management of Modernization, 1876–1911* (DeKalb: Northern Illinois Press, 1994), 62–78.

4 Lear, *Workers, Neighbors, and Citizens,* 53.

5 Vicente Hernández, *Arquitectura doméstica de la Ciudad de México (1890–1925)* (Ciudad de México: Universidad Nacional Autónoma de México, 1981), 99; Lear, *Workers, Neighbors, and Citizens,* 37.

6 Agostoni, *Monuments of Progress,* 52; Vitz, *City on a Lake,* 40–41.

7 Johns, *City of Mexico,* 14–30.

8 Johns, *City of Mexico,* 32–33.

9 Hernández, *Arquitectura doméstica*, 99–100; Laurence J. Rohlfes, "Police and Penal Correction in Mexico City, 1876–1911: A Study of Order and Progress in Porfirian Mexico" (PhD dissertation, Tulane University, 1983), 88; Johns, *City of Mexico*, 39.

10 Rohlfes, "Police and Penal Correction in Mexico City," 88.

11 Philip T. Terry, *Terry's Guide to Mexico* (Boston: Houghton Mifflin, 1911), 257.

12 On the privatization of Church and community properties to wealthy investors who transformed them into tenements, see Ernesto Aréchiga Córdoba, *Tepito: Del antiguo barrio de indios al arrabal* (Ciudad de México: Ediciones Uníos, 2003); Sergio Miranda Pacheco, *Tacubaya: De suburbia veraniego a ciudad* (Ciudad de México: Universidad Nacional Autónoma de México, 2007).

13 On *vecindades*, see Mauricio Tenorio-Trillo, *I Speak of the City: Mexico City at the Turn of the Twentieth Century* (Chicago: University of Chicago Press, 2012), 64–76.

14 Miguel Macedo, *Mi barrio* (Ciudad de México: Editorial "Cultura," 1930), 50; Elisa Speckman Guerra, "De barrios y arrabales: entorno, cultura material y quehacer cotidiano (Ciudad de México 1890–1910)," in *Historia de la vida cotidiana en México*, edited by Pilar Gonzalbo Aizpuru (Ciudad de México: Fondo de Cultura Económica, 2006), Vol 5, 24–25; Hernández, *Arquitectura doméstica*, 112–113.

15 Hernández, *Arquitectura doméstica*, 104–106.

16 Johns, *City of Mexico*, 32.

17 Lear, *Workers, Neighbors, and Citizens*, 36; Navarro, *La vida social*, 84.

18 Hernández, *Arquitectura doméstica*, 101, 106; Agostoni, "Discurso médico."

19 Schell Jr., *Integral Outsiders.*

20 See Wells and Joseph, "Modernizing Visions"; Tenorio-Trillo, *Mexico at the World's Fairs*; Agostini, *Monuments of Progress*; Lear, *Workers, Neighbors, and Citizens*; Wakild, "Naturalizing Modernity"; Alexander, *City on Fire*; Montaño, *Electrifying Mexico.*

21 Bliss, *Compromised Positions*, 29.

22 Luis Lara y Pardo, *La prostitución en México* (Ciudad de México: Librería de Ch. Bouret, 1908), 19–20, 27; Bliss, *Compromised Positions*, 25, 32.

23 José Juan Tablada, *La feria de la vida (memorias)* (Ciudad de México: Ediciones Botas, 1937), Vol 1, 87–88.

24 Navarro, *La vida social*, 413.

25 Lara y Pardo, *La prostitución*, 99; Garza, "Dominance and Submission," 82.

26 Archivo Histórico del Distrito Federal (hereafter, AHDF), Municipalidades, Tlalpan, Justicia, [1906], caja 188, exp. 40.

27 Lara y Pardo, *La prostitución*, 56, 72.

28 Navarro, *La vida social*, 408; Tablada, *La feria de la vida*, Vol 1, 86.

29 AHDF, Gobierno del Distrito, bandos, leyes, decretos, 1900, caja 85, exp. 6; *La Voz de México*, October 1, 1908.

30 AHDF, Gobierno del Distrito, diversions, v. 1387, exp. 446 [1910-11].

31 See, for example, *Nacional*, November 6, 1891; Navarro, *La vida social*, 408.

32 Julia Tuñón Pablos, *Women in Mexico* (Austin: University of Texas Press, 1999), 82–83.

33 Buffington, *Sentimental Education*, 126, 152–153, 158–159.

34 Bertram G. Goodhue, *Mexican Memories: The Record of a Slight Sojourn Below the Yellow Rio Grande* (New York: The Alley-Allen Press, 1892), 134.

35 Beezley, *Judas at the Jockey Club,* 16.

36 Steven B. Bunker, *Creating Mexican Consumer Culture in the Age of Porfirio Díaz, 1876–1911* (Albuquerque: University of New Mexico Press, 2012), 131, 137; Lear, *Workers, Neighbors, and Citizens,* 16.

37 Navarro, *La vida social,* 706–707; Buffington, *Sentimental Education.*

38 María Áurea Toxqui Garay, "'*El recreo de los amigos*': Mexico City's *Pulquerías* during the Liberal Republic (1856–1911)" (PhD dissertation, University of Arizona, 2008), 48–50.

39 Navarro, *La vida social,* 786; William H. Beezley, *Mexican National Identity: Memory, Innuendo, and Popular Culture* (Tucson: University of Arizona Press, 2008), 104.

40 Lear, *Workers, Neighbors, and Citizens,* 28; Navarro, *La vida social,* 775.

41 Navarro, *La vida social,* 788–790.

42 Christine Stansell, *City of Women: Sex and Class in New York, 1789–1960* (Chicago: University of Illinois Press, 1987), 42.

43 On the mixed commercial and residential use of vecindad space, see María Dolores Morales and María Gayón, "Viviendas, casas y usos de suelo en la Ciudad de México, 1848–1882," in *Casas, viviendas y hogares en la historia de México,* edited by Rosalva Loreto López (Ciudad de México: El Colegio de Mexico, Centro de Estudios Históricos, 2001), 350–351.

44 TSJDF, sXX, 1900, caja 0020, exp. 003238.

45 Speckman Guerra, "De barrios y arrabales," 30.

46 TSJDF, sXX, 1905, caja 0382, exp. 069142.

47 TSJDF, sXX, 1901, caja 0097, exp. 019183.

48 TSJDF, sXX, 1907, caja 0636, exp. 112131.

49 Tenorio-Trillo, *I Speak of the City,* 65–66.

50 Lara y Pardo, *La prostitución,* 74–75; Tablada, *La feria de la vida,* Vol 1, 86; Buffington, *Sentimental Education,* 183.

51 AHDF, Gobierno del Distrito, diversiones, v. 1387. exp. 375.

52 *El Monitor Republicano,* August 12, 1888.

53 Tablada, *La feria de la vida,* Vol 1, 136.

54 *El Diablito Bromista,* May 17, 1908, cited in Buffington, *Sentimental Education,* 138.

55 Archivo del Tribunal Superior de Justicia de la Ciudad de México, Siglo XIX, 1898, legajo 260300, caja 1541 (hereafter, TSJCM/sXIX/leg./caja).

56 D. Domingo Orvañanos, *Algo sobre legislacion sanitaria relative á las habitaciones en México* (Ciudad de México: Secretaría de Fomento, 1895), 7–8; Julio Guerrero, *La génesis del crimen en México: Estudio de psiquiatría social* (Ciudad de México: Librería de Ch. Bouret, 1901); Lara y Pardo, *La prostitución,* 119; Bliss, *Compromised Positions.*

57 TSJDF, sXX, 1904, caja 0327, exp. 057342.

58 TSJCM, sXIX, 1889, leg. 123628, caja 1143.

59 Arrom, *Women of Mexico City,* 188.

60 Domestics were seen as one step away from prostitution. See Porter, *Working Women in Mexico City*, 64–65.

61 Navarro, *La vida social*, 391–392.

62 Blum, *Domestic Economies*, 208–209.

63 TSJCM, sXIX, 1893, leg. 180859, caja 1354.

64 TSJDF, sXX, 1904, caja 0296, exp. 052721.

65 TSJCM, sXIX, 1888, leg. 89002, caja 1093.

66 TSJCM, sXIX, 1893, leg. 180859, caja 1354.

67 TSJCM, sXIX, 1893, leg. 180854, caja 1354.

68 *El Diablito Bromista*, May 3, 1908.

69 TSJCM, sXIX, 1893, leg. 180857, caja 1354.

70 TSJCM, sXIX, 1889, leg. 132114, caja 1145.

71 Arrom, *Women of Mexico City*, 188.

72 TSJCM, sXIX, 1898, leg. 260280, caja 1541.

73 TSJDF, sXX, 1902, caja 0185, exp. 034240.

74 TSJCM, sXIX, 1888, leg. 88589, caja 1092.

75 TSJCM, sXIX, 1893, leg. 180860, caja 1354.

76 TSJCM, sXIX, 1889, leg. 110629, caja 1148.

77 Lear, *Workers, Neighbors, and Citizens*, 60.

78 Lear, *Workers, Neighbors, and Citizens*, 62–63; Hart, *Revolutionary Mexico*, 167.

79 Lear, *Workers, Neighbors, and Citizens*, 73–74.

80 Porter, *Working Women in Mexico City*, xvii, xix-xx.

81 TSJCM, sXIX, 1898, leg. 260269, caja 1541.

82 TSJCM, sXIX, 1889, leg. 132109, caja 1145.

83 TSJDF, sXX, 1906, caja 0532, exp. 093573.

84 Pablos, *Women in Mexico*, 75.

85 Stansell, *City of Women*, 83, 125–126.

86 See, for example, Edward Shorter, "Female Emancipation, Birth Control, and Fertility in European History," *American Historical Review* 78, no. 3 (1973): 605–640; Edward Shorter, "Illegitimacy, sexual revolution and social change in modern Europe," *Journal of Interdisciplinary History* 2, no. 1 (1971): 237–272; Emma Griffin, "Sex, illegitimacy and social change in industrializing Britain," *Social History* 38, no. 2 (2013): 139–161.

87 As Julie Hardwick notes for pre-revolutionary France, strolling was an important public performance to establish community knowledge of a legitimate romantic relationship. See *Sex in an Old Regime City: Young Workers and Intimacy in France, 1660-1789* (New York: Oxford University Press, 2020), 47.

88 Condesa de Tramar, *El amor obligatorio* (Ciudad de México: Librería de Ch. Bouret, 1910), 182–183.

89 Mary Blake and Margaret Sullivan, *Mexico: Picturesque, Political, Progressive* (Boston: Lee and Shepard, 1888), 89; Robert S. Barrett, *The Standard Guide to the City of Mexico and Vicinity* (Ciudad de México: Modern Mexico Publishing Company, 1900), 39–40.

90 *La Patria,* August 22, 1897.

91 Lipsett-Rivera, *Origins of Macho,* 66–67. Beyond Mexico, in nineteenth-century London, couples strolling together was a marker of courtship and could be interpreted as the "explicitly sexual." See Rebecca Solnit, *Wanderlust: A History of Walking* (New York: Penguin Books, 2000), 232.

92 Instituto de Investigaciones Dr. José María Luis Mora, Biblioteca "Ernesto de la Torre Villar," Proyecto de Historia Oral (PHO), 1/18, interview of Roque González Garza by Daniel Cazes, 1960, Ciudad de México.

93 TSJDF, sXX, 1905, caja 0382, exp. 069142.

94 TSJDF, sXX, 1901, caja 0092, exp. 016685.

95 TSJCM, sXIX, 1898, leg. 260302, caja 1541.

96 TSJCM, sXIX, 1889, leg. 107508, caja 1152.

97 TSJDF, sXX, 1900, caja 0020, exp. 003238.

98 Lear, *Workers, Neighbors, and Citizens,* 37, 48.

99 TSJDF, sXX, 1900, caja 0047, exp. 008871.

100 TSJDF, sXX, 1904, caja 0305, exp. 055383.

101 TSJDF, sXX, 1906, caja 0550, exp. 096602.

102 TSJDF, sXX, 1907, caja 0597, exp. 105681.

103 Pulquerías were larger and more popular venues than cantinas.

104 This is especially true for *La Guacamaya*'s recurring humorous segments "*Desde la estaca,*" "*Entre cotorras,*" and "*Desde la jaula.*"

105 Áurea Toxqui notes that pulquerías, or *casillas,* were male and female spaces. See "Breadwinners or Entrepreneurs? Women's Involvement in the *Pulquería* World of Mexico City, 1850–1910," in *Alcohol in Latin America: A Social and Cultural History,* edited by Gretchen Pierce and Áurea Toxqui (Tucson: University of Arizona Press, 2014), 108.

106 Sandra Lauderdale Graham, *House and Street: The Domestic World of Servants and Masters in Nineteenth-Century Rio de Janeiro* (Austin: University of Texas Press, 1988), 63.

107 Navarro, *La vida social,* 73–74.

108 Carlos Monsívais, *Mexican Postcards* (London: Verso, 1997), 3.

109 Toxqui Garay, "*El recreo de los amigos,*" 157.

110 Buffington, *Criminal and Citizen;* Piccato, *City of Suspects;* Speckman Guerra, *Crimen y castigo.*

111 Speckman Guerra, "De barrios y arrabales," 39; Toxqui Garay, "*El recreo de los amigos,*" 148–151.

112 Buffington, *Sentimental Education; La Guacamaya.*

113 TSJCM, sXIX, 1888, leg. 88998, caja 1093.

114 TSJDF, sXX, 1905, caja 0393, exp. 068460.

115 TSJCM, sXIX, 1898, leg. 260276, caja 1541.

116 TSJCM, sXIX, 1898, leg. 260274, caja 1541.

117 TSJDF, sXX, 1903, caja 0211, exp. 037604.

118 TSJDF, sXX, 1906, caja 0480, exp. 081859.

119 TSJDF, sXX, 1908, caja 1420, exp. 121673.

120 TSJDF, sXX, 1902, caja 0145, exp. 024691.

121 TSJDF, sXX, 1904, caja 0348, exp. 063222.

122 TSJDF, sXX, 1909, caja 0878, exp. 151930.

123 Pablo Piccato notes that the working class held their own directional pathways throughout the city that corresponded to landmarks such as buildings and markets rather than street names and addresses. See *City of Suspects*, 46–47.

124 TSJDF, sXX, 1908, caja 0693, exp. 122071.

125 TSJDF, sXX, 1902, caja 0152, exp. 025420.

126 TSJDF, sXX, 1911, caja 1077, exp. 191236.

127 TSJDF, sXX, 1906, caja 0477, exp. 085740.

128 TSJDF, sXX, 1909, caja 0912, exp. 159596.

129 TSJDF, sXX, 1908, caja 0693, exp. 122071.

130 TSJCM, sXIX, 1898, leg. 260277, caja 1541.

131 TSJCM, sXIX, 1893, leg. 180847, caja 1354.

132 Melanie Tebbutt, *Women's Talk? A Social History of 'Gossip' in Working-Class Neighborhoods, 1880–1960* (Aldershot: Scolar Press, 1995), 9, 95.

133 As demonstrated, even into the 1950s and 1960s, working- and middle-class families held great concern over the lost chastity of daughters who stayed out late or all night. See Oscar Lewis, *The Children of Sánchez: Autobiography of a Mexican Family* (New York: Vintage Books, 1963), 149.

134 Johns, *City of Mexico*, 37.

135 Tebbutt, *Women's Talk?*, 77.

136 Abreu Esteves, *Meninas perdidas*, 198–199.

137 Arlette Farge, *Fragile Lives: Violence, Power, and Solidarity in Eighteenth-Century Paris*, translated by Carol Shelton. (Cambridge: Harvard University Press, 1993), 19–20.

138 TSJDF, sXX, 1908, caja 0729, exp. 128437.

139 TSJDF, sXX, 1906, caja 0468, exp. 083235.

140 TSJCM, sXIX, 1889, leg. 119568, caja 1148.

141 TSJDF, sXX, 1906, caja 0506, exp. 088739.

142 TSJDF, sXX, 1904, caja 0369, exp. 066380.

143 TSJCM, sXIX, 1888, leg. 83712, caja 1092.

144 TSJDF, sXX, 1904, caja 0305, exp. 055383.

145 TSJCM, sXIX, 1889, leg. 132082, caja 1151.

146 TSJDF, sXX 1909, caja 0846, exp. 149797.

147 TSJCM, sXIX, 1889, leg. 132099, caja 1151.

148 TSJDF, sXX, 1909, caja 0879, exp. 152091.

149 *La Guacamaya*, November 17, 1904.

150 TSJCM, sXIX, 1890, leg. 150488, caja 1193.

151 TSJCM, sXIX, 1889, leg. 132099, caja 1151.

152 Foreign visitors also noted the role of middle- and upper-class family's domestic staff in the love affairs of young couples. See Fanny Chambers Gooch, *Face to Face with the Mexicans* (New York: Fords, Howard, & Hulbert, 1887), 280.

153 TSJCM, sXIX, 1889, leg. 134264, caja 1150.

154 TSJCM, sXIX, 1898, leg. 260302, caja 1541.
155 TSJDF, sXX, 1904, caja 0345, exp. 062352.
156 Tebbutt, *Women's Talk?*, 77, 95.

Chapter 2. Love, Sex, and Vigilance

1 Piccato, *City of Suspects;* Rohlfes, "Police and Penal Correction in Mexico City."
2 Gilles Deleuze, *Foucault,* translated by Hand Seán (Minneapolis: University of Minnesota Press, 1988), 27; Hubert L. Dreyfus and Paul Rabinow, *Michel Foucault: Beyond Structuralism and Hermeneutics* (Chicago: University of Chicago Press, 1983), 184–185.
3 For an examination of early policing in Mexico, see Nicole von Germeten, *The Enlightened Patrolman: Early Law Enforcement in Mexico City* (Lincoln: University of Nebraska Press, 2022).
4 Rohlfes, "Police and Penal Correction in Mexico City," 9, 41–45.
5 Piccato, *City of Suspects,* 43.
6 Rohlfes, "Police and Penal Correction in Mexico City," 9, 94–95; Piccato, *City of Suspects,* 42
7 Rohlfes, "Police and Penal Correction in Mexico City," 9, 76–77, 86.
8 Piccato, *City of Suspects,* 45.
9 Piccato, *City of Suspects,* 7.
10 Piccato, *City of Suspects,* 43.
11 Rohlfes, "Police and Penal Correction in Mexico City," 27.
12 Speckman Guerra, *Crimen y castigo,* 253–254.
13 French, *A Peaceful and Working People;* Overmyer-Velázquez, *Visions of the Emerald City.*
14 Speckman Guerra, *Crimen y castigo,* 309.
15 Speckman Guerra, *Crimen y castigo,* 31–34.
16 French, *A Peaceful and Working People;* Matthews, *The Civilizing Machine,* 11–13.
17 Agostoni, "Discurso médico," 1, 8. A similar vision was articulated by turn-of-the-century Brazilian reformers. See Abreu Esteves, *Meninas perdidas,* 29, 31.
18 Francisco A. Flores, *El hímen en México* (Mexico City: Secretaría de Fomento, 1885), 20.
19 Buffington, *Criminal and Citizen,* 54, 59; Guerrero, *La génesis del crimen en México,* 316–333.
20 Guerrero, *La génesis del crimen en México,* 335, 344. Guerrero was far from the only social reformer to link lower-class sexual values to social degeneration. See Juan Arellano, *La prostitución en Mexico* (Mexico City: Secretaría de Fomento, 1895), 17–18; Domingo Orvañano, *Algo sobre legislación sanitaria . . . ,* 7–8; Miguel S. Macedo, *La criminalidad en México* (Mexico City: Oficina Tip. De la Secretaría de Fomento, 1897), 30; Lara y Pardo, *La prostitución,* 11–12, 43, 57–58, 87, 148. Carlos Rougmagnac, in several of his studies of Mexican criminality, highlighted the wantonness of the poor as a precursor to criminal behavior. See *Los criminales en México: Ensayo de psicología criminal* (Ciudad de México: Tipografía El Fénix, 1904); *Crímenes sexuales y pasionales: Estudios de psicología morbosa* (Ciudad de

México: Librería de Ch. Bouret, 1906); *La prostitución reglamentada: Sus inconvenientes, su inutilidad y sus peligros* (Ciudad de México: Tipografía Económica, 1909); *Matadores de mujeres* (Ciudad de México: Librería de Ch. Bouret, 1910).

21 Abreu Esteves, *Meninas perdidas,* 30.

22 Arrom, *Women of Mexico City,* 71.

23 Komisaruk, *Labor and Love,* 210.

24 French, *Heart in the Glass Jar,* 63.

25 Piccato, *City of Suspects,* 123–124.

26 On the role of women and mothers as the natural allies of social reformers in hygienic campaigns, see Agostoni, "Discurso médico," 4, 20.

27 Buffington, *Sentimental Education,* 150.

28 Robert Buffington, "Introduction: Conceptualizing Criminality in Latin America," in *Reconstructing Criminality in Latin America*, edited by Carlos A. Aguirre and Robert Buffington (Wilmington: Scholarly Resources, 2000), xvi; Carlos Aguirre and Ricardo D. Salvatore, "Writing the History of Law, Crime, and Punishment in Latin America," in *Crime and Punishment in Latin America: Law and Society since Late Colonial Times*, edited by Ricardo D. Salvatore, Carlos Aguirre, and Gilbert M. Joseph (Durham: Duke University Press, 2001), 14–17.

29 Overmyer-Velázquez, *Visions of the Emerald City,* 66.

30 TSJCM, sXIX, 1898, leg. 260301, caja 1541.

31 TSJDF, sXX, 1900, caja 0020, exp. 003254.

32 TSJCM, sXIX, 1889, leg. 142049, caja 1152.

33 TSJCM, sXIX, 1889, leg. 119568, caja 1148.

34 TSJCM, sXIX, 1888, leg. 88730, caja 1095.

35 TSJDF, sXX, 1901, caja 0099, exp. 014546.

36 For a discussion of the limits of instilling order and discipline among subaltern groups, see Neufeld, *Blood Contingent,* chapter 6.

37 Rohlfes, "Police and Penal Correction," 27–31; Piccato, *City of Suspects,* 43–45.

38 *Diario del Hogar,* September 1, 1896.

39 French, *A Peaceful and Working People,* 64.

40 TSJCM, sXIX, 1889, leg. 119572, caja 1148.

41 TSJDF, sXX, 1909, caja 0879, exp. 152091.

42 Agostoni, "Discurso médico,"; Dreyfus and Rabinow, *Michel Foucault,* 139–141.

43 Deleuze, *Foucault,* 27–28.

44 TSJCM, sXIX, 1893, leg. 180875, caja 1354.

45 TSJDF, sXX, 1903, caja 0276, exp. 044619.

46 TSJCM, sXIX, 1893, leg. 180857, caja 1354.

47 TSJDF, sXX, 1908, caja 0693, exp. 122077.

48 TSJCM, sXIX, 1894, leg. 196578, caja 1394.

49 TSJDF, sXX, 1904, caja 0348, exp. 063229.

50 Findlay, "Courtroom Tales of Sex and Honor," 201.

51 TSJDF, sXX, 1908, caja 0690, exp. 121699.

52 TSJDF, sXX, 1908, caja 0693, exp. 122071.

53 TSJDF, sXX, 1910, caja 0964, exp. 169471.

54 Buffington, *Criminal and Citizen*, 94–95, 106; Neufeld, *Blood Contingent*, 45.

55 Arrom, *Women of Mexico City*, 78–79. For example, fathers no longer had the right to murder adulterous daughters, sell children due to poverty, or force a child to marry.

56 Sloan, *Runaway Daughters*, 135–136; Silvia M. Arrom, "Changes in Mexican Family Law in the Nineteenth Century: The Civil Codes of 1870 and 1884," *Journal of Family History* 10, no. 3 (1985): 305–306.

57 Seed, *To Love, Honor, and Obey*, 200.

58 Stern, *Secret History*, 97–98.

59 Sloan, *Runaway Daughters*, 136; Arrom, "Changes in Mexican Family Law," 305–306.

60 Jeffrey M. Shumway, *The Case of the Ugly Suitor and other Histories of Love, Gender, and Nation in Buenos Aires, 1776–1870* (Lincoln: University of Nebraska Press, 2005), 82.

61 Abreu Esteves, *Meninas perdidas*, 132, 198–199.

62 María Odila Silva Dias, *Power and Everyday Life: The Lives of Working Women in Nineteenth-Century Brazil*, translated by Ann Frost (New Brunswick: Rutgers University Press, 1995), 122.

63 Findlay demonstrates a similar phenomenon in Puerto Rico, "Courtroom Tales of Sex and Honor," 206. Similarly, in her examination of ancien régime France, Julie Hardwick notes that mitigating the risks for young women's reputations and ensuring a better future for younger generations was central to the promotion and protection of licit intimacy. See *Sex in an Old Regime City*, 46.

64 TSJCM, sXIX, 1888, leg. 83717, caja 1092.

65 Blum, *Domestic Economies*, 24–25.

66 Buffington, *Sentimental Education*, 197.

67 Elise Speckman Guerra concludes that the main goal of a rapto allegation was for families to force marriage between the youths. In the cases examined here, securing a financial settlement was just as common as seeking a marriage proposal. See Speckman Guerra, "De barrios y arrabales," 33.

68 Speckman Guerra, "De barrios y arrabales," 34.

69 TSJDF, sXX, 1902, caja 0150, exp. 023961.

70 TSJCM, sXIX, 1889, leg. 142371, caja 1152.

71 TSJDF, sXX, 1906, caja 0468, exp. 083245.

72 Dirección General de Estadística, *Estadísticas sociales del Porfiriato, 1877–1910* (Mexico City: Dirección General de Estadística, 1956), 19–21; Jaffary, *Reproduction and Its Discontents*, 37.

73 French, *Heart in the Glass Jar*, 63.

74 TSJDF, sXX, 1901, caja 0077, exp. 015095.

75 TSJDF, sXX, 1901, caja 0067, exp. 011958.

76 For a discussion of the *casa chica* throughout Mexican history, see Stern, *Secret History*, 256; Matthew C. Gutmann, *The Meanings of Macho: Being a Man in Mexico City* (Berkeley: University of California Press, 1996), 138–141; Lewis, *Children of Sánchez*.

77 TSJCM, sXIX, 1889, leg. 132080, caja 1151.

78 TSJCM, sXIX, 1893, leg. 180873, caja 1354.

79 *Código Penal para el Distrito Federal y Territorio de la Baja California sobre Delitos del Fuero Común, y para toda la República Mexicana, sobre Delitos Contra la Federación* (Chihuahua: Librería de Donato Miramontes, 1883), Art. 811.

80 French, *Heart in the Glass Jar*, 33; Stern, *Secret History*, 17; Sloan, *Runaway Daughters*, 2; Findlay, "Courtroom Tales of Sex and Honor," 210.

81 Sloan finds a similar pattern in Porfirian Oaxaca. See *Runaway Daughters*, 4.

82 Michel Foucault, *Discipline and Punish: The Birth of the Prison*, translated by Alan Sheridan (New York: Vintage Books, 1977), 27.

83 TSJCM, sXIX, 1889, leg. 132114, caja 1145.

84 TSJCM, sXIX, 1894, leg. 196579, caja 1394.

85 TSJDF, sXX, 1905, caja 0377, exp. 066902.

86 Caulfield, "The Changing Politics of Freedom and Virginity," 236.

87 Sloan, *Runaway Daughters*, 6–7.

88 TSJCM, sXIX, 1889, leg. 119565, caja 1148.

89 TSJDF, sXX, 1906, caja 0468, exp. 083199

90 TSJDF, sXX, 1907, caja 0605, exp. 106104.

91 Putnam, Chambers, and Caulfield, "Introduction," 13.

92 TSJDF, sXX, 1904, caja 0296, exp. 052721.

93 Sloan, *Runaway Daughters*, 132.

94 TSJDF, sXX, 1907, caja 0639, exp. 112687.

95 TSJDF, sXX, 1906, caja 0482, exp. 084724.

96 TSJDF, sXX, 1906, caja 0482, exp. 084727.

97 TSJCM, sXIX, 1893, leg. 180827, caja 1354.

98 Stern, *Secret History*, 80; Sloan, *Runaway Daughters*, 35.

99 Sloan, *Runaway Daughters*, 177.

100 Findlay, "Courtroom Tales of Sex and Honor," 205–206; Abreu Esteves, *Meninas perdidas*, 15–16.

101 Flores, *El hímen en México*, 23; Caulfield, *In Defense of Honor*, 19, 97.

102 TSJCM, sXIX, 1885, leg. 65190, caja 940.

103 TSJDF, sXX, 1908, caja 0693, exp. 122077.

104 Flores, *El hímen en México*, 27.

105 Catherine Komisaruk makes a similar point. See "Rape Narratives, Rape Silences," 396.

106 *Código Penal para el Distrito Federal*, Art. 793.

107 *Código Penal para el Distrito Federal*, Art. 808.

108 For example, TSJDF, sXX, 1910, caja 1010, exp. 179620.

109 TSJCM, sXIX, 1893, leg. 180847, caja 1354.

110 TSJDF, sXX, 1900, caja 0020, exp. 002292.

111 Parents and guardians could either provide a birth certificate or, more commonly, a baptismal record from a parish church. TSJDF, sXX, 1904, caja 0369, exp. 066380.

112 TSJCM, sXIX, 1889, leg. 132095, caja 1151.

113 TSJDF, sXX, 1910, caja 0949, exp. 166955.
114 Abreu Esteves, *Meninas perdidas,* 47, 82.

Chapter 3. Consent, Coercion, and True Romance

1 French, *Heart in the Glass Jar,* 64, 84–85.
2 For a discussion of how sexual crimes in the colonial era were tied to male honor, see Lipsett-Rivera, "A Slap in the Face of Honor," 194–197; Seed, *To Love, Honor, and Obey,* 63; Gutiérrez, *When Jesus Came,* 209.
3 For a discussion of how this phenomenon continued under the liberal legal code, see Speckman Guerra, *Crimen y castigo,* 44; French, *Heart in the Glass Jar,* 30–31.
4 Arrom, *Women of Mexico City,* 97; Dore, "One Step Forward, Two Steps Back," 17–25.
5 *Siete Partidas,* Ley III del Título XX de la Partida VII.
6 See *Código Penal para el Distrito Federal,* Art. 793 (estupro); Art. 795 and 796 (violación); Art. 808 (rapto).
7 For example, Ann Twinam notes that the legal protection of honor was reserved exclusively to the elite. See *Public Lives, Private Secrets,* 33. While colonial laws targeting the deflowering of virgins protected the inheritance, legitimacy, and racial purity of elite families, thereby making their adjudication much more common among the well-to-do, plebian women reported rapes as attacks against their honor. See Lipsett-Rivera, "A Slap in the Face of Honor," 194–196.
8 French, *Heart in the Glass Jar,* 86. For a comprehensive discussion of what kinds of female agency can and cannot exist under Liberal states as a result of entrenched patriarchy and misogyny see, Catherine A. MacKinnon, *Toward a Feminist Theory of the State* (New York: Oxford University Press, 1989), chapter 8.
9 Looking at Porfirian Chihuahua, William French notes that parents often "granted" the exercise of agency to their daughters while also noting that women exercised their will when leaving home for a novio. See *Heart in the Glass Jar,* 80–81, 84. Cases from Mexico City suggest that parents were most often forced to grant that agency by the willful decision-making of daughters.
10 In cases of estupro, the 1871 Penal Code for the Federal District privileged written promises of marriage to girls over the age of fourteen over verbal ones. See *Código Penal para el Distrito Federal,* Capítulo III, Título III, 198. Also, see French, *Heart in the Glass Jar,* 28–29.
11 Scholars focusing on nineteenth-century Latin America have noted how court testimony reveals gendered scripts that assumed female sexual passivity. See, for example, Findlay, "Courtroom Tales of Sex and Honor," 202; Martínez-Alier, *Marriage, Class and Colour,* 111; Putnam, Chambers, and Caulfield, "Introduction," 13; Speckman Guerra, "De barrios y arrabales," 33. On gendered sexual violence see Stern, *Secret History,* 57–59, 63. Stern argues that in late-colonial Mexico, gender-rooted violence represented the most common form of violent episodes and, within that category, rape represents one-third of the cases of violence against women.
12 TSJCM, sXIX, 1889, leg. 132093, caja 1151.
13 TSJCM, sXIX, 1889, leg. 114303, caja 1145.

14 TSJCM, sXIX, 1889, leg. 134264, caja 1150.

15 TSJDF, sXX, 1905, caja 0373, exp. 064847.

16 Looking at Mexican migrants in the 1990s, Jennifer Hirsch identifies the rise of trust and affection as examples of modern, companionate relationships as well as a shift away from traditional courtship practice a generation earlier. See *A Courtship after Marriage: Sexuality and Love in Mexican Transnational* Families (Berkeley: University of California Press, 2003), 105, 110–111. As examples from this chapter demonstrate, Mexico City's urban environment allowed for early articulations of notably modern behaviors and values.

17 TSJDF, sXX, 1910, caja 0977, exp. 171827.

18 TSJCM, sXIX, 1898, leg. 260300, caja 1541.

19 TSJDF, sXX, 1900, caja 0020, exp. 003255.

20 Mark Padilla, et al., "Introduction: Cross-Cultural Reflections on an Intimate Intersection," in *Love and Globalization: Transformations of Intimacy in the Contemporary World,* edited by Mark B. Padilla, Jennifer S. Hirsch, Miguel Muñoz-Laboy, Robert E. Sember, and Richard G. Parker (Nashville: Vanderbilt University Press, 2007), xv. Indeed, such examples are a stark contrast to the children of the upper classes who showed a desire to appease parents with their marriage choices. See Donald Fithian Stevens, *Mexico in the Time of Cholera* (Albuquerque: University of New Mexico Press, 2019), 220.

21 TSJCM, sXIX, 1889, leg. 132112, caja 1145.

22 TSJDF, sXX, 1908, caja 0691, exp. 121722.

23 TSJDF, sXX, 1904, caja 0306, exp. 054624.

24 Sloan, *Runaway Daughters,* 6–7.

25 TSJDF, sXX, 1902, caja 0132, exp. 023515.

26 TSJDF, sXX, 1902, caja 0150, exp. 023968.

27 On the canal systems that linked Chalco to Mexico City, see Tortolero Villaseñor, "Canales de riego y canales navegables."

28 TSJCM, sXIX, 1895, leg. 206453, caja 1434.

29 TSJCM, sXIX, 1893, leg. 180838, caja 1354.

30 Indeed, current feminist debates on liberal consent theory highlight the onus the law places on women despite unequal social relations and access to the law. See MacKinnon, *Toward a Feminist Theory of the State,* 174–177; Ann Cahill, *Rethinking Rape* (Ithaca: Cornell University Press, 2001), 169–176.

31 TSJDF, sXX, 1900, caja 0042, exp. 011068.

32 TSJDF, sXX, 1905, caja 0376, exp. 066682.

33 TSJDF, sXX, 1905, caja 0376, exp. 066680.

34 TSJDF, sXX, 1907, caja 0577, exp. 100016.

35 French, *Heart in the Glass Jar,* 207.

36 Nicole Sanders, "Gender and Consumption in Porfirian Mexico: Images of Women in Advertising, *El Imparcial,* 1897–1910," *Frontiers* 38, no. 1 (2017): 1–30; Bunker, *Creating Mexican Consumer Culture.*

37 A similar phenomenon is depicted in the late-nineteenth-century United States. See John D'Emilio and Estelle B. Freeman, *Intimate Matters: A History of Sexuality in*

America, (Chicago: University of Chicago Press, 2012), 194–201, and Kathy Peiss, *Cheap Amusements: Working Women and Leisure in Turn-of-the-Century New York* (Philadelphia: Temple University Press, 1986), 56–67.

38 There was a sustained critique of *coquetismo* throughout the Porfiriato in newspapers as well as etiquette manuals. See, for example, *La Familia,* November 8, 1888; *El Mundo Ilustrado,* April 23, 1899; *El Popular,* February 8, 1903; *El Diario,* February 1, 1907. Also, see Condesa de Tramar, *El amor obligatorio,* 178–179.

39 *Código Penal para el Distrito Federal,* Art. 795 and 796, respectively.

40 Piccato, *City of Suspects,* 123.

41 Findlay, "Courtroom Tales of Sex and Honor," 212.

42 Sloan, *Runaway Daughters,* 3.

43 Putnam, Chambers, and Caulfield, "Introduction," 13.

44 Contemporary feminist discussions of liberal consent theory have highlighted its failure as rooted in the simultaneous assumption of gender neutrality and the distinctly gendered ways that laws and social expectations are applied. Placing the ethical spotlight on women's actions—such as whether they attempted to notify a police officer on the street—represents an example of why scholars have criticized a reliance on the standard of consent. See, for example, Cahill, *Rethinking Rape,* 169–176.

45 TSJCM, sXIX, 1889, leg. 107508, caja 1152.

46 TSJDF, sXX, 1908, caja 0733, exp. 129078. Both cases were adjudicated in one file.

47 See, for example, Lauderdale Graham, *House and Street,* 45; Abreu Esteves, *Meninas perdidas,* 45; Porter, *Working Women in Mexico City,* 64–65.

48 Sloan, *Runaway Daughters,* 34.

49 TSJDF, sXX, 1909, caja 0846, exp. 149797.

50 Komisaruk, "Rape Narratives, Rape Silences," 388.

51 TSJDF, sXX, 1901, caja 0097, exp. 019183.

52 See, for example, *Diario del Hogar,* June 14, 1892; *La Patria,* July 3, 1897; *El Popular,* November 12, 1897, November 21, 1907.

53 TSJDF, sXX, 1907, caja 0638, exp. 112560.

54 TSJDF, sXX, 1903, caja 0276, exp. 044655.

55 TSJDF, sXX, 1900, caja 0047, exp. 008852.

56 TSJDF, sXX, 1907, caja 0596, exp. 105242.

57 Stern, *Secret History,* 6–7; Ana Lidia García Peña, *El fracaso del amor: Género e individualismo el siglo XIX mexicano* (Ciudad de México: El Colegio de México, Centro de Estudios Históricos: Toluca, Estado de México, México: Universidad Autónoma del Estado de México, 2006), 55, 61–67.

58 Padilla, et al., "Cross-Cultural Reflections on an Intimate Intersection," xv, xvii.

59 For a discussion of masculine identity, especially the articulation of *macho,* and violence, see Gutmann, *The Meanings of Macho,* 235–236; Macías-González and Rubenstein, "Introduction," 11–14.

60 TSJCM, sXIX, 1889, leg. 114303, caja 1145.

61 French, *Heart in the Glass Jar,* 84.

62 TSJCM, sXIX, 1885, leg. 53962, caja 941.

63 TSJDF, sXX, 1907, caja 1354, exp. 180873.

64 TSJDF, sXX, 1900, caja 0042, exp. 011068.

65 TSJCM, sXIX, 1889, leg. 119564, caja 1148.

66 TSJCM, sXIX, 1889, leg. 119569, caja 1148.

67 TSJDF, sXX, 1907, caja 0636, exp. 112131.

68 TSJCM, sXIX, 1893, leg. 180885, caja 1354.

69 William M. Reddy, *The Making of Romantic Love: Longing and Sexuality in Europe, South Asia, and Japan, 900-1200 CE* (Chicago: University of Chicago Press, 2012). 6. Reddy uses the term "longing for association" as opposed to desire or love to avoid an overemphasis on lust and sexual gratification, although those may well be central to a given relationship.

70 TSJDF, sXX, 1900, caja 0030, exp. 002306.

71 TSJCM, sXIX, 1898, leg. 260301, caja 1541.

72 TSJDF, sXX, 1907, caja 0587, exp. 103499.

73 TSJDF, sXX, 1908, caja 0683, exp. 119513.

74 TSJDF, sXX, 1911, caja 1078, exp. 191429.

75 French, *Heart in the Glass Jar,* 252.

76 French, *Heart in the Glass Jar,* 84.

Chapter 4. Being Together

1 Federal agencies recorded that in Mexico City, between 1900 and 1905, for example, 33–40 percent of births were illegitimate. Similarly, in 1900, when the city's population hovered at around 540,000 residents, only 1,500 marriages were registered that year. See Direción General de Estadísticas, *Estadísticas sociales del Porfiriato, 1877–1910* (Ciudad de México: Secretaría de Economía, 1956), 1, 20–21, 30.

2 Robert McCaa, "Marriageways in Mexico and Spain, 1500–1900," *Continuity and Change* 9, no. 1 (1994): 30.

3 Navarro, *La vida social,* 16–17, 410.

4 Sloan, *Runaway Daughters,* 170.

5 García Peña, *El fracaso del amor,* 18–19. On how the elimination of colonial era protections affected women, see Dore, "One Step Forward, Two Steps Back," 22–25.

6 French, *Heart in the Glass Jar,* 64–65.

7 Komisaruk, *Labor and Love,* 210.

8 TSJDF, sXX, 1908, caja 0879, exp. 152003.

9 TSJDF, sXX, 1908, caja 0693, exp. 122071.

10 TSJDF, sXX, 1910, caja 0964, exp. 169471.

11 TSJDF, sXX, 1910, caja 0966, exp. 170508.

12 TSJCM, sXIX, 1888, leg. 88589, caja 1092.

13 Arrom, "Changes in Mexican Family Law," 95; García Peña, *El fracaso del amor.*

14 A similar claim is made for nineteenth-century working-class couples in France. See Farge, *Fragile Lives,* 22–23.

15 TSJDF, sXX, 1901, caja 0073, exp. 016186.

16 In 58 of 234 (24.8 percent) cases, women specifically noted *mala vida* at home, to either authorities or their partners, as their reason for running away.

17 Sloan, *Runaway Daughters,* 170; Findlay, "Courtroom Tales of Sex and Honor," 207.

18 TSJCM, sXIX, 1889, leg. 142371, caja 1152.

19 TSJDF, sXX, 1904, caja 0305, exp. 055380.

20 TSJDF, sXX, 1910, caja 1010, exp. 179620.

21 See, for example, French, *Heart in the Glass Jar,* 65.

22 *El Faro,* February 13, 1906.

23 Navarro, *La vida social,* 410.

24 Indeed, as Robert McCaa notes for nineteenth-century Mexico: "Rising illegitimacy rates testify to the many who wagered their sex in a mating game whose prize was more likely a child than a spouse." See "The Peopling of 19th century Mexico: Critical scrutiny of a censured century," *Statistical Abstract of Latin America* vol. 30 (1993): 10.

25 TSJDF, sXX, 1904, caja 0348, exp. 063229.

26 TSJCM, sXIX, 1889, leg. 129474, caja 1145.

27 TSJCM, sXIX, 1888, leg. 88998, caja 1093.

28 *Código Penal para el Distrito Federal,* Art. 816.

29 TSJCM, sXIX, 1893, leg. 180847, caja 1354.

30 TSJDF, sXX, 1906, caja 0550, exp. 096602.

31 TSJDF, sXX, 1905, caja 0376, exp. 066663.

32 Silvia M. Arrom asks whether poor families relied on kinship networks as readily as elite groups. This case provides an example of how they did. See "Historia de la mujer y de la familia latinoamericanas," *Historia Mexicana* 42, no. 2 (1992): 396.

33 TSJCM, sXIX, 1888, leg. 88730, caja 1095.

34 TSJDF, sXX, 1909, caja 0879, exp. 152091.

35 TSJDF, sXX, 1906, caja 0468, exp. 083245.

36 Arrom, *Women of Mexico City,* 250–256; Navarro, *La vida social,* 411, García Peña, *El fracaso del amor,* 72–73. It was not until 1915 that divorced people could remarry. See Stephanie Smith, "'If Love Enslaves . . . Love Be Damned!': Divorce and Revolutionary State Formation in the Yucatán," in *Gender, Politics, and Power in Modern Mexico,* edited by Jocelyn Olcott, Mary Kay Vaughan, and Gabriela Cano (Durham: Duke University Press, 2006), 101–102.

37 Lear, *Workers, Neighbors, and Citizens,* 79–80. For a similar discussion in different nineteenth-century Latin American urban environments see Abreu Esteves, *Meninas perdidas,* 190 and Komisaruk, *Labor and Love,* 205–206, 210.

38 Vaughan, "Women, Class, and Education," 140.

39 Navarro, *La vida social,* 410.

40 French, *Heart in the Glass Jar,* 64.

41 TSJDF, sXX, 1906, caja 0477, exp. 085740.

42 *El Diario,* January 6, 1909.

43 *El Faro,* March 15, 1906.

44 *El Faro,* February 13, 1906.

45 TSJCM, sXIX, 1889, leg. 111533, caja 1150.

46 *La Guacamaya,* June 22, 1905.

47 *La Guacamaya,* October 11, 1906.

48 Arrom, *Women of Mexico City,* 71.

49 French, *Heart in the Glass Jar,* 35.

50 TSJCM, sXIX, 1889, leg. 142371, caja 1152.

51 TSJCM, sXIX, 1896, leg. 1039597, caja 1473.

52 Ann Twinam, *Public Lives, Private Secrets,* 39; Lipsett-Rivera, *Origins of Macho,* 57.

53 TSJCM, sXIX, 1889, leg. 114303, caja 1145.

54 TSJDF, sXX, 1902, caja 0152, exp. 025435.

55 A similar phenomenon is discussed for the colonial period in Boyer, *Lives of the Bigamists,* 4–6. Boyer notes how itinerancy allowed some men the opportunity to make a "new life," which could include a bigamist marriage.

56 TSJCM, sXIX, 1889, leg. 134264, caja 1150.

57 TSJCM, sXIX, 1893, leg. 180824, caja 1354.

58 TSJDF, sXX, 1909, caja 0878, exp. 151930.

59 *Código Civil del Distrito Federal y Territorio de la Baja California,* Título V, Capítulo I, Art. 161 (1870).

60 TSJDF, sXX, 1901, caja 0088, exp. 013901.

61 Navarro, *La vida social,* 411–412.

62 A similar conclusion is reached by Eileen Findlay in her examination of late-nineteenth-century Puerto Rico. See "Courtroom Tales of Sex and Honor," 207.

63 TSJCM, sXIX, 1891, leg. 143539, caja 1249.

64 Peiss, *Cheap Amusements;* Joanne Meyerowitz, *Women Adrift: Independent Wage Earners in Chicago, 1880–1930* (Chicago: University of Chicago Press, 1988); Ruth Alexander, *The Girl Problem: Female Sexual Delinquency in New York, 1900–1930* (Ithaca: Cornell University Press, 1995); Mary Oden, *Delinquent Daughters: Protecting and Policing Adolescent Female Sexuality, 1885–1920* (Chapel Hill: University of North Carolina Press, 1995).

65 TSJDF, sXX, 1904, caja 0306, exp. 054624.

66 Sloan, *Runaway Daughters,* 47.

67 TSJCM, sXIX, 1888, leg. 83712, caja 1092.

68 TSJDF, sXX, 1907, caja 0597, exp. 105681.

69 TSJCM, sXIX, 1891, leg. 143540, caja 1249.

70 TSJCM, sXIX, 1898, leg. 260298, caja 1541.

71 TSJDF, sXX, 1907, caja 0586, exp. 103098.

72 Families dropping charges after a promise of marriage represented the second most common outcome: 56 of 234 cases (24 percent).

73 TSJDF, sXX, 1904, caja 0327, exp. 057342.

74 TSJDF, sXX, 1907, caja 0586, exp. 103118.

75 Komisaruk, *Labor and Love,* 221.

76 See *The Famous 41,* edited by McKee Irwin, McCaughan, and Nasser.

77 Buffington, "Homophobia and the Mexican Working Class," 194–195. Buffington shows that middle-class periodicals invoked a homosexual panic that intended to reinforce heteronormativity. The penny press used homosexuality to challenge bourgeois social control by contrasting their effeminate masculinity to working-class patriotism and manliness.

78 Pablo Piccato, "Interpretations of Sexuality in Mexico City Prisons: A Critical Ver-

sion of Roumagnac," in *The Famous 41*, edited by McKee Irwin, McCaughan, and Nasser. 252–253; Buffington, *Criminal and Citizen*, 130–140; Carlos Rougmanac, *Los criminales en Mexico: Ensayo de psicología criminal* (Ciudad de México: Tipografía El Fénix, 1904). Carlos Roumagnac, *Crímenes sexuales y pasionales: Estudio de psicología morbosa* (Ciudad de México: Librería de Ch. Bouret, 1906). Carlos Roumagnac, *Matadores de mujeres* (Ciudad de México: Librería de Ch. Bouret, 1910).

79 *El Colmillo Público*, June 24, 1907.

80 See, for example, *La Guacamaya*, April 25, 1901.

81 Françoise Barret-Ducrocq, *Love in the Time of Victoria: Sexuality and Desire among Working-Class Men and Women in Nineteenth-Century London*, translated by John Howe (New York: Penguin Books, 1992), 64.

Chapter 5. Using Sex

1 Lear, *Workers, Neighbors, and Citizens*, 95–96; Blum, *Domestic Economies*, 86–87; French, *A Peaceful and Working People*, 78–80; Buffington, *Criminal and Citizen*, 75–77; Piccato, *City of Suspects*, 58–60; Rodney Anderson, *Outcasts in their Own Land: Mexican Industrial Workers, 1906–1911* (DeKalb: Northern Illinois University Press, 1976), 45–46.

2 Stern, *Secret History*, 93; For a discussion of the motivations that caused young men and women to run away in the colonial period, see Boyer, *Lives of the Bigamists*, 54, 133–134.

3 Lear, *Workers, Neighbors, and Citizens*, 76; Porter, *Working Women in Mexico City*, 64.

4 TSJCM, sXIX, 1895, leg. 206452, caja 1434.

5 TSJDF, sXX, 1905, caja 0377, exp. 066883.

6 Martínez-Alier makes this claim for nineteenth-century Cuba, although in contrast to Mexico City, she details a high value of virginity among both the white and black population. See *Marriage, Class and Colour*, 110–113.

7 TSJDF, sXX, 1905, caja 0372, exp. 064817.

8 Padilla, et al., "Cross-Cultural Reflections on an Intimate Intersection," xv.

9 García Peña details how marriage in nineteenth-century Mexico, especially the entrenched divide between the public and private sphere and the strengthening of male authority in the household, furthered domestic violence against women who asserted public, financial, or sexual independence. See *El fracaso del amor*, 55, 66–70.

10 Condesa de Tramar, *El amor obligatorio*, 26; Stevens, *Mexico in the Time of Cholera*, 209.

11 TSJCM, sXIX, 1885, leg. 53966, caja 941.

12 TSJCM, sXIX, 1893, leg. 180876, caja 1354.

13 TSJCM, sXIX, 1885, leg. 53962, caja 941.

14 TSJCM, sXIX, 1898, leg. 260302, caja 1541.

15 TSJCM, sXIX, 1889, leg. 132080, caja 1151.

16 TSJDF, sXX, 1905, caja 0382, exp. 069142.

17 Porter, *Working Women in Mexico City,* 30–31.

18 TSJDF, sXX, 1900, caja 0042, exp. 011068.

19 TSJCM, sXIX, 1888, leg. 88588, caja 1092.

20 TSJCM, sXIX, 1889, leg. 142363, caja 1152.

21 TSJCM, sXIX, 1898, leg. 260304, caja 1541.

22 For a discussion of female-headed households in colonial Mexico City see Stern, *Secret History,* 262. Abreu Esteves finds a similar dynamic in belle époque Rio de Janeiro, see *Meninas perdidas,* 137. For a broader discussion of female-headed households in Latin America, see Dore, "The Holy Family."

23 TSJDF, sXX, 1900, caja 0020, exp. 002292.

24 The term "*mala vida*" has long been used in Mexico, dating back to colonial times. See, for example, Richard Boyer, "Women, *La Mala Vida,* and the Politics of Marriage," in *Sexuality and Marriage in Colonial Latin America,* edited by Lavrin. 252–286.

25 Soledad González Montes and Pilar Iracheta Cenegorta, "La violencia en la vida de las mujeres campesinas: El Distrito de Tenango, 1880–1910," in *Presencia y transparencia: La mujer en la historia de México,* edited by Carmen Ramos Escandón (Ciudad de México: Colegio de México, 1992), 126.

26 In one-quarter of the cases examined in this study, women noted their *mala vida* as the primary reason they ran away. Similarly, in her examination of late nineteenth-century Puerto Rico, Eileen Findlay found that in 35 percent of the rapto cases she studied, women noted family violence as the reason they eloped. See "Courtroom Tales of Sex and Honor," 210.

27 Findlay, "Courtroom Tales of Sex and Honor," 209.

28 TSJCM, sXIX, 1889, leg. 114303, caja 1145.

29 Montes and Cenegorta, "La violencia en la vida de las mujeres campesinas," 126.

30 TSJCM, sXIX, 1898, leg. 260301, caja 1541.

31 TSJDF, sXX, 1907, caja 0568, exp. 096799.

32 On the tensions between stepmothers, economic precarity, and child abuse, see Robert Darton, *The Great Cat Massacre and Other Episodes in French Cultural History* (New York: Vintage Books, 1984), 341–342. In the eleven cases where stepparents are mentioned in the case file, ten of those reported abuse or unwanted sexual attention (exclusively by stepfathers).

33 TSJCM, sXIX, 1890, leg. 150499, caja 1193.

34 TSJCM, sXIX, 1889, leg. 132109, caja 1145.

35 TSJCM, sXIX, 1893, leg. 180875, caja 1354.

36 TSJDF, sXX, 1902, caja 0132, exp. 023515.

37 TSJCM, sXIX, 1885, leg. 53997, caja 941.

38 TSJCM, sXIX, 1889, leg. 132116, caja 1145.

39 TSJCM, sXIX, 1889, leg. 119571, caja 1148.

40 García Peña, *El fracaso del amor,* 214.

41 *The Mexican Herald,* November 4, 1906, September 29, 1909; *El Popular,* February 26, 1907; *El Diario,* August 23, 1909; *La Patria,* September 15, 1909.

42 *El Tiempo,* March 7, 1885.

43 TSJDF, sXX, 1910, caja 0935, exp. 163612.

44 Gamboa, *Santa*.

45 TSJDF, sXX, 1906, caja 0506, exp. 088739.

46 García Peña, *El fracaso del amor,* 220–221.

47 Bliss, *Compromised Positions,* 33. A similar claim is made about women in colonial Mexico City. See Stern, *Secret History,* 261.

48 TSJDF, sXX, 1908, caja 0690, exp. 121689.

49 Lara y Pardo, *La prostitución en México,* 108–113.

50 Barret-Ducrocq makes this claim about working-class girls in Victorian London. See *Love in the Time of Victoria,* 73.

51 Stern outlines this practice in colonial Mexico City. See *Secret History,* 261. And, as has been argued for ancien régime France, the line between accepting gifts and money from a sexual partner, on the one hand, and prostitution, on the other, was difficult to discern. See Hardwick, *Sex in an Old Regime City,* 63.

52 Stansell, *City of Women,* 172.

53 On nineteenth-century abortion practice and its criminalization in Mexico see Jaffary, *Reproduction and Its Discontents,* 84–87, 89–91.

54 TSJDF, sXX, 1900, caja 0020, exp. 003238.

55 On the classist inequalities of the Porfirian justice system, see Garza, *Imagined Underworld,* 159–161; Buffington, *Criminal and Citizen,* 53–54.

56 TSJCM, sXIX, 1889, leg. 132099, caja 1151.

57 TSJCM, sXIX, 1888, leg. 88591, caja 1092.

58 Bliss, *Compromised Positions,* 38–39; Porter, *Working Women in Mexico City,* 64.

59 TSJCM, sXIX, 1888, leg. 88592, caja 1092.

60 Nicole Sanders highlights how Porfirian advertising commodified female sexuality while social reformers promoted middle-class domesticity as the ideal for women as citizens and consumers. See "Gender and Consumption," 12–13.

61 Peiss, *Cheap Amusements,* 110.

62 TSJDF, sXX, 1900, caja 0030, exp. 002293.

63 Porter, *Working Women in Mexico City,* 64; Lara y Pardo, *La prostitución en México,* 108–113.

64 Bliss, *Compromised Positions,* 33–34.

65 Buffington, *Sentimental Education,* 9.

66 Condesa de Tramar, *El amor obligatorio,* 198.

67 *Don Cucufate,* August 20, 1906.

68 For a discussion of Don Juan and *tenorios del barrio,* see Buffington, *Sentimental Education,* 170–173.

69 *Don Cucufate,* August 27, 1906.

70 *El Chile Piquín,* January 19, 1905.

71 Buffington, *Sentimental* Education, 174.

72 *La Guacamaya,* August 6, 1908.

73 Lipsett-Rivera, *Origins of Macho,* 52–53; Arrom, *Women of Mexico City,* chapter 2.

74 TSJDF, sXX, 1905, caja 0375, exp. 066510.

75 See, for example, Arrom, *Women of Mexico City,* 64–66; Sloan, *Runaway Daughters,* 35; French, *Heart in the Glass Jar,* 30–31; Bliss, *Compromised Positions,* 28, 46.

76 The culture of "treating" is examined in turn-of-the-century New York where working-class "charity girls" traded sexual favors for male attention, gifts, and various forms of adventure. See Peiss, *Cheap Amusements,* 107–111.

77 TSJDF, sXX, 1902, caja 0152, exp. 025420.

78 Barret-Ducrocq, *Love in the Time of Victoria,* 64.

Chapter 6. Shameless Love

1 Lavrin, "Introduction," 10; Patricia Seed, *To Love, Honor, and Obey,* 64; Komisaruk, *Labor and Love,* 206.

2 For an examination of middle- and upper-class courtship in mid-nineteenth-century Mexico, as well as how it was shaped by literary culture, see Stevens, *Mexico in the Time of Cholera.*

3 Condesa de Tramar, *El amor obligatorio,* 170–189; Manuel Antonio Carreño, *Manual de urbanidad y buenas maneras de la juventud de ambos sexos* (New York: D. Appleton and Company, 1894). For more on the popularity of Carreño's self-improvement manual in Porfirian Mexico, see Víctor M. Macías-González, "*Hombres del mundo:* La masculinidad, el consume, y los manuals de urbanidad y buenas maneras," in *Orden social e identidad de género. México, siglos XIX y XX,* edited by María Teresa Fernández Aceves, Carmen Ramos Escandón, and Susie Porter (Ciudad de México: CIESAS/Universidad de Guadalajara, 2006), 267–297.

4 Charles Macomb Flandrau, *Viva Mexico!* (New York: D. Appleton and Company, 1908), 90.

5 Blake and Sullivan, *Mexico: Picturesque, Political, Progressive,* 61; Thomas L. Rodgers, *Mexico? Si, Señor* (Boston: Mexican Central Railway Company, 1894), 138–139; Thomas Unett Brocklehurst, *Mexico To-Day: A Country with a Great Future* (London: John Murray, 1883), 199; J.H. Bates, *Notes on a Tour in Mexico and California* (New York: Burr Printing House, 1887), 64; William Henry Bishop, *Old Mexico and Her Lost Provinces* (New York: Harper & Brothers, 1883), 110; J.R. Flippin, *Sketches from the Mountains of Mexico* (Cincinnati: Standard Publishing Company, 1889), 256–257, 280–282; Barrett, *The Standard Guide to the City of Mexico and Vicinity,* 39; A. Gringo, *Through the Land of the Aztecs* (London: Sampson Low, Marston & Company, 1892), 74–75.

6 Flippin, *Sketches,* 281–282.

7 Rodgers, *Mexico?,* 139; Gringo, *Through the Land of the Aztecs,* 74.

8 Rodgers, *Mexico?,* 138.

9 Gringo, *Through the Land of the Aztecs,* 75; Brocklehurst, *Mexico To-Day,* 199; Chambers Gooch, *Face to Face with the Mexicans,* 278–280.

10 In his classic study, *The Civilizing Process,* Norbert Elias noted that in the transition from feudalism to the modern era in European society, personal behaviors related to etiquette, bodily propriety, and living conditions were central to middle-class attempts to create new social practices opposed to the Middle Ages as well as to dis-

tinguish themselves from the lower orders. See Norbert Elias, *The Civilizing Process: Sociogenetic and Psychogenetic Investigations,* translated by Edmund Jephcott, rev. ed. (Malden: Blackwell, 2000), 180–182, 189, 307. For a further discussion of how bourgeois civilizing sensibilities aimed to differentiate social class and instill their social superiority in Western Europe and the United States, see Peter Gay, *The Bourgeois Experience: Victoria to Freud. Vol. 1, Education of the Senses* (Oxford: Oxford University Press, 1984) and *The Bourgeois Experience: Victoria to Freud. Vol. 2, The Tender Passion* (Oxford: Oxford University Press, 1986).

11 There is considerable literature on this for both the colonial and modern eras. See, for example, Lavrin, "Introduction," 10; Gutiérrez, *"When Jesus Came,"* 209–226; Seed, *To Love, Honor, and Obey,* 157; Piccato, *Tyranny of Opinion,* 12; Putnam, Chambers, and Caulfield, "Introduction," 3.

12 Flores, *El hímen en México;* Also, Jaffary argues that by the late-nineteenth century, women from all classes showed greater concern for the preservation of female virginity and the defense of sexual virtue. The 234 cases from Mexico City and its surrounding municipalities examined in this study contradict that claim. See *Reproduction and Its Discontents,* 36–37, 132.

13 Caulfield, *In Defense of Honor,* 14. Even this claim is difficult to uphold because it proves a challenge to determine how much investigating judges and their scribes shaped plebian testimony, whether denying them the language of honor or superimposing their own vocabulary into the legal record.

14 Sloan, *Runaway Daughters,* 2–3, 38, 176; Blum, *Domestic Economies,* 30; Abreu Esteves, *Meninas perdidas,* 118, 131, 166.

15 Anthony Giddens, *Modernity and Self-Identity: Self and Society in the Late Modern Age* (Stanford: Stanford University Press, 1991), 54.

16 For a discussion of the authenticity of judicial depositions and how scribes, notaries, and judicial authorities filtered testimony, see Farge, *Allure of the Archives,* 29; Kathryn Burns, *Into the Archive: Writing and Power in Colonial Peru* (Durham: Duke University Press, 2010), 34; Tortorici, *Sins against Nature,* 14–15.

17 Abreu Esteves, *Meninas perdidas,* 199; Tebbutt, *Women's Talk?,* 77, 149.

18 Elizbeth Dore demonstrates how poor female-headed households differed significantly from the patriarchal models set by the elite. See "The Holy Family," 111–114.

19 James Scott, *Domination and the Arts of Resistance: Hidden Transcripts* (New Haven: Yale University Press, 1990), 158.

20 TSJCM, sXIX, 1888, leg. 88591, caja 1092.

21 TSJCM, sXIX, 1889, leg. 132111, caja 1145.

22 TSJCM, sXIX, 1889, leg. 132099, caja 1151.

23 TSJDF, sXX, 1908, caja 0699, exp. 123594.

24 TSJDF, sXX, 1903, caja 0276, exp. 044654.

25 TSJDF, sXX, 1907 caja 0666, exp. 117269.

26 TSJDF, sXX, 1910, caja 0935, exp. 163612.

27 TSJDF, sXX, 1906, caja 0537, exp. 094311.

28 TSJCM, sXIX, 1888, leg. 88998, caja 1093.

29 TSJDF, sXX, 1910, caja 0953, exp. 167624.

30 TSJCM, sXIX, 1893, leg. 180838, caja 1354.

31 TSJDF, sXX, 1902, caja 0152, exp. 025435.

32 TSJCM, sXIX, 1891, leg. 143541, caja 1249.

33 TSJCM, sXIX, 1889, leg. 119568, caja 1148. As has been noted, working woman made claims to honor and dignity as workers and not as "repositories of sexual morality." See Porter, *Working Women in Mexico City*, 132.

34 TSJDF, sXX, 1904, caja 0369, exp. 066380.

35 TSJDF, sXX, 1906, caja 0477, exp. 085740.

36 French, *A Peaceful and Working People*, 84–85.

37 Of the 234 cases examined in this study, I have identified twenty cases where both litigants were distinctly members of the middle or upper class. Admittedly an imperfect science, a variety of indicators were used to determine social rank such as: residential address, dwelling type, level of literacy, employment, salary, clothing, and use of the honorific title "don" or "doña."

38 *Diario del Hogar*, September 1, 1896.

39 See, for example, *El Imparcial*, August 11, 1898; *El Cómico*, January 20, 1901.

40 *El Nacional*, April 23, 1898.

41 Piccato, *Tyranny of Opinion*, 15–16, 226–228.

42 *La Araña*, August 24, 1905.

43 *El Papagayo*, August 7, 1904.

44 *La Guacamaya*, January 18, 1906.

45 See, for example, *Hijo del Fandango*, September 9, 1901.

46 TSJCM, sXIX, 1888, leg. 88589, caja 1092.

47 TSJCM, sXIX, 1898, leg. 260298, caja 1541.

48 TSJDF, sXX, 1901, caja 0097, exp. 019183.

49 TSJDF, sXX, 1906, caja 0482, exp. 084727.

50 TSJCM, sXIX, 1894, leg. 196578, caja 1394.

51 TSJDF, sXX, 1902, caja 0205, exp. 037533.

52 TSJDF, sXX, 1905, caja 0377, exp. 066883.

53 William French found twelve cases from Parral, Chihuahua where men explicitly cited that sex had failed to show bodily proof of virginity as a justification to not marry. See French, *Heart in the Glass Jar*, 61.

54 These numbers stand in sharp contrast to late nineteenth-century Puerto Rico where Eileen Findlay finds that the majority of men arrested for rapto claimed that their lovers were virgins. See Findlay, "Courtroom Tales of Sex and Honor," 209.

55 TSJCM, sXIX, 1888, leg. 88588, caja 1092.

56 TSJCM, sXIX, 1898, leg. 260304, caja 1541.

57 TSJCM, sXIX, 1889, leg. 111533, caja 1150.

58 TSJCM, sXIX, 1889, leg. 111535, caja 1050.

59 TSJDF, sXX, 1902, caja 0132, exp. 023518.

60 TSJDF, sXX, 1903, caja 0264, exp. 047381.

61 TSJDF, sXX, 1904, caja 0369, exp. 066380.

62 TSJDF, sXX, 1909, caja 0878, exp. 151930.

63 TSJCM, sXIX, 1898, leg. 260277, caja 1541.

64 TSJDF, sXX, 1900, caja 0049, exp. 008752.

65 TSJCM, sXIX, 1898, leg. 260270, caja 1541.

66 TSJDF, sXX, 1905, caja 0393, exp 068460.

67 TSJDF, sXX, 1909, caja 0879, exp. 152003.

68 TSJDF, sXX, 1902, caja 0185, exp. 034240

69 TSJCM, sXIX, 1893, leg. 180873, caja 1354.

70 TSJCM, sXIX, 1898, leg. 260277, caja 1541.

71 TSJCM, sXIX, 1895, leg. 206453, caja 1434.

72 Tebbutt, *Women's Talk?*, 148.

73 TSJDF, sXX, 1906, caja 0468, exp. 083245.

74 TSJDF, sXX, 1909, caja 0846, exp. 149797.

75 TSJDF, sXX, 1908, caja 0690, exp. 121699.

76 TSJDF, sXX, 1908, caja 0693, exp. 122077.

77 Stevens, *Mexico in the Time of Cholera*, 209, 220.

78 TSJCM, sXIX, 1898, leg. 260280, caja 1541.

79 TSJDF, sXX, 1907, caja 0586, exp. 103285.

80 TSJDF, sXX, 1904, caja 0345, exp. 062329.

81 TSJDF, sXX, 1910, caja 0958, exp. 168428.

82 TSJDF, sXX, 1902, caja 0132, exp. 023515.

83 TSJDF, sXX, 1908, caja 0693, exp. 122077.

84 Flores, *El hímen en México*, 65.

85 *Código Penal para el Distrito Federal*, Art. 793.

86 *Código Penal para el Distrito Federal*, p. 59.

87 TSJDF, sXX, 1908, caja 0693, exp. 122071.

88 TSJCM, sXIX, 1898, leg. 260302, caja 1541.

89 TSJDF, sXX, 1907, caja 0577, exp. 100016.

90 TSJDF, sXX, 1906, caja 0532, exp. 093573.

91 TSJCM, sXIX, 1893, leg. 180859, caja 1354.

92 Sonya Lipsett-Rivera notes that wearing a shawl was a sign of sexual modesty. That Gala took the time to mention why she did not bring it suggests that she worried about the assumption the judge might make about her lack of virtue, going into public without one. See *Gender and the Negotiation of Daily Life in Mexico*, 224.

93 TSJDF, sXX, 1905, caja 0376, exp. 066792.

94 TSJDF, sXX, 1905, caja 0376, exp. 066680.

95 This has been demonstrated in various contexts. For the colonial era, see Twinam, "Honor, Sexuality, and Illegitimacy," 147. For twentieth-century Brazil, see Caulfield, "The Changing Politics of Freedom and Virginity," 231. For Porfirian Chihuahua, see French, *Heart in the Glass Jar*, 61.

96 Buffington, *Sentimental Education*, 26–27.

97 Buffington, *Sentimental Education*, 184–185.

98 *Don Cucufate*, September 3, 1906.

99 *El Diablito Bromista*, July 14, 1907.

100 *La Guacamaya*, October 1, 1903.

101 *La Guacamaya,* November 27, 1902.

102 *La Guacamaya,* April 21, 1905.

103 *La Guacamaya,* February 15, 1906.

104 Buffington, *Sentimental Education,* 26–34.

105 Richard Terdiman, *Discourse/Counter-Discourse: The Theory and Practice of Symbolic Resistance in Nineteenth-Century France* (Ithaca: Cornell University Press, 1989), 149–150.

106 *La Guacamaya,* June 14, 1904.

107 TSJCM, sXIX, 1893, leg. 180854, caja 1354.

108 TSJCM, sXIX, 1889, leg. 121891, caja 1147.

109 William French finds a similar phenomenon. See *Heart in the Glass Jar,* 59.

110 TSJDF, sXX, 1903, caja 0264, exp. 047381.

111 TSJDF, sXX, 1907, caja 0588, exp. 103641.

112 *El Chile Piquín,* January 12, 1905.

113 *El Chile Piquín,* January 19, 1905.

114 For example, *La Guacamaya,* September 3, 1903.

115 *La Guacamaya,* January 28, 1904.

116 Buffington, *Sentimental Education,* 184.

117 *El Pinche,* July 21, 1904.

118 Buffington, *Sentimental Education,* 184–185.

119 *El Diablito Bromista,* November 17, 1907

120 Medical exams of the hymen most often categorized deflowering as recent (*reciente*), not recent (*no es reciente*), or old (*antigua*). TSJDF, sXX, 1902, caja 0150, exp. 023968.

121 Buffington, *Sentimental Education,* 167–168; Giddens, *Modernity and Self-Identity,* 54, 70.

122 Hubert L. Dreyfus, *Being-in-the-World: A Commentary on Heidegger's* Being and Time, *Division I* (Cambridge: MIT Press, 1990). 26–27.

123 Martin Heidegger, *Being and Time,* translated by John Macquarrie and Edward Robinson (New York: Harper Perennial/Modern Thought, 2008), 312–317; Michael Gelven, *A Commentary on Heidegger's "Being and Time:" A Section-by-Section Interpretation* (New York: Harper & Row, 1970), 160–166.

124 Heidegger, *Being and Time,* 165.

Conclusion

1 Barret-Ducrocq, *Love in the Time of Victoria,* 183.

2 In *Wayward Lives, Beautiful Experiments: Intimate Histories of Social Upheaval* (New York: W.W. Norton & Company, 2019), Saidiya Hartman examines the lives of Black women and girls that, while constrained by white supremacy and poverty in New York and Philadelphia, were characterized by their refusal and opposition—through everyday acts of living—to behave in ways expected of them. In so doing, Hartman lays bare the ways that marginalized lives come to be seen as deviant and dysfunctional according to hegemonic norms.

3 Abreu Esteves, *Meninas perdidas,* 205.

4 See, for example, Putnam, Chambers, and Caulfield, "Introduction," 13. The authors argue: "Sexual morality mattered to [working-class] women, for their personal and family status depended on it . . . virginity was basic to female marriageability." Similarly, Nora Jaffary has argued: "In [Porfirian Mexico] the pressure for plebian women to adhere to the mores of sexual purity that had earlier been more strongly represented in elite classes increased" and "By the late nineteenth century, the public reputation of sexual honor had become more imperative for woman of *all* social classes [my emphasis]." See *Reproduction and Its Discontents,* 37, 132.

5 Anthony Giddens, *The Transformation of Intimacy: Sexuality, Love & Eroticism in Modern Societies* (Stanford: Stanford University Press, 1992).

6 Lawrence Stone, *The Family, Sex and Marriage in England 1500–1800* (New York: Harper Perennial, 1983). 417.

7 D'Emilio and Freedman, *Intimate Matters,* 302–305. The authors discuss the influence of Hugh Hefner and Helen Gurley Brown on shaping the sexual revolution.

8 Olga Lorena Rojas, *Hombres y relaciones de género en México* (Ciudad de México: El Colegio de México, 2022), 34–41; María Lucero Jiménez Guzmán, "Sexualidad, vida conyugal y relaciones de pareja. Experiencias de algunos varones de los sectores medio y alto de México," in *Sucede que me canso de ser hombre . . . Relatos y reflexiones sobre hombres y masculinidades en México,* edited by Ana Amuchástegui and Ivonne Szasz (Ciudad de México: El Colegio de México, 2007), 233; Catherine Menkes and Leticia Suárez, "Prácticas sexuales y reproductivas de las jóvenes en México," in *Los jóovenes ante el siglo XXI,* edited by Emma Liliana Navarrete López (Ciudad de México: El Colegio Mexiquense, 2004), 24; Noemí Ehrenfeld Lenkiewicz, "Un mosaico de experiencias: Embarazo y maternidad en adolescentes urbano-marginales," in *Los jóvenes ante el siglo XXI,* 48, 62; Patricio Solís, Cecilia Gayet, and Fátima Juárez, "Las transiciones a la vida sexual, a la unión y a la maternidad en Mexico: Cambios en el tiempo y estratificación social," in *Salud reproductiva y condiciones de vida en México,* vol. I, edited by Susana Lerner and Ivonne Szasz (Ciudad de México: El Colegio de México, 2008), 400, 417; Ivonne Szasz, "Relaciones de género y desigualdad socioeconómica en la construcción social de las normas sobre la sexualidad en México," in *Salud reproductiva y condiciones de vida en México,* vol. I, 443–456.

9 Rojas, *Hombres y relaciones de género,* 48–49; Jiménez Guzmán, "Sexualidad, vida conyugal y relaciones de pareja," 207; Ivonne Szasz, "Sexualidad y género: Algunas experiencias de investigación en México," *Debate Feminista* 18 (1998): 80–81; Solís, Gayet, and Juárez, "Las transiciones a la vida sexual," 417; Szasz, "Relaciones de género y desigualdad socioeconómica," 438, 467.

10 María Eugenia Mídena and Zuanilda Mendoza, *Géneros y generaciones: Etnografía de las relaciones entre hombre y mujeres de la Ciudad de México* (Ciudad de México: EDAMEX, 2001), 55–62; Navarrete López, *Los jóvenes ante el siglo XXI,* 48, 62.

11 Ivonne Szasz, "Relaciones de género y desigualdad socioeconómica," 457–467. See, also, Ana Amuchástegui Herrera, "Virginidad e iniciación sexual en México: la so-

brevivencia de saberes sexuales subyugados frente a la modernidad," *Debate Feminista* 18 (1998): 131–151.

12 Daniel Nehring, "Negotiated Familism: Intimate Life and Individualization Among Young Female Professionals from Mexico City," *Canadian Journal of Latin American and Caribbean Studies/ Revue canadienne des études latino-américaines et caraïbes* 36, no. 71 (2011): 165–196.

13 Gutmann, *The Meanings of Macho*, 133; Rojas, *Hombres y relaciones de género*, 46; Solís, Gayet, and Juárez, "Las transiciones a la vida sexual," 400; Szasz, "Relaciones de género y desigualdad socioeconómica," 445–447.

14 Dore, "One Step Forward, Two Steps Back," 25–26.

REFERENCES

Archives and Libraries

Archivo General de la Nación (AGN), Ciudad de México, México
Archivo del Tribunal Superior de Justicia de la Ciudad de México, Archivo General de la Nación
Archivo del Tribunal Superior de Justicia del Distrito Federal, Archivo General de la Nación
Archivo Histórico del Distrito Federal (AHDF), Ciudad de México, México
Gobierno del Distrito, Archivo Histórico del Distrito Federal
Municipalidades, Archivo Histórico del Distrito Federal
University of Texas, Austin, Texas, United States of America
Benson Latin American Collection, Texas, United States of America
Biblioteca Miguel Lerdo de Tejada, Ciudad de México, México
Universidad Autónoma de México, Ciudad de México, México
Hemeroteca Nacional, Ciudad de México, México
Instituto de Investigaciones Dr. José María Luis Mora, Ciudad de México, México
Biblioteca "Ernesto de la Torre Villar," Instituto de Investigaciones Dr. José María Luis Mora
Proyecto de Historia Oral, Instituto de Investigaciones Dr. José María Luis Mora

Periodicals

Diario del Hogar
Don Cucufate
El Chango
El Chile Piquín
El Colmillo Público
El Diablito Bromista
El Diario
El Faro
El Mundo Ilustrado
El Papagayo
El Pinche

El Popular
El Tiempo
Hijo del Fandango
La Araña
La Familia
La Guacamaya
La Patria
Nacional
The Mexican Herald

Secondary Sources

Abreu Esteves, Martha. *Meninas perdidas: Os populares e o cotidiano do amor no Rio De Janeiro da belle époque*. Rio de Janeiro: Paz e Terra, 1989.

Agostoni, Claudia. *Monuments of Progress: Modernization and Public Health in Mexico, 1876–1910*. Calgary: University of Calgary Press, 2003.

Agostoni, Claudia. "Discurso médico, cultura higiénica y la mujer en la Ciudad de México al cambio de siglo (XIX-XX)," *Mexican Studies/Estudios Mexicanos* 18, no. 1 (2002): 1–22.

Aguirre, Carlos, and Ricardo D. Salvatore. "Writing the History of Law, Crime, and Punishment in Latin America." In *Crime and Punishment in Latin America: Law and Society since Late Colonial Times,* edited by Ricardo D. Salvatore, Carlos Aguirre, and Gilbert M. Joseph. Durham: Duke University Press, 2001.

Aguirre, Carlos A., and Robert Buffington (eds.) *Reconstructing Criminality in Latin America*. Wilmington: Scholarly Resources, 2000.

Alexander, Anna Rose. *City on Fire: Technology, Social Change, and the Hazards of Progress in Mexico City, 1860–1910*. Pittsburgh: University of Pittsburgh Press, 2016.

Alexander, Ruth. *The Girl Problem: Female Sexual Delinquency in New York, 1900–1930*. Ithaca: Cornell University Press, 1995.

Amuchástegui Herrera, Ana. "Virgindad e iniciación sexual en México: La sobrevivencia de saberes sexuales subyugados frente a la modernidad," *Debate Feminista* 18 (1998): 131–151.

Anderson, Rodney. *Outcasts in their Own Land: Mexican Industrial Workers, 1906–1911*. DeKalb: Northern Illinois University Press, 1976.

Aréchiga Córdoba, Ernesto. *Tepito: Del antiguo barrio de indios al arrabal*. Ciudad de México: Ediciones Uníos, 2003.

Arellano, Juan. *La prostitución en México*. Ciudad de México: Secretaría de Fomento, 1895.

Arrom, Silvia. *The Women of Mexico City, 1790–1857*. Stanford: Stanford University Press, 1985.

Arrom, Silvia. "Historia de la mujer y de la familia latinoamericanas," *Historia Mexicana* 42, no. 2 (1992): 379–418.

Arrom, Silvia. "Changes in Mexican Family Law in the Nineteenth Century: The Civil Codes of 1870 and 1884," *Journal of Family History* 10, no. 3 (1985): 305–317.

Barret-Ducrocq, Françoise. *Love in the Time of Victoria: Sexuality and Desire among Working-Class Men and Women in Nineteenth-Century London.* Translated by John Howe. New York: Penguin Books, 1992.

Barrett, Robert S. *The Standard Guide to the City of Mexico 1900.* Ciudad de México: Modern Mexico Publishing Company, 1900.

Bates, J.H. *Notes on a Tour in Mexico and California.* New York: Burr Printing House, 1887.

Beezley, William. *Judas at the Jockey Club and other Episodes in Porfirian Mexico.* Lincoln: University of Nebraska Press, 2018.

Beezley, William. *Mexican National Identity: Memory, Innuendo, and Popular Culture.* Tucson: University of Arizona Press, 2008.

Beezley, William. "The Porfirian Smart Set Anticipates Thorstein Veblen in Guadalajara." In *Rituals of Rule, Rituals of Resistance: Public Celebrations and Popular Culture in Mexico,* edited by William Beezley, Cheryl English Martin, and William E. French. Wilmington: Scholarly Resources, 1994.

Besse, Susan K. *Restructuring Patriarchy: The Modernization of Gender Inequality in Brazil, 1914–1940.* Chapel Hill: University of North Carolina Press, 1996.

Bishop, William Henry. *Old Mexico and Her Lost Provinces.* New York: Harper & Brothers, 1883.

Blake, Mary, and Margaret Sullivan. *Mexico: Picturesque, Political, Progressive.* Boston: Lee and Shepard, 1888.

Bleynat, Ingrid. *Vendors' Capitalism: A Political Economy of Public Markets in Mexico City.* Stanford: Stanford University Press, 2021.

Bliss, Katherine Elaine. *Compromised Positions: Prostitution, Public Health, and Gender Politics in Revolutionary Mexico City.* University Park: Pennsylvania State University Press, 2001.

Blum, Ann. *Domestic Economies: Family, Work, and Welfare in Mexico City, 1884–1943.* Lincoln: University of Nebraska Press, 2009.

Boyer, Richard. *Lives of the Bigamists: Marriage, Family, and Community in Colonial Mexico.* Albuquerque: University of New Mexico Press, 1995.

Boyer, Richard. "Honor among Plebians: *Mala Sangre* and Social Reputation." In *The Faces of Honor: Sex, Shame, and Violence in Colonial Latin America,* edited by Lyman L. Johnson and Sonya Lipsett-Rivera, 152–178. Albuquerque: University of New Mexico Press, 1998.

Boyer, Richard. "Women, *La Mala Vida,* and the Politics of Marriage." In *Sexuality and Marriage in Colonial Latin America,* edited by Asunción Lavrin. Lincoln: University of Nebraska Press, 1989.

Brocklehurst, Thomas Unett. *Mexico To-Day: A Country with a Great Future.* London: John Murray, Albemarle Street, 1883.

Buffington, Robert. *A Sentimental Education for the Working Man: The Mexico City Penny Press, 1900–1910.* Durham: Duke University Press, 2015.

Buffington, Robert. *Criminal and Citizen in Modern Mexico.* Lincoln: University of Nebraska Press, 2000.

Buffington, Robert. "Homophobia and the Mexican Working Class, 1900–1910." In *The Famous 41: Sexuality and Social Control in Mexico, 1901,* edited by Robert McKee Irwin, Edward J. McCaughan, and Michelle Rocío Nasser. New York: Palgrave Macmillan, 2003.

Buffington, Robert. "Introduction." In *A Global History of Sexuality: The Modern Era,* edited by Robert M. Buffington, Eithne Luibhéid, and Donna J. Guy. Chichester: Wiley Blackwell, 2014.

Buffington, Robert. "Introduction: Conceptualizing Criminality in Latin America." In *Reconstructing Criminality in Latin America,* edited by Carlos A. Aguirre and Robert Buffington. Wilmington: Scholarly Resources, 2000.

Buffington, Robert, and Pablo Piccato. "Tales of Two Women: The Narrative Construction of Porfirian Reality." In *True Stories of Crime in Modern Mexico,* edited by Robert Buffington and Pablo Piccato. Albuquerque: University of New Mexico Press, 2009.

Bunker, Steven B. *Creating Mexican Consumer Culture in the Age of Porfirio Díaz, 1876–1911.* Albuquerque: University of New Mexico Press, 2012.

Burns, Kathryn. *Into the Archive: Writing and Power in Colonial Peru.* Durham: Duke University Press, 2010.

Butler, Judith. *Gender Trouble: Feminism and the Subversion of Identity.* New York: Routledge, 1990.

Buve, Raymond, and Romana Falcón (eds.) *Don Porfirio presidente . . . nunca omnipotente: Hallazgos, reflexiones y debates, 1876–1911.* Ciudad de México: Universidad Iberoamericana, 1998.

Cahill, Ann. *Rethinking Rape.* Ithaca: Cornell University Press, 2001.

Cano, Gabriela, Pamela J. Fuentes, Anne Rubenstein, and Nicole Sanders. "On the History of Sexuality in Modern Mexico City," *Mexican Studies/Estudios Mexicanos* 36, no. 1–2 (2020): 150–166.

Carreño, Manuel Antonio. *Manual de urbanidad y buenas maneras de la juventud de ambos sexos.* New York: D. Appleton y Compañía, 1894.

Castillo, Debra A. "Meat Shop Memories: Federico Gamboa's *Santa,*" *Inti* 40–41 (1995): 175–192.

Caulfield, Sueann. *In Defense of Honor: Sexual Morality, Modernity, and Nation in Early-Twentieth-Century Brazil.* Durham: Duke University Press, 2000.

Caulfield, Sueann. "The Changing Politics of Freedom and Virginity in Rio de Janeiro, 1920–1940." In *Honor, Status, and Law in Modern Latin America,* edited by Sueann Caulfield, Sarah C. Chambers, and Lara Putnam. Durham: Duke University Press, 2005.

Caulfield, Sueann, Sarah C. Chambers, and Lara Putnam (eds.) *Honor, Status, and Law in Modern Latin America.* Durham: Duke University Press, 2005.

Chambers, Sarah C. *From Subjects to Citizens: Honor, Gender, and Politics in Arequipa, Peru 1780–1854.* University Park: Pennsylvania State University Press, 1999.

Código Civil del Distrito Federal y Territorio de la Baja California. Ciudad de México: Imprenta de Francisco Díaz de León, 1884.

Código Penal para el Distrito Federal y Territorio de la Baja California sobre Delitos del Fuero Común, y para toda la República Mexicana, sobre Delitos contra la Federación. Chihuahua: Librería de Donato Miramontes, 1883.

Cosío Villegas, Daniel (ed.) *Historia Moderna de México.* Ciudad de México: Editorial Hermes, 1955–1972, 10 volúmenes.

Darton, Robert. *The Great Cat Massacre and Other Episodes in French Cultural History.* New York: Vintage Books, 1984.

Davis, Natalie Zemon. *Fiction in the Archives: Pardon Tales and Their Tellers in Sixteenth-Century France.* Stanford: Stanford University Press, 1987.

Deleuze, Gilles. *Foucault.* Translated by Hand Seán. Minneapolis: University of Minnesota Press, 1988.

De los Reyes, Aurelio (ed.) "Siglo XX: Campo y ciudad." In *Historia de la vida cotidiana en México,* edited by Pilar Gonzalbo Aizpuru, Vol. 5. Ciudad de México: El Colegio de México, Fondo de Cultura Económica, 2006.

D'Emilio, John, and Estelle B Freedman. *Intimate Matters: A History of Sexuality in America.* Chicago: University of Chicago Press, 2012.

Díaz, Arlene J. *Female Citizens, Patriarchs, and the Law in Venezuela, 1786–1904.* Lincoln: University of Nebraska Press, 2004.

Dirección General de Estadística *Estadísticas Sociales del Porfiriato, 1877–1910.* Ciudad de México: Dirección General de Estadística, 1956.

Dore, Elizabeth. *Myths of Modernity: Peonage and Patriarchy in Nicaragua.* Durham: Duke University Press, 2006.

Dore, Elizabeth. "One Step Forward, Two Steps Back: Gender and the State in the Long Nineteenth Century." In *Hidden Histories of Gender and the State in Latin America,* edited by Elizabeth Dore and Maxine Molyneux. Durham: Duke University Press, 2000.

Dore, Elizabeth. "The Holy Family: The Imagined Households in Latin American History." In *Gender Politics in Latin America,* edited by Elizabeth Dore. New York: Monthly Review Press, 1997.

Dreyfus, Hubert L. *Being-in-the-World: A Commentary on Heidegger's Being and Time, Division I.* Cambridge: MIT Press, 1990.

Dreyfus, Hubert L., and Paul Rabinow. *Michel Foucault: Beyond Structuralism and Hermeneutics.* Chicago: University of Chicago Press, 1983.

Elias, Norbert. *The Civilizing Process: Sociogenetic and Psychogenetic Investigations.* Translated by Edmund Jephcott. Malden: Blackwell, 2000.

Farge, Arlette. *The Allure of the Archives.* Translated by Thomas Scott-Railton. New Haven: Yale University Press, 2013.

Farge, Arlette. *Fragile Lives: Violence, Power and Solidarity in Eighteenth-Century Paris.* Translated by Carol Shelton. Cambridge: Harvard University Press, 1993.

Fernández Aceves, María Teresa, Carmen Ramos Escandón, and Susie Porter (eds.) *Orden social e identidad de género. México, siglos XIX y XX.* Ciudad de México: CIESAS/Universidad de Guadalajara, 2006.

Findlay, Eileen J. *Imposing Decency: The Politics of Sexuality and Race in Puerto Rico, 1870–1920.* Durham: Duke University Press, 1999.

Findlay, Eileen J. "Courtroom Tales of Sex and Honor: *Rapto* and Rape in Late Nineteenth- Century Puerto Rico." In *Honor, Status, and Law in Modern Latin America*, edited by Sueann Caulfield, Sarah C. Chambers, and Lara Putnam. Durham: Duke University Press, 2005.

Flandrau, Charles Macomb. *Viva Mexico!* New York: D. Appleton and Company, 1908.

Flippin, J.R. *Sketches from the Mountains of Mexico.* Cincinnati: Standard Publishing Company, 1889.

Flores, Francisco A. *El hímen en México.* Ciudad de México: Secretaría de Fomento, 1885.

Foucault, Michel. *The Birth of Biopolitics: Lectures at the Collège de France*, edited by Michel Senellart and translated by Graham Burchell. New York: Picador, 2008.

Foucault, Michel. *The History of Sexuality: Volume One: An Introduction*, edited by Gros Frédéric and translated by Robert Hurley. New York: Vintage Books, 1990.

Foucault, Michel. *Discipline and Punish: The Birth of the Prison.* Translated by Alan Sheridan. New York: Vintage Books, 1977.

French, William E. *The Heart in the Glass Jar: Love Letters, Bodies, and the Law in Mexico.* Lincoln: University of Nebraska Press, 2015.

French, William E. *A Peaceful and Working People: Manners, Morals, and Class Formation in Northern Mexico.* Albuquerque: University of New Mexico Press, 1996.

French, William E. "*Progreso Forzado:* Workers and the Inculcation of the Capitalist Work Ethic in the Parral Mining District." In *Rituals of Rule, Rituals of Resistance: Public Celebrations and Popular Culture in Mexico*, edited by William H. Beezley, Cheryl English Martin, and William E. French. Wilmington: Scholarly Resources, 1994.

French, William E., and Katherine Elaine Bliss (eds.) *Gender, Sexuality, and Power in Latin America since Independence.* Lanham: Rowman & Littlefield, 2007.

Gamboa, Federico. *Santa: A Novel of Mexico City* [1903]. Translated and edited by John Charles Chasteen. Chapel Hill: University of North Carolina Press, 2010.

Gamboa, Federico. *Santa.* Ciudad de México: Ediciones Botas México, 1938 [1903].

García Peña, Ana Lidia. *El fracaso del amor: Género e individualismo en el siglo XIX mexicano.* Ciudad de México: El Colegio de México, Centro de Estudios Históricos; Toluca: Universidad Autónoma del Estado de México, 2006.

Garza, James Alex. *The Imagined Underworld: Sex, Crime, and Vice in Porfirian Mexico City.* Lincoln: University of Nebraska Press, 2008.

Garza, James Alex. "Dominance and Submission in Don Porfirio's Belle Époque: The Case of Luis and Piedad." In *Masculinity and Sexuality in Modern Mexico*, edited by Víctor M. Macías-González and Anne Rubenstein. Albuquerque: University of New Mexico Press, 2012.

Garner, Paul. *Porfirio Díaz.* London: Longman, 2001.

Gay, Peter. *The Bourgeois Experience: Victoria to Freud. Vol. 1, Education of the Senses.* Oxford: Oxford University Press, 1984.

Gay, Peter. *The Bourgeois Experience: Victoria to Freud. Vol. 2, The Tender Passion.* Oxford: Oxford University Press, 1986.

Gelven, Michael. *A Commentary on Heidegger's "Being and Time:" A Section-by-Section Interpretation*. New York: Harper & Row, 1970.

Giddens, Anthony. *The Transformation of Intimacy: Sexuality, Love & Eroticism in Modern Societies*. Stanford: Stanford University Press, 1992.

Giddens, Anthony. *Modernity and Self-Identity: Self and Society in the Late Modern Age*. Stanford: Stanford University Press, 1991.

Gooch, Fanny Chambers. *Face to Face with the Mexicans*. New York: Fords, Howard, & Hulbert, 1887.

Goodhue, Bertram G. *Mexican Memories*. New York: The Alley-Allen Press, 1892.

González Montes, Soledad, and Pilar Iracheta. "La violencia en la vida de las mujeres campesinas: El Distrito de Tenango, 1880–1910." In *Presencia y transparencia: La mujer en la historia de México*, edited by Carmen Ramos Escandón. Ciudad de México: Colegio de México, 1992.

González Navarro, Moisés. "La vida social." In *La historia moderna de México*, Vol. 4, edited by Daniel Cosío Villegas. Ciudad de México: Editorial Hermes, 1955–1972.

Greenleaf, Richard. *The Mexican Inquisition of the Sixteenth Century*. Albuquerque: University of New Mexico Press, 1969.

Griffin, Emma. "Sex, illegitimacy and social change in industrializing Britain," *Social History* 38, no. 2 (2013): 139–161.

Gringo, A. *Through the Land of the Aztecs*. London: Sampson Low, Marston & Company, 1892.

Guerrero, Julio. *La génesis del crimen en México: Estudio de psiquiatría social*. Ciudad de México: Librería de Ch. Bouret, 1901.

Gutiérrez, Ramón A. *When Jesus Came, the Corn Mothers Went Away: Marriage, Sexuality, and Powers in New Mexico, 1500–1846*. Stanford: Stanford University Press, 1991.

Gutmann, Matthew C. *The Meanings of Macho: Being a Man in Mexico City*. Berkeley: University of California Press, 1996.

Guy, Donna J. *White Slavery and Mothers Alive and Dead: The Troubled Meeting of Sex, Gender, Public Health, and Progress in Latin America*. Lincoln: University of Nebraska Press, 2000.

Hardwick, Julie. *Sex in an Old Regime City: Young Workers and Intimacy in France, 1660–1789*. Oxford: Oxford University Press, 2020.

Hart, John M. *Empire and Revolution: The Americans in Mexico since the Civil War*. Berkeley: University of California Press, 2002.

Hart, John M. *Revolutionary Mexico: The Coming and Process of the Mexican Revolution*. Berkeley: University of California Press, 1987.

Hartman, Saidiya. *Wayward Lives, Beautiful Experiments: Intimate Histories of Social Upheaval*. New York: W.W. Norton & Company, 2019.

Heidegger, Martin. *Being and Time*. Translated by John Macquarrie and Edward Robinson. New York: Harper Perennial/Modern Thought, 2008.

Hernández, Vicente. *Arquitectura doméstica de la Ciudad de México (1890–1925)*. Ciudad de México: Universidad Nacional Autónoma de México, 1981.

Hirsch, Jennifer. *Courtship after Marriage: Sexuality and Love in Mexican Transnational Families*. Berkeley: University of California Press, 2003.

Holden Robert H. *Mexico and the Survey of Public Lands: The Management of Modernization, 1876–1911.* DeKalb: Northern Illinois Press, 1994.

Hutchison, Elizabeth Quay. *Labors Appropriate to Their Sex: Gender, Labor, and Politics in Urban Chile, 1900–1930.* Durham: Duke University Press, 2001.

Illadies, Carlos, and Marion Barbosa (eds.) *Los trabajadores de la Ciudad de México, 1860–1950.* Ciudad de México: El Colegio de México, Universidad Autónoma Metropolitana-Cuajimalpa, 2013.

Irwin, Robert McKee, Edward J. McCaughan, and Michelle Rocío Nasser (eds.) *The Famous 41: Sexuality and Social Control in Mexico, 1901.* New York: Palgrave Macmillan, 2003.

Jaffary, Nora E. *Reproduction and Its Discontents in Mexico: Childbirth and Contraception from 1750 to 1905.* Chapel Hill: University of North Carolina Press, 2016.

Jiménez Guzmán, María Lucero. "Sexualidad, vida conyugal y relaciones de pareja. Experiencias de algunos varones de los sectores medio y alto de México." In *Sucede que me canso de ser hombre . . . Relatos y reflexiones sobre hombres y masculinidades en México,* edited by Ana Amuchástegui and Ivonne Szasz. Ciudad de México: El Colegio de México, 2007.

Johns, Michael. *The City of Mexico in the Age of Díaz.* Austin: University of Texas Press, 1997.

Joseph, Gilbert M., and Daniel Nugent (eds.) *Everyday Forms of State Formation: Revolution and the Negotiation of Rule in Modern Mexico.* Durham: University of Durham Press, 1994.

Knight, Alan. *The Mexican Revolution,* 2 Volumes. Cambridge: Cambridge University Press, 1986.

Komisaruk, Catherine. *Labor and Love in Guatemala: The Eve of Independence.* Stanford: Stanford University Press, 2013.

Komisaruk, Catherine. "Rape Narratives, Rape Silences: Sexual Violence and Judicial Testimony in Colonial Guatemala," *Biography* 31, no. 3 (2008): 369–396.

Kuntz Ficker, Sandra. *Empresa extranjera y mercado interno: El Ferrocarril Central Mexicano, 1880–1907.* Ciudad de México: El Colegio de México, 1995.

Lara y Pardo, Luis. *La prostitución en México.* Ciudad de México: Librería de Ch. Bouret, 1908.

Las siete partidas del Sabio Rey D. Alfonso el IX: Cotejados con variantes de más interés y con glosa. Barcelona: Imprenta de Antonio Bergnes y Compañía, 1843.

Lauderdale Graham, Sandra. *House and Street: The Domestic World of Servants and Masters in Nineteenth-Century Rio de Janeiro.* Austin: University of Texas Press, 1992.

Lavrin, Asunción, ed. *Sexuality and Marriage in Colonial Latin America.* Lincoln: University of Nebraska Press, 1989.

Lavrin, Asunción. "Introduction: The Scenario, the Actors, and the Issues." In *Sexuality and Marriage in Colonial Latin America,* edited by Asunción Lavrin. Lincoln: University of Nebraska Press, 1989.

Lear, John. *Workers, Neighbors, and Citizens: The Revolution in Mexico City.* Lincoln: University of Nebraska Press, 2001.

Lenkiewicz, Noemí Ehrenfeld. "Un mosaico de experiencias: Embarazo y maternidad en adolescentes urbano-marginales." In *Los jóvenes ante el siglo XXI*, edited by Emma Liliana Navarrete López. Ciudad de México: El Colegio Mexiquense, 2004.

Lewis, Oscar. *The Children of Sanchez: Autobiography of a Mexican Family.* New York: Vintage Books, 1963.

Lipsett-Rivera, Sonya. *The Origins of Macho: Men and Masculinity in Colonial Mexico.* Albuquerque: University of New Mexico Press, 2019.

Lipsett-Rivera, Sonya. "A Slap in the Face of Honor." In *The Faces of Honor: Sex, Shame, and Violence in Colonial Latin America,* edited by Lyman L. Johnson and Sonya Lipsett-Rivera, 179–200. Albuquerque: University of New Mexico Press, 1998.

Loreto López, Rosalva. *Casas, viviendas y hogares en la historia de México.* Ciudad de México: El Colegio de México, Centro de Estudios Históricos, 2001.

Macedo, Miguel S. *La criminalidad en México.* Ciudad de México: Oficina Tip. de la Secretaría de Fomento, 1897.

Macedo, Miguel S. *Mi barrio.* Ciudad de México: Editorial "Cultura," 1930.

Macías-González, Víctor M. "*Hombres del mundo:* La masculinidad, el consumo, y los manuales de urbanidad y buenas maneras." In *Orden social e identidad de género. México, siglos XIX y XX,* edited by María Teresa Fernández Aceves, Carmen Ramos Escandón, and Susie Porter. Ciudad de México: CIESAS/Universidad de Guadalajara, 2006.

Macías-González, Víctor M., and Anne Rubenstein. "Introduction: Masculinity and History in Modern Mexico." In *Masculinity and Sexuality in Modern Mexico,* edited by Víctor M. Macías-González and Anne Rubenstein. Albuquerque: University of New Mexico Press, 2012.

Macías-González, Víctor M., and Anne Rubenstein, eds. *Masculinity and Sexuality in Modern Mexico.* Albuquerque: University of New Mexico Press, 2012.

MacKinnon, Catherine A. *Toward a Feminist Theory of the State.* New York: Oxford University Press, 1989.

Martin, Cheryl English. "Popular Speech and Social Order in Northern Mexico, 1650–1830," *Comparative Studies in History and Society* 32, no. 2 (1990): 305–324.

Martínez-Alier, Verena. *Marriage, Class and Colour in Nineteenth Century Cuba: A Study of Racist Attitudes and Sexual Values in a Slave Society.* Cambridge: Cambridge University Press, 1974.

Matthews, Michael. *The Civilizing Machine: A Cultural History of Mexican Railroads, 1876–1910.* Lincoln: University of Nebraska Press, 2013.

Matthews, Michael. "Deadly Words, Deadly Deeds: Honor, Sexuality, and Uxoricide in Porfirian Mexico," *Journal of Social History* 51, no. 2 (2017): 341–363.

McCaa, Robert. "Marriage ways in Mexico and Spain, 1500–1900," *Continuity and Change* 9, no. 1 (1994).

McCaa, Robert. "The Peopling of 19th Century Mexico: Critical Scrutiny of a Censured Century," *Statistical Abstract of Latin America* 30 (1993): 1–33.

McKee Irwin, Robert, Edward J. McCaughan, and Michelle Rocío Nasser (eds.) *The Famous 41: Sexuality and Social Control in Mexico, 1901.* New York: Palgrave Macmillan, 2003.

Menkes, Catherine, and Leticia Suárez. "Prácticas sexuales y reproductivas de las jóvenes en México." In *Los jóvenes ante el siglo XXI,* edited by Emma Liliana Navarrete López. Ciudad de México: El Colegio Mexiquense, 2004.

Meyerowitz, Joanne, *Women Adrift: Independent Wage Earners in Chicago, 1880–1930.* Chicago: University of Chicago Press, 1988.

Mídena, María Eugenia, and Zuanilda Mendoza. *Géneros y generaciones: Etnografía de las relaciones entre hombres y mujeres de la Ciudad de México.* Ciudad de México: EDAMEX, 2001.

Miranda Pacheco, Sergio. *Tacubaya: De suburbio veraniego a ciudad.* Ciudad de México: Universidad Nacional Autónoma de México, 2007.

Monsívais, Carlos. *Mexican Postcards.* London: Verso, 1997.

Montaño, Diana J. *Electrifying Mexico: Technology and the Transformation of a Modern City.* Austin: University of Texas Press, 2021.

Mora, Carl J. *Mexican Cinema: Reflections of a Society, 1896–2004.* Jefferson: McFarland & Co. Inc, 2005.

Morales, Ma. Dolores y María Gayón. "Viviendas, casas y usos de suelo en la Ciudad de México, 1848–1882." In *Casas, viviendas y hogares en la historia de México,* edited by Rosalva Loreto López. Ciudad de México: El Colegio de México, Centro de Estudios Históricos, 2001.

Morgan, Tony. "Proletarians, Politicos, and Patriarchs: The Use and Abuse of Cultural Customs in the Early Industrialization of Mexico City, 1880–1910." In *Rituals of Rule, Rituals of Resistance: Public Celebrations and Popular Culture in Mexico,* edited by William H. Beezley, Cheryl English Martin, and William E. French. Wilmington: Scholarly Resources, 1994.

Nehring, Daniel. "Negotiated Familism: Intimate Life and Individualization Among Young Female Professionals from Mexico City," *Canadian Journal of Latin American and Caribbean Studies/ Revue canadienne des études latino-américaines et caraïbes* 36, no. 71 (2011): 165–196.

Neufeld, Stephen B. *The Blood Contingent: The Military and the Making of Modern Mexico, 1876–1911.* Albuquerque: University of New Mexico Press, 2017.

Oden, Mary. *Delinquent Daughters: Protecting and Policing Adolescent Female Sexuality, 1885–1920.* Chapel Hill: University of North Carolina Press, 1995.

Orvañanos, D. Domingo. *Algo sobre legislación sanitaria relative á las habitaciones en México.* Ciudad de México: Secretaría de Fomento, 1895.

Overmyer-Velázquez, Mark. *Visions of the Emerald City: Modernity, Tradition, and the Formation of Porfirian Oaxaca, Mexico.* Durham: Duke University Press, 2006.

Padilla, Mark B., Jennifer S. Hirsch, Miguel Muñoz-Laboy, Robert E. Sember, and Richard G. Parker, eds. *Love and Globalization: Transformations of Intimacy in the Contemporary World.* Nashville: Vanderbilt University Press, 2007.

Padilla, Mark B., Jennifer S. Hirsch, Miguel Muñoz-Laboy, Robert E. Sember, and Richard G. Parker. "Introduction: Cross-Cultural Reflections on an Intimate Intersection." In *Love and Globalization: Transformations of Intimacy in the Contemporary World,* edited by Mark B. Padilla, Jennifer S. Hirsch, Miguel Muñoz-Laboy, Robert E. Sember, and Richard G. Parker. Nashville: Vanderbilt University Press, 2007.

Peiss, Kathy. *Cheap Amusements: Working Women and Leisure in Turn-of-the-Century New York*. Philadelphia: Temple University Press, 1986.

Piccato, Pablo. *A History of Infamy: Crime, Truth, and Justice in Mexico*. Berkeley: University of California Press, 2017.

Piccato, Pablo. *The Tyranny of Opinion: Honor in the Construction of the Mexican Public Sphere*. Durham: Duke University Press, 2010.

Piccato, Pablo. *City of Suspects: Crime in Mexico City, 1900–1931*. Durham: Duke University Press, 2001.

Piccato, Pablo. "Interpretations of Sexuality in Mexico City Prisons: A Critical Version of Roumagnac." In *The Famous 41: Sexuality and Social Control in Mexico, 1901*, edited by Robert McKee Irwin, Edward J. McCaughan, and Michelle Rocío Nasser. New York: Palgrave Macmillan, 2003.

Pierce, Gretchen, and Áurea Toxqui (eds.) *Alcohol in Latin America: A Social and Cultural History*. Tucson: University of Arizona Press, 2014.

Pitt-Rivers, Julian A. "Honour and Social Status." In *Honour and Shame: The Values of Mediterranean Society*, edited by Jean Peristiany. London: Weidenfeld and Nicolson, 1965.

Porter, Susie S. *Working Women in Mexico City: Public Discourses and Material Conditions, 1879–1931*. Tucson: University of Arizona Press, 2003.

Putnam, Lara, Sarah C. Chambers, and Sueann Caulfield. "Introduction: Transformations in Honor, Status, and Law over the Long Nineteenth Century." In *Honor, Status, and Law in Modern Latin America*, edited by Sueann Caulfield, Sarah C. Chambers, and Lara Putnam. Durham: Duke University Press, 2005.

Ramos Escandón, Carmen (ed.) *Presencia y transparencia: La mujer en la historia de México*. Ciudad de México: Colegio de México, 1992.

Reddy, William M. *The Making of Romantic Love: Longing and Sexuality in Europe, South Asia, and Japan, 900–1200 Ce*. Chicago: University of Chicago Press, 2012.

Rodgers, Thomas L. *Mexico? Si, Señor*. Boston: Mexican Central Railway Company, 1894.

Rohlfes, Laurence J. "Police and Penal Correction in Mexico City, 1876–1911: A Study of Order and Progress in Porfirian Mexico." Ph.D. dissertation, Tulane University, 1983.

Rojas, Olga Lorena. *Hombres y relaciones de género en México*. Ciudad de México: El Colegio de México, 2022.

Rosemblatt, Karin Alejandra. *Gendered Compromises: Political Cultures and the State in Chile, 1920–1950*. Chapel Hill: University of North Carolina Press, 2000.

Roumagnac, Carlos. *Matadores de mujeres*. Ciudad de México: Librería de Ch. Bouret, 1910.

Roumagnac, Carlos. *La prostitución reglamentada: Sus inconvenientes, su inutilidad y sus peligros*. Ciudad de México: Tipografía Económica, 1909.

Roumagnac, Carlos. *Crímenes sexuales y pasionales: Estudios de psicología morbosa*. Ciudad de México: Librería de Ch. Bouret, 1906.

Roumagnac, Carlos. *Los criminales en México: Ensayo de psicología criminal*. Ciudad de México: Tipografía El Fénix, 1904.

Salvatore, Ricardo D., Carlos Aguirre, and Gilbert M. Joseph (eds.) *Crime and Punish-*

ment in Latin America: Law and Society since Late Colonial Times. Durham: Duke University Press, 2001.

Sanders, Nichole. *Gender and Welfare in Mexico: The Consolidation of a Postrevolutionary State*. University Park: Pennsylvania State University Press, 2011.

Sanders, Nichole. "Gender and Consumption in Porfirian Mexico: Images of Women in Advertising, *El Imparcial,* 1897–1910," *Frontiers* 38, no. 1 (2017): 1–30.

Schell, William, Jr. *Integral Outsiders: The American Colony in Mexico City, 1876–1911.* Wilmington: Scholarly Resources, 2001.

Scott, James. *Domination and the Arts of Resistance: Hidden Transcripts.* New Haven: Yale University Press, 1990.

Scott, Joan Wallach. *Gender and the Politics of History.* New York: Columbia University Press, 1988.

Scott, Joan Wallach. "Gender: A Useful Category of Historical Analysis," *American Historical Review* 91, no. 5 (1986): 1053–75.

Seed, Patricia. *To Love, Honor, and Obey in Colonial Mexico: Conflicts over Marriage Choice, 1574–1821.* Stanford: Stanford University Press, 1988.

Shorter, Edward. "Female Emancipation, Birth Control, and Fertility in European History," *American Historical Review* 78, no. 3 (1973): 605–640.

Shorter, Edward. "Illegitimacy, sexual revolution and social change in modern Europe," *Journal of Interdisciplinary History* 2, no. 1 (1971): 237–272.

Shumway, Jeffrey M. *The Case of the Ugly Suitor and other Histories of Love, Gender, and Nation in Buenos Aires, 1776–1870.* Lincoln: University of Nebraska Press, 2005.

Silva Dias, Maria Odila. *Power and Everyday Life: The Lives of Working Women in Nineteenth- Century Brazil.* Translated by Ann Frost. New Brunswick: Rutgers University Press, 1995.

Sloan, Kathryn A. *Runaway Daughters: Seduction, Elopement, and Honor in Nineteenth-Century Mexico.* Albuquerque: University of New Mexico Press, 2008.

Smith, Stephanie. "'If Love Enslaves . . . Love Be Damned!': Divorce and Revolutionary State Formation in the Yucatán." In *Gender, Politics, and Power in Modern Mexico,* edited by Jocelyn Olcott, Mary Kay Vaughan, and Gabriela Cano. Durham: Duke University Press, 2006.

Solís, Patricio, Cecilia Gayet y Fátima Juárez. "Las transiciones a la vida sexual, a la unión y a la maternidad en Mexico: Cambios en el tiempo y estratificación social." In *Salud reproductiva y condiciones de vida en México,* Vol. 1, edited by Susana Lerner and Ivonne Szasz. Ciudad de México: El Colegio de México, 2008.

Solnit, Rebecca. *Wanderlust: A History of Walking.* New York: Penguin Books, 2000.

Speckman Guerra, Elisa. *Crimen y castigo: Legislación penal, interpretaciones de la criminalidad y administración de justicia, Ciudad de México, 1872–1910.* Ciudad de México: El Colegio de México; Centro de Estudios Históricos, Universidad Nacional Autónoma de México; Instituto de Investigaciones Históricas, 2007.

Speckman Guerra, Elisa. "De barrios y arrabales: Entorno, cultura material y quehacer cotidiano (Ciudad de México 1890–1910)." In *Historia de la vida cotidiana en México*, edited by Pilar Gonzalbo Aizpuru. Ciudad de México: Fondo de Cultura Económica, 2006.

Stansell, Christine. *City of Women: Sex and Class in New York, 1789–1960.* Chicago: University of Illinois Press, 1987.

Stern, Steve J. *The Secret History of Gender: Women, Men, and Power in Late Colonial Mexico.* Chapel Hill: University of North Carolina Press, 1995.

Stevens, Donald Fithian. *Mexico in the Time of Cholera.* Albuquerque: University of New Mexico Press, 2019.

Stone, Lawrence. *The Family, Sex and Marriage in England 1500–1800.* New York: Harper Perennial, 1983.

Szasz, Ivonne. "Relaciones de género y desigualdad socioeconómica en la construcción social de las normas sobre la sexualidad en México." In *Salud reproductiva y condiciones de vida en México*, Vol. 1, edited by Susana Lerner and Ivonne Szasz. Ciudad de México: El Colegio de México, 2008.

Szasz, Ivonne. "Sexualidad y género: Algunas experiencias de *investigación* en México," *Debate Feminista* 18 (1998): 80–81.

Tablada, José Juan. *La feria de la vida (memorias).* Ciudad de México: Ediciones Botas, 1937.

Tebbutt, Melanie. *Women's Talk? A Social History of 'Gossip' in Working-Class Neighborhoods, 1880–1960.* Aldershot: Scolar Press, 1995.

Tenenbaum, Barbara A. "Streetwise History: The Paseo de la Reforma and the Porfirian State, 1876–1910." In *Rituals of Rule, Rituals of Resistance: Public Celebrations and Popular Culture in Mexico*, edited by William Beezley, Cheryl English Martin, and William E. French. Wilmington: Scholarly Resources, 1994.

Tenorio-Trillo, Mauricio. *I Speak of the City: Mexico City at the Turn of the Twentieth Century.* Chicago: University of Chicago Press, 2012.

Tenorio-Trillo, Mauricio. *Mexico at the World's Fairs: Crafting a Modern Nation.* Berkeley: University of California Press, 1996.

Terdiman, Richard. *Discourse/Counter-discourse: The Theory and Practice of Symbolic Resistance in Nineteenth Century France.* Ithaca: Cornell University Press, 1989.

Terry, Philip T. *Terry's Guide to Mexico.* Boston: Houghton Mifflin, 1911.

Tinsman, Heidi. *Partners in Conflict: The Politics of Sexuality, Gender, and Labor in the Chilean Agrarian Reform, 1950–1973.* Durham: Duke University Press, 2002.

Tortolero Villaseñor, Alejandro. *Notarios y agricultores: Crecimiento y atraso en el campo mexicano, 1780–1920.* Iztapalapa: Universidad Autónoma Metropolitana, 2008.

Tortolero Villaseñor, Alejandro. "Canales de riego y canales navegables en la Cuenca de México: Economía, patrimonio y paisaje en el México porfirista," *Historia Caribe* 10, no. 26 (2015): 75–105.

Tortorici, Zeb. *Sins against Nature: Sex and Archives in Colonial New Spain.* Durham: Duke University Press, 2018.

Toxqui, Áurea. "Breadwinners or Entrepreneurs? Women's Involvement in the *Pulquería* World of Mexico City, 1850–1910." In *Alcohol in Latin America: A Social and Cultural History*, edited by Gretchen Pierce and Áurea Toxqui. Tucson: University of Arizona Press, 2014.

Toxqui Garay, María Áurea. "'*El recreo de los amigos*': Mexico City's *Pulquerías* during the Liberal Republic (1856–1911)." Ph.D. dissertation, University of Arizona, 2008.

Tramar, Condesa de. *El amor obligatorio.* Ciudad de México: Librería de Ch. Bouret, 1910.

Tuñón Pablos, Julia. *Women in Mexico.* Austin: University of Texas Press, 1999.

Tutino, John. "Power, Marginality, and Participation in Mexico City, 1870–2000." In *New World Cities: Challenges to Urbanization and Globalization in the Americas,* edited by John Tutino and Martin V. Melosi. Chapel Hill: University of North Carolina Press, 2019.

Twinam, Ann. *Public Lives, Private Secrets: Gender, Honor, Sexuality, and Illegitimacy in Colonial Spanish America.* Stanford: Stanford University Press, 1999.

Twinam, Ann. "Honor, Sexuality, and Illegitimacy in Colonial Spanish America." In *Sexuality and Marriage in Colonial Latin America,* edited by Asunción Lavrin. Lincoln: University of Nebraska Press, 1989.

Vaughan, Mary Kay. *Cultural Politics in Revolution: Teachers, Peasants, and Schools in Mexico, 1930–1940.* Tucson: University of Arizona Press, 1997.

Vaughan, Mary Kay. "Modernizing Patriarchy: State Policies, Rural Households, and Women in Mexico, 1930–1940." In *Hidden Histories of Gender and the State in Latin America* edited by Elizabeth Dore and Maxine Molyneux. Durham: Duke University Press, 2000.

Vaughan, Mary Kay. "Women, Class, and Education in Mexico, 1880–1928," *Latin American Perspectives* 4, no 1–2 (1977): 135–152.

Van Deusen, Nancy E. "Determining the Boundaries of Virtue: The Discourse of *Recogimiento* among Women in Seventeenth-Century Lima," *Journal of Family History* 22, no. 4 (1997): 373–389.

Von Germeten, Nicole. *The Enlightened Patrolman: Early Law Enforcement in Mexico City.* Lincoln: University of Nebraska Press, 2022.

Von Germeten, Nicole. *Violent Delights, Violent End: Sex, Race, and Honor in Colonial Cartagena de Indias.* Albuquerque: University of New Mexico Press, 2013.

Viqueira Albán, Juan Pedro. *Propriety and Permissiveness in Bourbon Mexico.* Wilmington: Scholarly Resources, 1999.

Vitz, Matthew. *A City on a Lake: Urban Political Ecology and the Growth of Mexico City.* Durham: Duke University Press, 2012.

Wakild, Emily. "Naturalizing Modernity: Urban Parks, Public Gardens and Drainage Projects in Porfirian Mexico City," *Mexican Studies/Estudios Mexicanos* 23, no. 1 (2007): 101–123.

Waldon, Kathy. "The Sinners and the Bishop in Colonial Venezuela: The *Visita* of Bishop Mariano Martí, 1771–1784." In *Sexuality and Marriage in Colonial Latin America,* edited by Asunción Lavrin. University of Nebraska Press, 1989.

Weeks, Jeffrey. *Sex, Politics and Society: The Regulation of Sexuality since 1800.* London: Longman, 1989.

Weinstein, Barbara, *For Social Peace in Brazil: Industrialists and the Remaking of the Work.* Chapel Hill: University of North Carolina Press, 1996.

Wells, Allen, and Gilbert M. Joseph. "Modernizing Visions, 'Chilango' Blueprints, and

Provincial Growing Pains: Mérida at the Turn of the Century." *Mexican Studies/Estudios Mexicanos* 8, no. 2 (1992): 167–215.

Weston, Kate. *Long Slow Burn: Sexuality and Social Science.* New York: Routledge, 1990.

INDEX

Michael Matthews is professor of history at Elon University. He is the author of *The Civilizing Machine: A Cultural History of Mexican Railroads, 1876–1910*, and is a coeditor and contributor for *Mexico in Verse: A History of Music, Rhyme, and Power.*